THE ENGINEER
IN THE INDUSTRIAL CORPORATION

THE ENGINEER IN THE INDUSTRIAL CORPORATION

R. RICHARD RITTI

COLUMBIA UNIVERSITY PRESS
NEW YORK AND LONDON

ISBN: 0-231-03373-7
Library of Congress Catalog Card Number: 73-133913
Printed in the United States of America

Preface

This book represents the cumulative knowledge of perhaps ten years of empirical study of engineers and engineering organization. In one sense it differs from other research studies in the field in that it has been motivated largely by problem/policy formation concerns. My attempt generally has been to look ahead toward problems promising to become crucial in the future rather than those currently identified by management. My reasoning was that once a problem becomes apparent it is difficult or impossible to research it properly, to hold off pending executive action until sufficient understanding of the problem can be gained. Properly diagnosing future problems gives more lead time in arriving at possible solutions. Furthermore, executives typically are too busy with the problems of today's operations to worry about the problems of tomorrow's. Though future market planning is given great emphasis, future operations planning is given little. I heard it said of one busy engineering executive, "Marsh's long-range plan runs from breakfast to lunch."

The result of this emphasis on future problems is that the focus of the book—underutilization of skills and lack of organizational influence—is placed in more general terms than that of the usual executive perspective. The problems are seen as a consequence of a form of organization rather than as the result of incompetence or poor execution. Because of this I want to reemphasize that the corporation involved—Electromech—is basically a healthy and prosperous organization, successfully competitive in its field. The problems I describe have been uncovered by systematically collecting data and comparing results from groups functioning under different organizational conditions. This gives a perspective quite different from that given by managerial experience alone. Put another way, the problems I describe I have in a sense created by providing the means through which these problems could be described and documented.

A major consideration in writing this book has been to speak to two different audiences: an administrative or executive management group directly or indirectly responsible for engineering activities, and an academic audience comprising students of the sociology or social psychology of organizations. This has created a few problems in organizing the material, primarily over the inclusion of basic conceptual material unneeded by academic readers, and the presentation of detailed empirical data that may seem unnecessary to the practitioner. Over-all, however, I think that the reading will not prove tedious to either group.

By way of acknowledgments I face a different sort of problem. Since the anonymity of Electromech is of crucial importance to me, I wish not to acknowledge directly my debt to the many people in Electromech who have made these studies possible. However, it must be obvious to the reader that the projects discussed herein could not have been successfully carried on by a single researcher. I would like to give special thanks to George Strauss and William F. Whyte, who read earlier drafts of the manuscript and made what I felt to be key suggestions for revision and additions. I would like also to thank Leonard Sayles for his advice and help in problems of publication. Finally, I owe an unspecific but clearly felt debt of gratitude to my colleague and friend, Fred H. Goldner, with whom I have collaborated on several earlier articles based on this material and whose general advice and whose intellect have continually stimulated new perspectives in my thinking.

Pennsylvania State University R. Richard Ritti
November, 1970

Contents

Figures

Tables

THE ENGINEER
IN THE INDUSTRIAL CORPORATION

1 The Unhappy Engineer?

"The engineer is asked to fill a 'little hole,' a small part in a 'big hole.' This goes with little salary, little recognition, little prestige, little contribution. Sure you're bitter." [1]

Engineers say things like this, and more engineers feel this way than management would like to believe. People involved in engineering administration find it difficult to accept the existence of pervasive discontent among engineers. Thus the question mark in the chapter heading, which is a phrase taken from a report that cites some very negative survey results; but the question mark implies that the editors have not quite accepted those results as truth.[2]

The research reported in this book is motivated by the kind of evidence presented in that report. I have tried to answer the questions "Is it really true that engineers are unhappy?" and "Why should they be so?" The answers are relative, of course. But the pages that follow will demonstrate that the answer to the first question is yes; engineers are more dissatisfied than one would expect. The answer to the second question is considerably more complicated, involving as it does problems that are inherent in the type of productive process employed as well as aspects of management philosophy and the control systems used by management in attempting to organize that

[1] This quotation is taken from an unpublished report, "The Engineer's Self-Image and His Image of [Electromech]," by Percy Black, a management consultant.

[2] The phrase occurs in Stevens Alumniletter, Vol. I (February, 1960), Stevens Institute of Technology, Hoboken, New Jersey.

productive process. A further point is that the kind of productive process likely to produce dissatisfaction will be found most commonly in organizations which may be described as technology-based.

MORE UNHAPPY THAN WHOM?

Dissatisfaction, of course, is a relative thing and so our question should be rephrased to read: "Are engineers more unhappy than others?" One answer, dating from 1955, comes from an analysis of the SRA employee inventory.

> In the Industrial Relations Center's surveys, professionals revealed only slightly more favorable attitudes than production workers and factory labor. Their feelings appeared to be about the same as routine office employees. They were definitely less satisfied than skilled workers, foremen, salesmen, and management. For high-status employees, their attitudes about the work situation in general were considerably less favorable than might be expected.[3]

Of special interest here is the fact that the rating engineers gave to effectiveness of administration was "lower than 85% of all employee groups surveyed." [4]

Again, in 1964 a report by the Opinion Research Corporation found that "general discontent with their work and the company they work for is usually higher among technical people than among other well educated groups that are closely identified with management." [5] This report shows that only 27 per cent of engineers gave their jobs a rating of "very good" as compared to 60 per cent of the sales force and 40 per cent of both the headquarters staff and the production group. My research in Electromech yields remarkably similar data in response to an identical question about job attitudes.[6] The pattern of responses in Figure 1.1 again shows engineers

[3] Moore and Renck, "The Professional Employee in Industry," p. 55, in Orth *et al., Administering Research and Development.*

[4] *Ibid.*, p. 58.

[5] Opinion Research Corporation, "The Complex Problems of Engineers in Industry," mimeographed report, p. 17.

[6] Electromech is a pseudonym for the corporation in which most of the research reported here was carried out.

Figure 1.1
Attitude Toward Job of Different Occupational Groups

QUESTION: "HOW DO YOU LIKE YOUR JOB—THE KIND OF WORK YOU DO?"

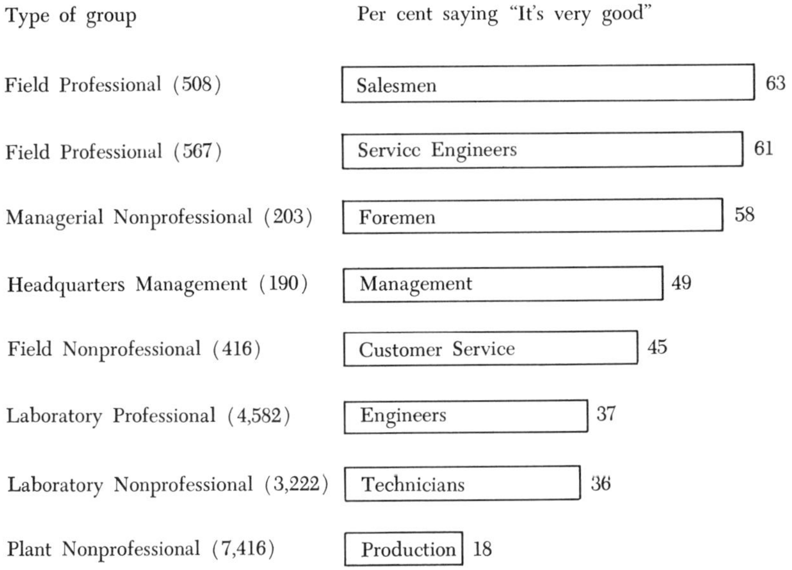

to be less satisfied with their work than any other group except those directly involved in production work—blue-collar workers.[7]

Thus a consistent pattern of dissatisfaction among engineers relative to other occupational groups suggests itself. Furthermore, this pattern seems to persist over a period of time and is not associated with some particular set of economic conditions. And of special interest is the fact that all the "field" employees express a higher level of satisfaction than do comparable laboratory workers. The "field"

[7] The percentages reported here are taken from various surveys of Electromech employees given in approximately the same time period—1963–65. Data for the field groups were taken from sample surveys while other data were taken from census surveys. Thus the group sizes do not reflect the relative proportions of the occupational groups in Electromech. While the figures have shifted somewhat in later surveys, the pattern remains the same. For example, a 1967 survey shows the figure for laboratory professionals at 28 per cent. Finally, the "Headquarters Management" group not described in the text comprises both staff and line management.

designation means that the employee works in direct contact with a customer. He may be selling equipment, helping the customer to install and learn to operate equipment (service engineer), or repairing and servicing equipment at customer installations (customer service). Differences between laboratory and field lie in the much smaller size of the local organization (e.g., sales office vs. laboratory) and in the amount of direct contact with what one technical manager terms "the real world"—the customer.

My contention is that the typical and necessary work organization of the laboratory is responsible for the dissatisfaction of engineers. The field groups—salesmen and service engineers—show similar attitudes although their background and training are different. The development laboratory workers—engineers and technicians—show very much the same attitudes although their background and training again are different. Furthermore, I believe that the attitudes toward their work held by development engineers are closer to those held by production workers because in many ways the development laboratory is organized like the production plant.

Work in the field allows more individual freedom of action. The service engineer or salesman usually has full responsibility for an account or installation. He has more individual influence. A sale or a successful installation is directly and visibly the result of his efforts. The work organization of the development laboratory is necessarily more hierarchical, more bureaucratic. In the development laboratory an engineer is seldom responsible for an entire project unless he is a project manager. On large projects the development engineer works on a small part of the final system. Perhaps he is assigned work that only provides a service to those who develop the system. In any event, the satisfaction that seems to be inherent in the full responsibility provided by the field environment is missing in the laboratory. The division of labor common in the production plant is more analogous.[8]

[8] Blauner presents an interesting example of the impact on job satisfaction of what he terms "fractionized" job assignments. He makes the point that while auto workers have a very good understanding of how their individual efforts fit into the final product, their tasks are so small a part of the total effort that they gain no satisfaction from this knowledge. I have the feeling that the same is true of engineering, that efforts to show engineers how their part fits in are useless. See Blauner, *Alienation and Freedom,* p. 108.

Figure 1.2
Reports of Underutilization by Different Occupational Groups

QUESTION: "HOW DO YOU FEEL ABOUT THE AMOUNT OF WORK YOU ARE EXPECTED TO DO?"

Per cent saying

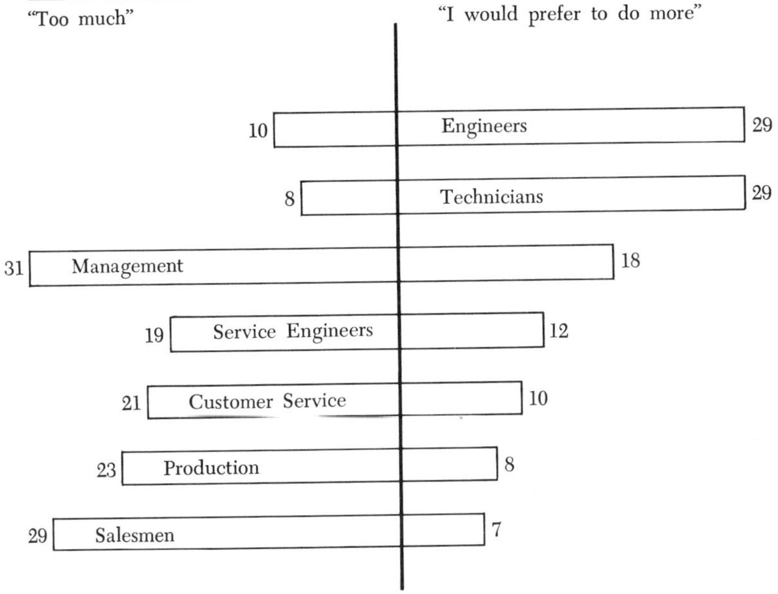

But the work expectations of development engineers are incompatible with the production plant environment. Performance is constrained by the environment.[9] Production workers do not expect to use their full skills or potential (though they may not like that situation). Engineers do. The consequence of this is an expressed desire to "do more," to be given the chance to perform. When asked how they felt about the amount of work expected of them, the various occupational groups responded as shown in Figure 1.2. (These groups are identical to those in Figure 1.1, although data for foremen are unavailable.) Note the close correspondence between satisfaction

[9] A 1969 newsletter of the National Society of Professional Engineers shows 42 per cent of their sample of members reporting that engineers are not properly utilized. See National Society of Professional Engineers, "Utilization of the Engineer," *Professional Engineer in Industry Newsletter,* XIV (May, 1969), 1.

with work as shown in Figure 1.1 and feelings of underutilization. Contrary to what might be expected, feelings of high work pressure and high work satisfaction go hand in hand for employees whose work affords them some measure of individual responsibility and influence. If achieving goals depends upon high performance, the opportunity to perform the job well is crucial.

THE TECHNOLOGY-BASED ENTERPRISE

Thus we see the core of the problem—the frustration and dissatisfaction that result from the mismatch of people and work. The reason for this state of affairs seems to me to be centered in the nature of the task. Yet I recognize that other explanations are possible. The task I have set for myself in the chapters that follow is that of examining the organizational problems inherent in large-scale systems development engineering activities whose primary production force comprises mainly college-educated professionals. My focus is the development end of the so-called research and development laboratory. And the work force, whom I call engineers for the sake of simplicity, are those engineers, metallurgists, or even programming specialists who are involved in coordinated activities leading to the development of new products, processes, or systems. I do not mean people involved in research—a distinction to be clarified in Chapter 3.

My first contact with systems development engineering came a number of years ago in the Electromech Corporation. I was pursuing a research project on engineering organization, and I had some questions and some answers based on my own past experience and work. For example, it seemed to me that boring work was a primary cause of dissatisfaction among engineers. Following this reasoning, it seemed to me also that low technology companies would have more boring work than high technology companies and thus exhibit a pattern of greater dissatisfaction. Now Electromech is certainly a high technology company. By this I mean that its products are continually evolving, and that these products are highly engineered and quite complex. This should be an ideal environment for a development engineer. Therefore, I was surprised to find quite the opposite.

In one of my first interviews an engineer described his anxiety on first coming to Electromech from a government job. He had not been entirely sure that he would be able to make good in such a high-powered organization, but he informed me with some disgust, "It's even worse here than it was in the government." A little later I had another discussion with a designer who told the same kind of story. As he talked of other jobs he had held, he spoke at some length of his experience as a toy designer. Designing toys, he said, was much more interesting and challenging than his current work! There were difficult and intriguing problems to work out and a high level of creativity was required. Not so in his present work! He concluded that while he liked the pay and prestige of Electromech much better, he had to admit that the work was far less interesting.

To understand how this can be we must first understand the nature of systems development engineering and the technology-based corporation which supports it. The key feature of the technology-based corporation is that its expansion, its growth into new fields, and its strategies for market competition are based on planned technological innovation. To survive, the technology-based corporation must offer products or systems that are superior in performance to those offered previously by itself or currently by competitors. Such innovation must be planned years in advance and programmed to meet the projected activities of competitors.[10] And this kind of activity must be differentiated from that of simply marketing products which have been developed by some on-going product development activity to fit some currently available market. For example, aircraft companies know that present designs will be made obsolete by competitors in a certain number of years. They can project that in, say, five years they must have a new aircraft with certain characteristics on the market. At the time this projection is made it is entirely likely that the technical knowledge required to attain those characteristics (in the sense of engineering, not science) is not known. In consequence of this, hordes of technical workers must be put in harness, informed only by some master plan, to spend the next five years ensuring that necessity becomes reality. I do not mean to

[10] A description of such activities and their necessity in the modern corporation is given in Galbraith, *The New Industrial State*.

imply that successful engineering development is sufficient to guarantee the success of the technology-based corporation, but simply that it is necessary, and necessary on a far larger scale than in some other industries where technical advances are perhaps marginal (for example, automobiles).

A second feature of the technology-based organization is that by and large it sells to institutional customers. This characteristic evolves from the fact that the technology-based organization is in the business of producing large, complex, high-technology machines or systems. Some examples of typical technology-based industries might be aerospace, military electronics, computers, and the like. Customers for these products are other corporations and the government, not the general public. Such customers can and do evaluate purchases on the basis of marginal differences in technical performance. Thus, to come full circle, there is a great deal of attention paid to the planning and the programming of future technological innovation.

THE ELECTROMECH CORPORATION

My model in the description of a technology-based organization is the engineering systems development function of a large company I have called the Electromech Corporation. The task of this development organization is the design development of electronic and electromechanical systems. I use the term "systems" instead of terms like "product" or "machine" because system better conveys the essential nature of the task being done in Electromech. That is, it conveys the unusual interdependence among engineering functions necessary to complete a design. A most familiar example of this kind of interdependence is the space vehicle. Large aircraft presents another example. So it is not only the systems interdependence but also the sheer magnitude and complexity of the task that creates a special organizational environment. Further examples may be found in missile detection and launch systems or electronic telephone switching systems.

And so in the ideal sense the term "system" conveys the notion that no single task of development can be done independently of another. The configuration adopted in one element of the system places constraints on the others. The design of an aircraft landing gear contributes weight to the over-all vehicle, but weight also sets constraints on the gear design. Finally, the true weight of the vehicle will not be known until the design is complete. In some cases estimates are sufficiently wrong enough to produce embarrassing consequences. Now, contrast this situation to the development, say, of new chemical plastic materials. In that industry it might be reasonable to turn ten engineers loose on a project and have them work independently of others in the organization—at least independent technically. To be sure, there are constraints of cost and competition, and there are marketing constraints. There are also constraints that derive from the fact that the organization itself is a system. That is, there are other project proposals which will compete for resources currently being used by projects under way. If a proposed project appears more deserving than an existing one, the existing one may be altered in some respects. But the technical goal is clear in that it is arrived at within the project. The technical configuration will not be modified because a group or groups working on other parts of the project have been unable or unwilling to create a design that is harmonious with that configuration. This is quite different from—to take a current example—the problems created by a shift from a swing-wing to a fixed delta-wing in a supersonic transport. All other aspects of the total vehicle design are affected, and it is certain that some designs already finished must be scrapped completely.

The idea that I am trying to convey is not that systems development organizations are totally different from other engineering endeavors but that the organizational problems they face are perhaps of an order of magnitude more difficult. Thus they serve to highlight problems that exist for all. I make no claim that the Electromech systems development organization is not unique in certain aspects; it is. But I know also that the problems it faces are already common in aerospace and electronics. Furthermore, it is my belief that this kind of organization is prototypical of organizations in the future. The application of systems concepts to organization management is already under way. M.B.A.'s are currently schooled in this way of thinking. These concepts, together with rapidly advancing information management and retrieval techniques, mean that organizations of a scale never before possible will soon become commonplace. Add to this the systems interdependence that results from the proliferation of organization specialties in planning, financial controls, and innumerable other specialties, and it would appear that the kind of systems complexities encountered in the Electromech development organization will not be special for long.

A sufficient description of the corporation itself can be given in a paragraph. Electromech is a corporation in the 100,000-employee class, with a number of R&D laboratories scattered throughout the country. Each of these is of a somewhat different character, different in size, and assigned a different part of a multiproduct systems development mission.[11] All are engaged in development that leads to the manufacturing and marketing of electronic and electromechanical systems and products. As I have already mentioned, these are high-technology products, and customers are for the most part institutions.

However, since I have set for myself the task of analyzing and elaborating on the problems that face the corporation, it seems only appropriate here to point out that Electromech is also a healthy and prosperous company. It has a past history of success, and anticipates continued success in the future. Electromech has always had harmonious relations with employees, and especially in engineering it offers a generally positive and attractive environment. I stress this because the problems I deal with are endemic to the situation, and not, it seems to me, products of poor management. In a way they are problems that Electromech faces ahead of others because its organizational form has already evolved to a state of complexity yet to be faced by others.

VIEWPOINT AND ORGANIZATION

Two themes will emerge in the analysis of the material presented in subsequent chapters, one dealing with problems directly associated with the nature of the productive process and another relat-

[11] A more detailed description of the various laboratories is given in Appendix A.

ing to the effect of management procedures or management attempts to control the productive process. Each of these I view as an independent factor acting to produce the consequences we have already reviewed. In understanding these effects we can see that management is confronted with the given conditions of the work itself and the people who must do it. These constitute the background of the problem. Therefore, my first task will be to describe what engineers do in a large systems development laboratory. A principal reason for this is to counteract some of the occupational myths that exist about the engineer-inventor, and to illustrate the fact that the problems of underutilization and consequent engineer dissatisfaction are inherent in the nature of the productive process. For what we shall see is that the microdivision of labor and the lack of individual responsibility are consequences of organizational necessity.

The second given, the work force of engineers employed to carry out the tasks of the laboratory, is the next topic for exploration. The question here is the match between individual goals, interests, and aspirations, and the characteristics of the work. So, for example, one set of explanations is plausible if engineers are professionally rather than organizationally oriented, as is claimed in much of the literature. But quite a different analysis results if engineers, like management, are generally oriented toward success in the organization and toward the practical matter of success in the marketplace. Therefore, since we find the latter to be true, since the professional model is largely inapplicable, our analysis points in the direction of problems associated with influence, mobility, and status within the organization, as opposed to autonomy, recognition, and status within the profession. Underutilization and its consequent dissatisfaction are not manifestations of the often cited professional-managerial conflict.

But if underutilization would be relatively easy to understand as a conflict between professional aspirations and business necessities, it is not so easy to comprehend in this new context. Why should underutilization exist where business management and engineers are basically in accord on the fundamental aims of engineering? I deal with this question in two chapters. First, I examine why an engineer expresses feelings of underutilization, why he says, "I would prefer to do more." And second, I look at some of the factors that explain why entire organizations differ considerably in the level of underutilization they exhibit. For in addition to the differences between laboratory and field organizations, we find that large differences exist among the various laboratory locations within the Electromech company.

Some of the answers provided by the analysis suggest the final questions to be asked. Thus it becomes clear that misutilization and underutilization are quite different situations. Engineers are misutilized when they are assigned to clerical or technical tasks beneath their capabilities, when they are assigned tasks that could be handled by technicians. Underutilization—wanting to do more—represents the fact that engineers literally have not enough to do. And while it is difficult to accept this fact, underutilization seems to be analogous to frictional unemployment on the level of an entire society. It seems also to be closely associated with the phenomenon of dissatisfaction among engineers.

But why should this be so? The answer lies in the two organizational factors we identified earlier. Thus part of the problem is inherent in the work process itself. The more complex the division of labor, the greater the problems of coordination and time sequencing. And since systems engineering is fundamentally a group effort, the failures of coordination and the out-of-sequence position of some projects will leave the engineer at times with no organizationally relevant tasks. The larger the system and the more complex the division of labor, the greater the probability of underutilization.

But the second part of the problem can be traced directly to management's control activities. For what emerges dramatically from the data is the fact that a good part of the underutilization and dissatisfaction mirrored in the responses of engineers can be traced directly to management's efforts to improve utilization and to increase the effectiveness with which it allocates the financial resources at its disposal. Management's attempts to allocate development effort to projects it deems most worthwhile result predictably in the removal of technical influence from lower levels of the organization to higher levels. And termination of projects and the reassignment of individuals contribute to the underutilization problem. For again it is quite clear from our data that higher satisfaction and less underutilization go hand in hand with greater local control or influence. Where local management, as opposed to division, is in a position to control the allocation of its own resources, the situation improves.

As a final task I will attempt, first, to relate these findings to certain systematic positions taken by other researchers in the field of organizations, and second, to explore the implications of these findings for management policy. This latter task I address by comparing some currently proposed solutions to the findings that emerge from this study. And if we find there is no panacea for the ills diagnosed, it is also well to remember that the solutions to new and difficult problems do not come without first specifying and redefining the problem.

RESEARCH IN THE TRADITION OF THE CASE STUDY

The data that form the basis of this study have been gathered at various times by various methods. However, they have one unifying feature. Each of the component studies was aimed in some way at helping the management of Electromech to understand better the problems it faced and what to do about them. Now, to some this may seem a disadvantage. It is certainly not "pure" research and there is definitely a desire on the part of management to attack problems as it sees them, not as the researcher might see them. But this management pressure can be handled, and at least one advantage follows from this situation; not the least of what a researcher learns comes through feeding back the research results to management and trying to answer the questions and the "so what" that result. That these questions are sometimes hostile—posed by a skeptical and occasionally threatened management—adds rather than detracts from the learning. This situation generates a healthy motivation to seek flaws and inconsistencies in the data, especially when the conclusions are at variance with reality as management has come to view it. Management is far from convinced that the behavioral attributes of organizations can be measured, and it seems as though management would be happier if it could dismiss the results as pure illusion.

But coexisting with this skepticism is a behavior pattern, especially true of the technical manager, that leads him to try to explain the results he sees. And the simpler this explanation the better. This is the real value of the process. For example, during one such research review, a group of managers was studying a set of data dealing with differences in manpower utilization in different laboratory locations. There were twelve geographically separate organizations involved. After looking at the data for a minute or so, an engineering executive said, "One thing I see is that labs managed by our older, more experienced managers look better than those with newer managers." He went on to point out that more effective utilization of the manpower in these laboratories was a consequence of the managers knowing their jobs better. Yet as we discussed that explanation, others in the room came up with exceptions, and I myself thought of others, enough to discredit the explanation. At this point someone said, "I'll tell you one thing that this chart proves, it shows that the farther you get from Corporate Staff executives the happier you are." Everyone laughed and I myself dismissed his observation as more or less a coincidence. But later analysis convinced me that a 1000-to-1 chance can hardly be dismissed as coincidence, that there are some very good reasons why the pattern should appear. And I will discuss those reasons in later chapters. But the point is this: I am not sure I ever would have thought of that by myself. Not because the idea is intellectually profound, but simply because it isn't the kind of thing a researcher is likely to look for. What happens is that the researcher builds up a store of very particular knowledge about the organization, suborganizations, and key people. This knowledge is certainly useless as formal research data, but is of enormous value in interpreting results from quantitative studies. The result, then, of this combination of surveys, interviews, and discussions with management is in the tradition of the case study combined with the methodology of the sample survey. And as the reader will see, at times the explanation of the quantitative analysis is based on knowledge gained through observation and knowledge of company folklore. Nevertheless, as with the case study, the aim is to arrive at generalizations that are applicable to a class of organizations.

METHODOLOGY

As I have stated, the analyses presented here are the results of a combination of questionnaire surveys and other less formal methods of gathering data. In fact, data from a number of different surveys are used, but where the survey is not described in more detail I refer to a company-wide survey of 4,582 nonsupervisory technical professionals in the Electromech Corporation. This group represents about a 70 per cent return in a total census survey of the development engineering activity in that company in the late fall of 1964. Of this group the large majority hold engineering degrees, though some have drifted into other kinds of support activity—for example, programming. Therefore, about 55 per cent report themselves as currently engaged in either electrical or mechanical engineering. Another 30 per cent report a current specialty in physics, mathematics, other applied science, or programming. The remaining 15 per cent are those who did not choose to classify themselves, or those in such specialties (discussed in Chapter 2) as engineering market planning or systems analysis. Finally, by degree level we have 3 per cent Ph.D.'s, 20 per cent Masters, 60 per cent Bachelors, and a remaining 17 per cent without any degree who have been classified by the company as professionals by way of experience and performance of job duties. In terms of service with the company, the group is relatively young. Eighty-five per cent have been with Electromech twelve years or less, while 25 per cent have been with the company less than two years.

The survey itself was administered to the respondents on company time and the booklets were filled in on the job. It is probably worth mentioning that for many of the respondents it was not the first time such a survey had been taken. This survey was simply one of a series of such given every other year or so.

In addition to the survey of nonsupervisory professionals, there was also an identical survey of all first-line supervisory engineers.

Data from this supervisory group are presented in several instances to reinforce the conclusions from the analysis of nonsupervisory data, but are never presented in combination with those data.

All survey booklets were identified by laboratory location and by project within that location. In this way each engineer could be guaranteed individual anonymity, but the analysis of different units within the locations could be performed. I have used an analysis by units only once, but the analysis of differences among the laboratory locations forms the basis for some of the more interesting conclusions arrived at in this research study. So, for example, while it might be assumed that different geographical locations within a company should be homogeneous, they are definitely not so. The importance of this is that correlations and other measures of association computed on the basis of the entire population comprise not one, but two sources of variation—differences among individuals within laboratories and some rather large differences among the laboratories.

Now the somewhat intriguing result of analyzing these effects separately is that some sizable correlations in the over-all population turn out to be the result almost entirely of differences among locations. That is, the association between two variables—for example, underutilization and influence—is almost wholly attributable to concomitant differences among the laboratory locations on mean levels of these two variables. For this reason any analysis of the association between variables reflecting attributes of individuals has been carried out *within* a given laboratory population. My procedure has been to use two typical, rather large laboratory locations and run identical analyses for each group. Each is a systems development laboratory engaged primarily at the time of the analysis in a schedule or time-oriented final design development mission. Each, however, is large enough to support varied activity. It is only where the results of these separate analyses turn out to be substantially the same that I have used the combined results to support the argument.

The rather large differences among the locations afford the opportunity to assess the effect of policies as opposed to individual situations. That is, individual responses can be (and often are) explained away as being the result of differences in perception, motivation, or expectations. This is not so easy to do when entire organizations are involved. So, for the analysis of these differences I have used twelve laboratory locations distributed geographically throughout this country. They vary considerably in size; still, the smallest has a population of over 100 technical professionals, the largest approximately 1000. Since these laboratories belong to different divisions of the Electromech Corporation, I have coded them by using the same initial letter for laboratories in the same division (e.g., Avondale and Aurora).

Finally, the reader will find few "tests of significance" herein. The reasons are simple. First, the group sizes are so large that conventional significance levels are reached well before the magnitudes are worthwhile looking at. And second, tests of significance are misleading in any event. I obviously have culled hundreds of tables and thousands of correlations and other assorted measures in arriving at the results presented here. Probability levels are consequently distorted. My point of view in presenting the data is that the real tests are plausibility, consistency, and reproducibility.

The rank correlations based on twelve observations present a different problem. The chance of observing a sample correlation as large as .50 between variables whose parent populations are in fact uncorrelated is about 1 in 10. Obviously, relatively large correlations in this situation can be the product of random processes. Thus, my criteria again must be consistency and pattern.

With this background complete, we are now ready to move on.

2 Engineers at Work

> Before we start I want to get it straight with you what I mean by an engineer. I think that a lot of the difficulty that the younger engineers have is that they don't know what an engineer does. There is a difference between an engineer and a scientist. An engineer works with hardware and schedules. In some respects he must compromise design with schedules. Practice is an important element in his success. The chance to make decisions is important because if you get the chance and make the right decision once, you will get the opportunity a second time. Young men right out of school don't know the difference between an engineer and a scientist and they are disappointed when they find out what an engineer does.[1]

This caveat was given me by an experienced engineer at the start of an interview. What he said is not true of all engineers, of course, but he pointed out a fact of life for the majority of development engineers. In this chapter I will try to uncover some of the reasons why this is so, why the majority of engineers use little advanced theory, little mathematics, and much practical sense and experience. For I have the feeling that the purpose and scope of engineering is largely misunderstood by the nonengineer. There is an occupational myth that engineering is precise, analytical, and mathematical. And some engineering work is. But it is also cut and try, derived from experience, and consequently nonmathematical.

Another myth is embodied in the logically satisfying belief that the development engineer translates current science into technology —a midwife between scientific knowledge and production. This

[1] Ritti, "Engineers and Managers," unpublished doctoral dissertation, p. 118.

again is largely untrue. Industrial research would be much easier to justify if this translation could be demonstrated. The fact is that the bulk of development engineering is art that builds on previous art. Principles established by science are used, no doubt. Yet the engineer relies more on his vendor's salesmen than he does on the resident scientist.[2]

Consequently, if systems development engineering is not what the occupational myths would have it to be, the task at hand is one of arriving at a better understanding of the work itself. For the core of the problem we are investigating apparently lies here. We know that engineers commonly cite "challenging work" as their primary job requirement. But what does this mean? How does the term "challenging work" translate into a specific set of work attributes, and what is it about the work organization of the development laboratory that creates "the unhappy engineer"?

WORKING IN THE DEVELOPMENT LABORATORY

Engineers are paid for their ability to achieve a practical end. They are fairly well specialized in a field of endeavor. Experience gives an engineer a feel for what will work and what will not work. The bulk of engineering development is done qualitatively first—from experience—then tested to determine the precise characteristics of the result. Modifications are made if the results do not meet specification. Engineering principles and relationships are used to inform the analysis—to suggest trial values—rather than to establish the design.

There are several good reasons for this. First, it is usually faster to do things this way. Second, because a machine, device, or system must operate under real as opposed to ideal conditions, the analyti-

[2] This is a personal observation, but I know of two studies that back it up. One shows "the vendor" providing twice the ideas of "company research." See Allen, "Sources of Ideas and Their Effectiveness in Parallel R&D Projects," Alfred P. Sloan School of Management, M.I.T., Working Paper #13065, 1965. Another study reported in "Career Comments," *Machine Design* xxxv (June 6, 1963), 114, shows that even when engineers recognize that a problem calls for considerable "basic or applied" research they generally work on the problem themselves rather than go to a researcher.

cal procedures that exist are not good enough or do not apply. There are too many interactions between components of the system or too many nonideal conditions to be coped with. Analytical formulas are derived under precisely controlled conditions, but engineering is done in the real world. Engineering is an art in its own right.

Many more engineering man-hours are spent in upgrading existing systems than in developing entirely new systems. The new system structure is very much in the pattern of the old, upgraded through experience, and with increased system performance. Furthermore, some development laboratory endeavors are not at all like engineering as the word is commonly used. Yet they are performed by graduate engineers because they must be—or because presumably no one else can perform them.

A large part of the engineering activity in the systems development laboratory is comprised of tasks that can be described as *formatted.*[3] The essential nature of the formatted task is that it can be learned as a self-contained specialty, independent of background knowledge. The familiarization of relevant background knowledge may help in the early stages of *learning* the task, but be of little or no value in *performing* it. A formatted task is one which is governed largely by relatively fixed procedures, standards, rules, which are relatively free of ambiguity and contingencies. Formatted tasks are not necessarily easy to learn—they may be quite complicated. Thus, the wiring rules for laying out the placement of modules and wires in newer technologies are very complex.

Performing some formatted tasks may demand considerable ingenuity and ability to commit procedures to memory. A nonengineering example is the solving of crossword puzzles. In education, solving the problems at the end of each chapter in a physics or engineering text is an example of a formatted task. All (or practically all) of the information necessary to solve the problem is contained in that chapter and preceding chapters. Computers can—and do—solve that class of problem.

What all this means is that the majority of engineers are occupied

[3] I am indebted to Dr. R. B. Miller for his concept of formatted tasks. In certain of the passages that follow I have used Miller's own language to describe the nature of formatted activities in systems development engineering.

in the performance of formatted tasks created for them by the innovations of the minority. Even a handful of innovators (at the right time or place and in the right pattern of ability) can generate discoveries and inventions *in concept* that will create a horde of formatted tasks for practical implementation.[4] In lesser number, innovations in concept (such as transistor technology in its first days) will require a number of rule-generators: people who can grasp an idea and translate it into standard practices for implementation. This translation itself can be formatted (as when standard transistor circuits are substituted in the standards manual for standard tube circuits). Large systems development projects thus tend to be carried out by a work force of engineers performing such specialized, formatted tasks. Entire specialist functions arise devoted to particular segments of the development effort.

In the next few pages I shall describe the nature of the work in a representative sample of these functions.

Systems Technology. The following examples are drawn from groups performing certain specialist functions that serve those who design the product itself. Each of these groups is made up of people who have knowledge and experience of a restricted area of engineering applicable to the development of large systems.

One such function is the design of special circuits that will perform operations requested by the systems designers. Each system will use relatively few of these as compared to the standard circuits. Instead of each systems group designing its own special circuits there is a central group that provides the service as well as maintaining some standardization of systems technology. They use standard components and work with a catalogue of circuits that have been designed previously. Past designs are used if they will meet current requirements. However, more often than not the identical circuit cannot be used.

Here is an example of a typical problem. The task involves designing a circuit to modify the signal coming from a unit designed

[4] This is not unique to systems engineering or to engineering for that matter. A former teacher of mine, Isadore Blumen, used the term "mathematical janitors" in describing the tasks of the multitude engaged in cleaning up the details of breakthroughs made by the few great mathematicians.

in one solid-state technology to be accepted by a remote unit in a different technology. The signal must be modified and the time required for transfer of the pulse taken into account. Past experience suggests the type of circuit and the configuration is then laid out. This takes perhaps two days, but there are problems.

First, the type of transistor chip specified for this circuit is scarce. Manufacturing has committed its entire output to previously established production requirements. Manufacturing argues that no part of the output can be spared. Given this attitude, the special circuit design group tries now to redesign the circuit using a different type of transistor. And the method of design itself is interesting. In this particular problem the analytic methods available to determine the circuit parameters are inadequate (as they apparently are in most cases) and the method of design is one of making estimates, building the circuit, and testing it to see what the results will be. In this case the process takes perhaps two weeks and produces only negative results. None of the alternatives that seem reasonable produce the desired effects. As the group leader describes the procedure: "Now we got political; we wrote memos about the transistors that we were going to need and got the systems people to back us up because they needed the circuit."

But the problem is not completely solved. Since the transistor chips are designed to be part of a compound solid logic circuit, they are not packaged as individual transistors and have no provision for accepting individual circuit input or output leads. Thus more effort is necessary to find someone in manufacturing who is willing to make a special run of transistor modules usable for the circuit test. Remember that testing the circuit is a necessary part of the design job. The group leader again points out the function of experience: "After doing the job for a couple of years you get to know who the right people are and who to go to when you have a problem. A new man could spend weeks [searching for help]." Writing the specifications of the circuit in complete form and documenting the circuit parameters for the system designer complete the design process.

Note the insignificant amount of "real engineering" in the total process. Experience dictates design and short-cuts analytical procedures. But bargaining and the exploration of alternative solutions take considerable time and energy. In this case the entire design process took between two and three months. Just laying out the appropriate circuits to meet the initial requirements took perhaps two or three days. I asked the group leader how long it would take a new electrical engineer to learn to design these circuits. He replied that about one and a half years would be sufficient. After about four and a half years an engineer starts performing his job by rote and learns very little that is new. At this point the assumption of greater responsibility as a group leader and then as a project manager provides opportunity for broader experience and continued career development.

Another example from the systems technology area serves to illustrate why engineering is often more art than precise analysis. Each engineer responsible for a part of the final system wants to make sure that his design will function well. One strategy is to inflate somewhat the requirements for designs that have a "common interface" with his own. Where a safety factor is required an engineer may exaggerate his requirements. The following example was given by an engineer working a heat transfer group.

> One thing you have to learn is that these specifications have a fudge-factor in them. You have to check on them. I remember getting one set of design specifications from the [systems designers] that specified 500 watts of power dissipation. That didn't sound right to me so I checked. What I found was that they have a power supply of only 400 watts, so how could they dissipate 500? This happens pretty often. We usually check on them.

Fudging specifications is clearly one way of ensuring success for your own designs, and perhaps at the expense of someone else. If you have forgotten something there is less to worry about. Unfortunately, the other man is also trying to ensure his own success and conflict occurs. Resolving such conflict takes time and energy in ascertaining the correct specifications and bargaining for a compromise.

One further example serves to illustrate the function of the vendor or salesman of engineered products. This example involves a chemical engineer who is responsible for the selection and evaluation of materials. In this case he was seeking an adhesive with special optical properties. I think I assumed that he would perform this function by cooking up some concoction in his test tubes, but it turns out that he never does this. First he consults his charts for the optical properties of different kinds of plastic resins, and then he writes to the manufacturers of these to find out if they have anything that will fit the specifications. The manufacturers, in turn, write back and often supply the names of other users who have requested similar materials. In this way he tracks down a suitable material, then proceeds to evaluate the material and document its properties. No test tubes, no concoction, no "creativity" required.

Systems Unit Design. The systems unit designer is a key figure in system development. Three or four designers usually work as a group on a project. The assignment to the designer is laid out in general terms by the systems planner who prepares the master plan or general flow chart of how the system is to work. The system is then divided into traditional "boxes" or functions. By "traditional" is meant what has been done in previous generations of this type of system. The manager of the design group then partitions a box into assignments for the individual designers.

The task of the designer is to describe the network and timing needed to perform the specified function. He will attempt to minimize the number of physical components needed for the job (in order to save dollar costs), minimize time lengths between elements, and minimize redundancies.

The correctness of his network depends on his knowledge of rules, the requirements of the function to be designed, and design "housekeeping"—keeping clerical track of what he has done and still has to do. As a specialist, he will be familiar with a history of alternatives on solving this class of problem. He may consult the library or other sources of precedent. The optimization of his design is mostly a matter of his skill, his diligence, and the project schedule.

The "state of the art" produces on occasion a "better general solution" for the design of a given class of system functions. However, the field of system design that we are dealing with here has no "theory": it is a set of practices and rules which can be applied with greater or lesser skill and facility. When I asked a design group about the importance of formal college training, one of them said this: "E.E. has been irrelevant to everything that I have done in this laboratory, and I have done almost everything there is to do." The others all agreed this was true.

The typical designer rarely thinks of detailed systems design as a lifetime career. His current activity therefore is regarded as one more assignment. It is a transition. As a consequence, he tends to lack the emotional involvement with the subject matter that many scientists feel about their domain of inquiry. Rather typically, the scientist is ready to dedicate a lifetime to a program in which his current research is a step. The engineer becomes engrossed in solving the specific task on which he is working during that day or week. But he is relatively uninterested in adding to the conceptual foundations of the state of the art.

When asked what career development meant, engineers showed no lack of agreement in this area. It means getting into management. It means more money. It means having an increased variety of work, working on a broader scope, and doing different things. As one engineer put it: "It means that your individual viewpoint on what should be done becomes more important and you get a better chance to use it."

Engineering Market Planning. A substantial segment of the laboratory work force is made up of engineers who interface between those actually designing systems and those marketing them. The planning function is involved in handling requests for special features to be added to "standard" systems. The job involves receiving a request from the field for a special feature and ultimately returning to the field a price quotation for the cost of that additional feature. In this role of go-between, the market planner tries to define and clarify what the customer wants. In the process he will attempt to modify or standardize an engineering design so that one design will serve as many different customers as possible. He acts as a protective buffer that keeps the customer at a distance.

> We pretty much classify the salesman as on the customer's side. I remember one case where the salesman was busy selling a product that didn't exist. When I called him about it, he told me, "We don't want to hear about your technical problems."

It seems that the special function of market planning has arisen in an attempt to manage the conflict inherent in the relations between marketing and engineering. But little engineering per se is necessary. A market planner told me, "I took calculus all the way up to the top; I never used any of it." He also pointed out the necessity of experience and knowledge of the company product in performing the job. "One of our top engineers could go some place else and be a dud. He's got to learn all over again."

Summary. These descriptions of the Electromech work environment counteract some of the occupational myths of engineering, in particular the myth of the engineer-inventor. Many engineers in any systems design environment must of necessity pursue routine, uninventive tasks. That there are also many engineering jobs in Electromech that can be described as innovative and exciting, jobs that do match the myth of the engineer-inventor, is true. However, these jobs are in the minority because they must be.

WORK ORGANIZATION: ACHIEVING THE GOALS OF THE BUSINESS

The business aims of the company dictate the system of work organization. The major resource of a development laboratory is manpower, and the major cost is manpower together with the physical plant necessary to house that manpower. Though we talk of allocating resources in terms of dollars, we are talking about allocating individuals. The social fact of resource allocation has very little to do with individual desires. Personnel involved in various projects often have no choice in their own assignments—they are assigned. And this is an important part of being a member of the work force as opposed to being a "professional." The work force is applied to meet the needs of the business in such ways as the policy-making members of the organization (i.e., "management") deem most effective. Only the politically astute engineer is able to prearrange his next work assignment through informal channels. All this means that an individual can get stuck on an undesirable project or in an undesirable function through no fault of his own, and have a great deal of difficulty in getting out. Military organizations and development laboratories have a lot in common—except that the latter have less equipment.

In this kind of environment work roles are established for both individuals and groups with the following objectives in view:

1. The organization must be responsive to market demands and changes in the market position of competitors.

2. The organization must have a pool of talent available on short notice that is able to perform required engineering functions.

3. The organization must maintain a current capability in the technologies required to produce new systems.

Predictability of performance is the chief requirement, and control is the primary motivator of administrative policy. The common supposition that creativity is wanted is misleading. Innovation that challenges control is sometimes tolerated, but seldom welcomed.[5] Meeting the schedule within the budget, turning out a product that does the job *only as well as it needs to be done:* these are the goals of laboratory management. The need for certainty as the product announcement or shipping dates approach forces engineering development to become a production operation. Efficiency and predictability in the engineering enterprise become more important than creativity, despite moralizing to the contrary.

I am not saying that innovation per se is unwelcome, but that innovation that upsets control is something no well-run development laboratory can tolerate. This is why laboratories will bureaucratize the function of creativity. Management designates groups (e.g., Advanced Technology) whose mission is innovation—subject to management scrutiny of budget and output. In this way the cost of innovation and its end products can be evaluated and controlled.

[5] This is a strong statement but again there are a few studies to back it up. Hansen and Marquis, "Can Creativity Be Predicted in Research Professionals?" Alfred P. Sloan School of Management, M.I.T., Working Paper #73-64, 1964, find a positive relationship between performance ratings and creative ability in research laboratories, but no correlation in development laboratories. In fact, for those rated in the lower half on performance in development there is a negative correlation between the measure of creative ability and performance rating. This suggests that creative engineers with few other redeeming features will be regarded as problems in the development laboratory. (Personal communication from D. G. Marquis.) See also Pelz and Andrews, *Scientists in Organizations*, p. 173.

Division of Labor among Organization Units. This emphasis on control and predictability through work organization has its impact on job activities. For one thing, specialization of functions leads to increased rationality of the division of labor and hence (so it is thought) to better control.

One of the most pervasive notions in industry is that task specialization leads to greater efficiency and better control. If a person or group is required to do only one task or specialty, and if he and others like him are the only ones performing this task or specialty, then not only will the job be done better but it will also be done more nearly alike in each job and for all projects. If one group designs all your electronic circuits, this group obviously should be more expert than any nonspecialist group. In addition, all your systems will have standard circuits, and if problems should develop you know who is "responsible."

Now, the effectiveness of this kind of specialization is often debated among managers. Different schemes are presented and find their adherents. Yet it seems to me that the most common outcome of such discussions is that, given the circumstances, there is really no other way to do the job. And that is my point. Specialization of departmental activities is a necessary consequence of the technological situation. In fact, recent evidence in the literature on organizations shows that successful firms tend to evolve systems of work organization that are similar to those typical of firms employing their own kind of productive process.[6] Put somewhat differently, the system of work organization is an outcome, a consequence of the technological factors involved. It is not an independent factor to be set in the "one best way" or to the taste or beliefs of the management. And so it seems to me that the issue here is not the relative effectiveness of different schemes of work organization; rather it is the satisfactoriness of the tasks that result from the technologically determined mode of work organization.

One such effect is on the social characteristics of the job. Less time is spent actually doing the task and more in "interfacing" or

[6] I refer here to the work of Woodward, *Industrial Organization,* and Lawrence and Lorsch, *Organization and Environment.* These works will be reviewed in more detail in Chapter 9.

finding the people who are supposed to do it for you. Consider, for example, the situation in which this engineer finds himself:

> I believe that service groups are used too much and as a result an engineer becomes more of a coordinator than anything else. As a result, the efficiency of the company goes down. For example: I once wanted to order a development level [device]. Here is a list of the people I had to contact to get it:
> 1. Purchasing
> 2. Manager of drafting
> 3. Drafting (artwork)
> 4. Photography lab
> 5. [Device] manufacturing group
> 6. [Device] layout group

The impact of this kind of thing on satisfaction is illustrated directly in our survey data. In Division F the three laboratories are organized along identical lines and it thus becomes possible to compare attitudes of engineers in different types of assignment. Since the data from each of the three locations show the same picture, we can have confidence that the results are attributable to the type of task. In this case I looked at three types of department groups:

1. Groups that are complete projects in themselves. That is, they may be parts of a larger system but in themselves they are integral projects.
2. Groups that are parts of larger projects.
3. Groups that are involved in providing specialized services to others.

There are slightly over 200 professionals representing each of these types.

When asked how often they found their work satisfying, 64 per cent of those on complete projects replied "usually," while 50 per cent and 43 per cent respectively of those in the part project and service groups felt the same way. Even larger differences resulted when these engineers were asked how often "your part of the project is of great importance in the final system." Seventy-two per cent on complete projects said "usually," while the figures for part project and service groups dropped to 55 per cent and 41 per cent respectively.

In summary, then, the need for effective work organization results in a division of labor among work groups that has a measurable effect on the job satisfaction of development engineers. The individual is not completely free to choose his task. Degree of specialization, importance of the work in total product development effort, and the currency of the technologies employed are dependent upon the mission of the group in the total effort of the laboratory or laboratory complex. And it is not only the intrinsic interest of the work that is involved. Careers are at stake—or so it may seem to the man who is caught in an unwanted work assignment. One engineer was concerned enough about his assignment to write this letter to his top management:

> [My concern] is that we who are phasing out [old technology] systems are apparently being left behind in several ways. The majority of effort in Electromech (that effort which I see) is being directed toward our [new technology] line. . . . What becomes of us who are phasing out [the old technology]? Do we remain stationary? Phasing out the [old technology] project is a large job requiring technically competent personnel, and as such I do not feel that such a job should be a drawback to them. By the time [the old technology project] is phased out, most of the promotions will have rightly been given to deserving and competent people. What of the others who were not involved early with the development and production of [new technology systems]? Are we not equally important . . . ?

The Development Cycle. A major factor in the work organization of project groups is the development cycle. Product development projects have a life cycle that may last from several months to a number of years. During this cycle the nature of work and the number of engineers required will vary considerably. Perhaps the most difficult problem in development laboratory administration is the allocation of human resources to the various development projects currently under way. The most bothersome feature of the development cycle is that the work load can take on some of the features of heavy auto traffic: jammed up here, thinned out to nothing over there, completely stalled, or going like hell to make up for lost time. This characteristic provoked the following comment from an obviously unhappy engineer:

> I think that better utilization of manpower should and can be achieved. In development work there seem to be just two speeds, mad haste or maddeningly slow. Perhaps some small projects can be kept available to serve a dual purpose,
> a) to enhance our position through diversification, and
> b) to provide a more even workload for the lab employees.

The development cycle can be described as a series of phases through which a project must pass.[7]

Phase 1. Funds have been committed to the project and engineers are being brought in as the project effort grows. Design specifications are not set and there is considerable exploratory work and testing of ideas. Cost and schedule pressures are at a minimum.

Phase 2. The design direction has been chosen and the design details are being worked out. The project is at maximum size and the work can still be described as challenging. However, there is little room for major new ideas at this point. Cost and schedule pressures are mounting and reach a maximum at the end of this phase.

Phase 3. The initial design work is complete and the major effort is being devoted to working the bugs out of the design through testing of prototype models. The work has become less challenging but the pressure remains high. The project continues at a maximum level of manpower.

Phase 4. The design is complete. The major bugs have been worked out and the "nitpicking" details of phasing out the development effort remain. Changes are still being made, however, and the documentation and engineering drawings must be completed and brought up to date. All this seems like an endless task and is described as "grunt work" or "dog work." The fortunate engineers have been reassigned to other projects and the ones who are left are generally unhappy.

Phase 5. "Empire" maintenance. Project groups tend to have a life of their own. Historically, it is less difficult to form a group than it is to dissolve one. For this reason project groups without current as-

[7] I think that there are other equally valid ways of describing the development cycle, and I am not suggesting that these phases exist as clearly marked stages of development. What I hope to show in this discussion is the dynamic nature of development work and the fact that the work itself changes considerably over a period of time.

signments remain for a time in what is politely called a "study phase." During this time a core of engineers remaining in the group will write proposals, casting about for new project commitments. This can be both an interesting and a demoralizing period. If no proposals are accepted the group will probably be broken up and reassigned in various areas of the development effort. This is generally seen as a step backward in career progress because the engineer must begin again building his reputation with new management.

Here is a partial account of what can happen when an engineering project moves from an earlier into a later phase. The writer is an Electromech engineer who was asked to describe a project cycle.[8] His account starts with his impressions of the relatively high morale of his associates at Electromech compared to other places he has worked. He then points out:

> Up to this time my management had encouraged individual thinking, and morale in the group was rather high. After the [documentation] process started, I found that my morale and the morale of others in the group decreased exponentially with the increase of paper that we handled each day. The tasks involved were sheer dog work. I found that my management's attitude changed, and that my manager was no longer receptive to suggestions to better the system and eliminate some routine dog work.
>
> It appalled me that it took a long time to convince the right people that a hand stamp should be made so that the pages would be hand-stamped and the location and part number written in. Even then it would have been easier to put the part number and location in a title block—but this of course was a major change and could not be done because no budget was approved to change the available [procedures]; even if this change meant a large decrease in engineering time essentially wasted so that the system could be perpetuated.
>
> It just startled me to see a complete change in my management's attitude, which, together with literally pounds of paper endlessly passing through my hands, led to a rather demoralizing state over a period of several months.

Through this description I have tried to illustrate that work assignments are very much a function of an inevitable cycle in the de-

[8] Again I am indebted to R. B. Miller for the quoted material. This section is taken from a term paper submitted in one of Dr. Miller's classes for Electromech engineers.

velopment process. There is no choice for these engineers. The job needs to be done and engineers are assigned to carry out that job. At times the work does not require their individual skills and abilities. But the primary goal is getting the job done within the allotted time and with the budgeted funds. Engineers realize this, and while they don't like it, they will generally concede that such work assignments are necessary and are justified because no one else is available to do them. Thus, though two thirds of our survey group felt that they had been assigned jobs during the past year that could have been handled by someone with less technical training than themselves, only one quarter of this group felt that assignment to such jobs was not justified. The nearly unanimous comment of those who felt the assignment was justified was that "there was no one else available to do it."

Superimposed on the development cycle are two other special circumstances which impact the work assignments of engineers and may cause considerable grief. These are decommitment of funds and scheduled overtime.

Decommitment. Projects are killed at various stages of development for several reasons. Projects compete for limited resources. When development projects are periodically reviewed there is generally a reallocation process. Lagging projects considered important receive funds and manpower from projects considered marginal. The marginal projects are then broken up. And this can be a demoralizing experience, especially if an engineer has identified himself and his career with a project. For it is not necessarily that the project has been unsuccessful. Resources are needed elsewhere and they have to come from somewhere—he is the lucky winner. Management is often forced to make these decisions on the most arbitrary bases. Such decisions are extremely difficult to explain reasonably.

The other major reason for decommitment, of course, is that the project is deemed unlikely to be successful. This may happen when market demand has disappeared during the intervening period, or perhaps because progress has not been sufficient to warrant a further gamble of resources. Trouble for engineers develops because decommitment is generally quicker than recommitment. It takes time to figure out how best to reassign personnel. And even then, the match between abilities and assignments is problematic. As one laboratory manager put it, "When are we going to learn that you can kill the project but you can't kill the people along with it?"

Overtime. Regularly scheduled overtime (e.g., putting in an extra day a week) is assigned because a project is in trouble. While this is a common way to bail out a project, I think most managers recognize that scheduled overtime is not necessarily the best way of solving the problem. Overtime necessarily results in underutilization of skills. Managers assign overtime when a project is in trouble to protect themselves. They must present the image of having done everything possible within their power to bring the project off successfully. This, together with a characteristic lack of coordination in crash programs, leads to the inevitable result of engineers sitting around on overtime looking for something to do.

Scheduled overtime and its consequences supply a good illustration of the work force strategies employed in managing the resources of the development laboratory.

In summary, development laboratories exist in industry to help companies achieve success in competitive business enterprise. Such business aims inform the policies of development laboratory administration, and lead to a type of work organization that stresses:

1. A rather complex and specialized division of labor among organizational units and the engineers within those units.

2. An emphasis on rationality of organization, with control a primary aim and effectiveness of individuals second to the effectiveness of the total coordinated effort.

All this means that the development laboratory work environment is considerably different from the field environment. The work organization of the development laboratory is a contrived blend of the factory and the academic, stressing the effectiveness of collective as opposed to individual effort, and yet relying primarily on intellectual rather than manual or social skills.

WORK ORGANIZATION: ACHIEVING THE GOALS OF THE WORKERS

Work is the instrument through which the engineer achieves his personal goals. A successful demonstration of the ability to perform a difficult assignment will usually lead to interesting new assignments, advancement to positions of increased responsibility, and accompanying financial benefits. The dissatisfied engineer, the engineer who says "I would prefer to do more," is asking for the chance to demonstrate his ability and thus qualify for the attendant rewards. This set of circumstances is illustrated by a number of studies in the literature that deal directly with the function of work in satisfying the personal goals of engineers.

The best known of these is a study by Herzberg and his colleagues dealing with the various sources of satisfaction and dissatisfaction associated with the work of engineers and accountants.[9] Herzberg's major thesis is that factors in the work environment act differently to produce the motivation to work. His theory is that the job content factors—achievement, recognition, advancement, responsibility, and the work itself—serve as sources of job satisfaction and are central elements in motivation. On the other hand, job context factors such as working conditions, company policy, and supervision serve primarily to lower satisfaction, and do not contribute to the motivation to work. In brief, performance and the satisfaction of personal goals should be positively related for the content factors but not for the context factors.

Avoiding some of the polemic discussion of this work, I believe the theory soundly represents the fact that the absence of challenging work—work leading to achievement and recognition—will mean that important personal goals are not satisfied. Company policy, working conditions, interpersonal relationships, and the quality of supervision cannot produce high levels of motivation and goal achievement in the absence of challenging work assignments. Data from Herzberg show achievement, the recognition of this achievement, the work itself, and responsibility as the most frequently mentioned themes associated with high job satisfaction by the engineers in his sample. Advancement and salary are also mentioned relatively frequently.[10]

Danielson reports similar results for a group of engineers and scientists.[11] Unfortunately, the scientists (including some biochemists,

[9] Herzberg *et al.*, *The Motivation to Work.* [10] *Ibid.*, p. 101.

[11] Danielson, *Characteristics of Engineers and Scientists.*

biologists, and physicians)[12] have not been separated from the sample. However, the major sources of lack of goal satisfaction for this group are categorized as follows:

1. Poor utilization of abilities and skill
2. Unable to prove one's self
3. Lesser trained person could do job
4. Boredom or monotony[13]

Since there seems to be little doubt that engineers expect recognition for a job well done, Raudsepp asked a group of engineers, "What form of recognition—other than money—should engineers receive for an outstanding job performance or accomplishment?" He reports the following results:

> The most meaningful form of recognition for excellence would be advancement in position or, at least, eligibility for promotion. They feel that engineers who have proved their extraordinary technical capacity should be advanced along technical lines to positions which would further challenge and tap their special abilities. In other words, recognition should be reflected in increased responsibility and greater authority with more freedom in making engineering decisions.[14]

These results reinforce our notion that challenging work assignments are the first event in a sequence leading to achievement, recognition of that achievement, and advancement to greater responsibility and authority. But "challenging work" is a slogan rather than a description. Thus, before we can isolate the aspects of a job that make it "challenging," we must first achieve a more detailed understanding of the way in which development engineers perceive the actual dimensions of their work. Table 2.1 provides an organization of these perceptions in the results of a factor analysis of some forty-five work description statements.[15]

Before getting into a detailed discussion of these results I think a note of caution is necessary. Do not interpret the *per cent indicating*

[12] The sample of engineers and scientists is described more fully in Riegel, *Collective Bargaining as Viewed by Unorganized Engineers and Scientists*, p. 10.

[13] Danielson, *Characteristics of Engineers and Scientists*, p. 42.

[14] Raudsepp, "Money Isn't Everything," *Machine Design*, XXXVI (March 12, 1964), 132–34.

[15] A brief description of the factor analysis used here is given in Appendix B.

"*usually*" too literally. This is derived from scales anchored at *always* or *never* true of the job in which the engineer is working.[16] In terms of these frequency descriptions it is one thing to respond to the general statement, "Your project offers you a real chance to show what you can do," and quite another to respond to the specific statement, "You communicate your ideas to others in your profession through papers delivered at professional meetings." My reasoning is that in responding somewhere between *always* and *never*, an engineer is much more likely to say that he usually has a chance to show what he can do than he is to say that he is usually communicating his ideas at professional meetings. However, if this is kept in mind the frequency figures do present some useful bases for comparison.

Most of the dimensions are self-explanatory, but a few comments are in order. First, it would be easy to misinterpret the meaning of the dimension I have labeled *Individual Responsibility* out of the context of the development laboratory. The freedom of direction implied by this factor does not imply the same kind of freedom that a research scientist might have in developing research proposals. An engineer is most certainly not free to work on anything he chooses —at least not the majority of engineers. Their projects are part of programs planned by laboratory management. What the dimension conveys to me is that within the constraints of the projected system and within the over-all planning of development laboratory management the engineer is relatively free to pursue his assigned task as he chooses. Furthermore, he has been accorded the responsibility and discretion to do so.

My second comment deals with the fifth dimension—*Visibility of Individual Contributions* (scoring low on this dimension is associated with high visibility). The common thread running through this dimension is that the engineer is working on a project in which he is but one of a large number of contributors, and that consequently the effort that he puts into his fragment of the project can-

[16] The work characteristics descriptions were presented in the form of Likert-type scales with 11 alternatives running from 0 (never) through 10 (always). Engineers responded in terms of how often they found themselves working on the type of job described in the statement. I have arbitrarily defined the per cent responding "usually" as the per cent indicating 7 or above on this scale.

Table 2.1

Major Dimensions of Engineers' Work Descriptions

	Per cent indicating "Usually"
I. UTILIZATION	
Your project offers you a real chance to show what you can do	55
How would you rate the time (as opposed to intellectual) demands of your present job?	39[a]
How would you rate the intellectual demands of your present job?	30[a]
You feel that your assignment is below your technical capability[b]	28
II. THEORETICAL CONTENT	
You are free to explore new ideas about technology or systems	41
Knowledge of the latest theoretical results in your speciality is required	36
You use theoretical formulations in developing problem solutions	33
Your work enables you to publish articles in technical journals	16
You have the opportunity to follow your own theoretical interests whether or not they promise a "payoff" for the company	11
You communicate your ideas to others in your profession through papers delivered at professional meetings	6
III. IMPORTANCE TO BUSINESS	
Your part of the project is of great importance in the final system	58
Your work has a direct impact on the business success of Electromech	36
You have the opportunity to discuss the results of your work directly with those in higher management	34
The work you are doing is of special interest to higher management	33
You participate in decisions that affect the future business of the company	22
IV. INDIVIDUAL RESPONSIBILITY	
You have the freedom to adopt your own approach to the job	65
You are making *all* the decisions on matters that directly concern your technical responsibility	36
You and only you determine the path of action that you shall follow	27
V. VISIBILITY OF INDIVIDUAL CONTRIBUTIONS[c]	
The specifications of your part of the job have already been decided by others	30
Every step you take must be agreed upon by those with whom you work	13
Your contribution to the project is hidden beneath the work of others	13
No one in laboratory management seems to know what you are doing	13
Your part of the project seems trivial or routine	12
You are given clear detailed instructions as to how to proceed with the job	8

	Per cent indicating "Usually"
VI. UNCERTAINTY OF OBJECTIVES	
Your scheduled objectives are changed	40
You work in a well-ordered job situation where the requirements are clear [d]	31
The initial information that you have been given turns out to be wrong	14
Your final results "die a slow death," unused on the shelf	11
Your project is canceled just when you are starting to make real progress	7

[a] Per cent saying "quite or extremely heavy."

[b] This item is negatively correlated with "utilization."

[c] These items are all scored in reverse.

[d] This item is negatively correlated with "uncertainty."

not easily be recognized by management. I would expect that this kind of situation arises primarily in the development of big systems. While the Visibility dimension conveys the idea of set, inflexible objectives, it is different from dimension six—*Uncertainty of Objectives.* Objectives can be clear and the proper information in hand (i.e., objectives *not* uncertain) without the implication of large group effort and the consequent fragmentation of work. Neither does the clarity of objectives imply that the *details* of the work are already specified. The factor analysis shows the two dimensions to be relatively uncorrelated.

The only dimensions correlated with one another to an appreciable extent are *Individual Responsibility* and *Theoretical Content.* The reason for this seems to come from engineers working in the applied science areas. Generally, scientific work is a more individual pursuit and does emphasize theory.

The Satisfaction of Personal Goals. Now to link these work characteristics with the personal goals of engineers. Each engineer is given a composite score on each of the major dimensions of the work characteristics. First we compute the individual's average score for each set of items comprising the dimension as shown in Table 2.1. The same procedure is now carried out for a scale of personal goal satisfaction derived from a factor analysis of another group of questionnaire items. This goal satisfaction scale contains the following items:

—In general, would you say that the work you are presently doing is helping you to achieve your more important personal goals?

—Do you feel that your personal goals are being satisfied in your present position with Electromech?

—In general, would you say the work description you have just given us represents a satisfying kind of job for you?

—How well would you say your job "measures up" to what you want of a job?

Table 2.2 shows the results of a correlational analysis between the over-all satisfaction scale and each of the six work characteristics. The analysis is repeated in two major laboratories. These laboratories are both representative of Electromech and yet are quite different in work organization. Similar results ensure some generality in the findings.

Table 2.2

Correlation Between Goal Satisfaction and Six Characteristics of Work

Work characteristic	Correlation coefficient	
	Ferndale laboratory (F1) (N=457)	Darby laboratory (D1) (N=858)
Utilization of skills	61 (47)[a]	65 (52)
Visibility of individual contributions	42 (17)	49 (18)
Importance to business	38 (12)	39 (8)
Theoretical content	38 (10)	29 (9)
Individual responsibility	36 (11)	34 (20)
Uncertainty of objectives	−24 (17)	−43 (30)
All characteristics combined	70	76

[a] Figures in parentheses are fifth-order partial correlation coefficients. Decimal points omitted.

The most striking result of this analysis is that the several work characteristics are such strong predictors of goal satisfaction.[17] The association between the best composite predictor from the work characteristics and goal satisfaction is .70 for Ferndale and .76 for Darby. This high degree of association confirms that the work itself is of crucial importance in satisfying the personal goals of development engineers.

A second major outcome of the analysis is the importance of utilization of skills. Utilization is by far the single most effective predictor of goal satisfaction, showing high levels of both full and unique association. This again is in keeping with the ideas we have been developing about the functions of work in meeting the goals of engineers. Visibility of Individual Contributions is also highly correlated with goal satisfaction in both laboratories, and this also is to be expected from what we know of the work role and goals of engineers. Nonetheless, this analysis clearly shows utilization to be the most important factor. The additional five work dimensions contribute only 30 to 40 percent to our success in predicting the goal satisfaction scores. One reason for this is that the scores for the other work dimensions are themselves correlated with the utilization score. These correlations with utilization range in size from .40 (Visibility) to .17 (Uncertainty).

The source of these correlations is not difficult to apprehend. Jobs that are perceived as utilizing skills are likely to be jobs affording visibility of one's individual efforts, jobs that are important in the over-all development effort, and jobs that have a higher than average theoretical content. By the very definition of our *utilization* concept, the intellectual demands will be higher than average. The utilization dimension is thus in some ways a more general concept than the others. It is also a characteristic of the work environment that seems clearly to differentiate the work organization of the laboratory from that associated with other types of endeavor, especially the field.

[17] A brief description of the multiple regression technique is given in Appendix B.

SUMMARY

At this point it seems proper to draw together the various conclusions reached in this chapter and use these to ask some specific questions about the roots of the several problems discussed.

Engineers express nearly the lowest work satisfaction of the various occupational groups for which we have comparable data. Only production workers are less satisfied. The counterpart finding is that engineers and their technicians—the laboratory workers—stand out from these other occupational groups in their feelings of underutilization. And we have just confirmed that utilization is a key factor in satisfying engineers' personal goals.

In consequence of these facts, it seems that the major factor responsible for the attitudes of engineers is the work organization of the development laboratory, and especially ways in which it is different from the work organization of the field groups—the service engineers, for example. Our inquiry into the nature of laboratory work has pointed to the work-force flavor of the laboratory work environment. The work role of the majority of engineers involves the performance of formatted tasks as opposed to innovative ones. Such tasks have little provision for growth beyond a limited sphere of expertise, and afford even less opportunity for making a significant impact on technical policy. Furthermore, the smaller, simpler field organizations afford a visibility of individual contributions that must be significantly greater than in the laboratory.

A consistent finding in the literature dealing with the job satisfaction of various occupational groups is that the higher status groups in an organization have higher job satisfaction.[18] Status means position or rank in the organization, and implies certain rights and duties that are associated with that position. Higher status members of the organization have—almost by definition—more influence in guiding the affairs of that organization than do lower status members. Therefore, I would like to turn this finding upside down, to suggest that the relative job satisfaction of our laboratory group im-

[18] French, "The Social Environment and Mental Health," *Journal of Social Issues*, XIX (October, 1963), 43.

plies its organizational status, and that this status is consistent with the rights and duties of engineers as organization members, members of a development laboratory work-force.

Now, what I want to demonstrate in the next chapter is that this work-force status is deeply in conflict with the aims and expectations of engineers. And while this conclusion seems obvious from the foregoing material, the analysis of the source of this conflict is not so obvious. For a difference of opinion exists centering on the imputation to engineers of different sets of work goals. The favored explanation holds that engineers, as professionals, are thwarted in the achievement of the professional goals of freedom from the business concerns of the firm, of contribution to basic knowledge, and of advancement in their chosen profession rather than in their organization. Dissatisfaction and underutilization reflect the unwillingness of management to meet these goals.

My contention is that exactly the opposite is true. What the majority of engineers desire is more influence in business-oriented decisions, not less. What they want is the achievement of practical results—they tend to be impatient with excessive abstraction. And their desire is for advancement and responsibility within the organization. Subsequent analysis and understanding of the problems of the systems development laboratory hinge directly on the acceptance of one or the other of these points of view. For this reason we proceed now to an analysis and description of the work goals of engineers.

3

The Work Goals of Engineers

> When I first entered engineering . . . I was just interested in doing what an engineer does. I like to see something built physically. . . . You like to see your ideas put into something physical, to see something work, do something, see the lights flash.[1]

Descriptions of the problems encountered in the administration of professionals in industrial organizations often contain discussions of the goals of engineers and scientists, and how these goals clash with those of the business. The task of this chapter is to demonstrate some flaws in these ideas, to show that the work goals of engineers are not those of scientists and do not conform to the well-known professional model. Furthermore, I want to demonstrate that this is not the result of faulty or incomplete professional identity, and to present evidence that work goals and expectations tend to be consistent with the productive process involved, appropriate for the necessary task. Beyond this, it seems that conflict develops between goals and task when the work activity or the mode of organization differs considerably from the occupational norm—a shared set of expectations held by members of the occupation.

Parts of this chapter are taken from an earlier paper, Ritti, "Work Goals of Scientists and Engineers," *Industrial Relations*, VII (1968), 118–31.

[1] Percy Black, "The Engineer's Self-Image and His Image of [Electromech]," unpublished report.

CONFLICT BETWEEN THE SCIENTIFIC MIND AND THE MANAGEMENT MIND

From personal experience I can attest to the fact that there is considerable confusion among engineering administrators over the work aims of professional people in their development laboratories. Companies want to present a professional image to the scientific community. Active participation in professional societies (such as holding office) and publication of results are encouraged in many large companies, but often the response is discouraging. Administrators want their engineers to be more professional, and are concerned and puzzled when programs aimed at encouraging publication and society activity yield but modest results.

Uncertainty about the work goals of engineers stems from at least two sources. The first of these is the blanket use of the term *professional.* Most companies have roughly four classes of employee: blue-collar workers, clerical or administrative workers, supervisory management, and several groups generally exempt from the provisions of the Wages and Hours Act, but not in supervisory management. One such group primarily engaged in technical activities is generally dubbed "professional." The confusion that consequently arises stems from taking this definition too literally, and thinking about technical specialists in terms of values imputed to the older established professions (e.g., medicine, law, etc.). Here is an example of this type of reasoning taken from the management literature.

> The professional man, in line with the standards of his specific profession, is trained to obtain certain goals along his path toward professional maturity. Often these professional goals, weighted heavily by ideas of independent research and broad social service, are in conflict with such specific organization goals as optimum profit planning, preeminence in the industry, and so on.[2]

There is a quick assumption that technical specialists, as professionals, and business must be uneasy bedfellows.

A second source of confusion about the goals of engineers stems

[2] Campfield, "Motivating the Professional Employee," *Personnel Journal,* XLIV (1965), 427.

from reports that refer directly to engineers and scientists as a group. For example, a report issued by the Opinion Research Corporation presents as its major thesis the idea that there is a basic conflict between the goals pursued by management and those pursued by engineers and scientists.[3] Knowledge for its own sake is a primary goal of scientists and engineers, and they are thwarted in achieving this goal by management pressure for practical results.

> At the heart of the problem are the engineers' and scientists' expectations and ideals that are hard to fulfill in a business organization.
>
> This shows up in the image scientists and engineers have of themselves in contrast with their image of management . . . notice that two major expectations that stand out are unrealistic for the vast majority of technical professionals: (a) freedom from pressure, and (b) pursuit of knowledge for its own sake.[4]

Apparently, the search for a generalization about professional goals has led in some cases to a distortion of the facts, and in others to misleading interpretations. Yet company management continues to urge engineers to accept a professional identity, and the management literature mirrors this viewpoint.

On the other hand, social scientists have also been led to misinterpretations by dependence upon the literature on professions. Even those correctly making the distinction between engineers and scientists discuss the problems of engineering organizations in terms of an unavoidable conflict between business organizations and professionals. Commenting on a study showing a lack of "professional identification" among engineers, Kornhauser sees the problem as one of "the differential capacity of professions to engender a type of person who is capable of upholding professional standards in the face of pressures from non-professional organizations, notably industry and government." [5]

LOCALS AND COSMOPOLITANS

This clash between business goals and professional goals has been elaborated in terms of the work motivations of engineers and scien-

[3] Opinion Research Corporation, "The Conflict Between the Scientific Mind and the Management Mind" (1959), mimeographed report.

[4] *Ibid.*, p. 11. [5] Kornhauser, *Scientists in Industry*, p. 154.

tists. The labels *local* and *cosmopolitan* have been used to differentiate individuals whose primary loyalties are to their employing organization (locals) from those whose loyalty is primarily to their profession or field of specialty (cosmopolitans).[6] "Cosmopolitans" are more likely to be engaged in basic research.[7] Their field of interest necessarily spans work being done in many organizations (academic as well as industrial). "Locals" are more interested in application, working on technology that is applicable to the business aims of the company. The "local" type is expected to pattern his behavior and to measure his success against internal or company standards, the "cosmopolitan" to pattern his behavior and to measure his success against the standards of his entire profession or field of specialty. One inference resulting from the use of these terms has been that the "cosmopolitan" will be a "problem person" and the "local" a good employee.[8] From this point of view, the discussion of conflict between the scientific mind and the management mind is one postulating an inevitable conflict between scientist cosmopolitans and management locals.

These ideas about career orientation can be useful in thinking about organizational problems, but they can also be misleading. While there are those whom the label "local" or "cosmopolitan" fits perfectly, it is also true that the majority fall somewhere between, or are both, or—more importantly—that success in the organization does not preclude success in the specialty when organization goals and the goals of the specialty are the same.[9] Furthermore, the goals of certain specialties are far more consonant with business goals than others. Basic scientific research—the advancement of fundamental knowledge—is usually peripheral to the business goals of the company. Strains between business goals and the "cosmopolitan" scientific goals are bound to arise. Engineering, on the other hand, requires the "local" outlook. The creation of technology is without meaning if the technology is not marketed or otherwise put to use. A

[6] See Shepard, "Nine Dilemmas in Industrial Research," *Administrative Science Quarterly*, I (1956), 298.

[7] Kornhauser, *Scientists in Industry*, pp. 122–23.

[8] Shepard, "Nine Dilemmas in Industrial Research," *Administrative Science Quarterly*, I (1956), 298.

[9] See, for example, Glaser, *Organizational Scientists: Their Professional Careers*.

successful design is tested ultimately by competition with other designs, not by exposure to one's colleagues.

Looking at career orientation in this way, we would expect to find that engineers who are working in engineering development laboratories are primarily "locals."

THE "LOCAL" ENGINEER

Survey data from the Electromech development laboratory population show that the goals of engineers are generally in harmony with the aims of the business. Table 3.1 shows six major clusters or dimensions of these goals, and the percentage of the total population indicating the goal is very important for them.[10] These dimen-

Table 3.1

Major Dimensions of Engineering Goals

	Per cent indicating "Very Important"
I. BUSINESS GOALS	
Have the opportunity to help the company build its reputation as a first-class organization	72
Have the opportunity to help the company increase its profits	69
Work on problems that have practical applications important to your company	67
Have the opportunity to see the concrete results of what you have done	65
Know what the goals of your division are	61
Work on projects that have a direct impact on the business success of your company	48
Participate in decisions that affect the future business of the company	41
Participate in decisions that set the direction of technical effort in the company	38
II. TECHNICAL GOALS	
Have the opportunity to explore new ideas about technology or systems	61

[10] As with the work characteristics, these goals were rated in importance on an 11-point Likert-type scale. The per cent responding "very important" is the percentage of individuals giving that goal a rating of 8, 9, or 10.

	Per cent indicating "Very Important"
Advance to a high-level staff technical position	57
Work with others who are outstanding in their technical achievements	54
Have the opportunity to work on complex technical problems	49
Work on projects that require learning new technical knowledge	47
Work on projects that utilize the latest theoretical results in your specialty	37
III. SECURITY GOALS	
Live in a location and community that are desirable to you and your family	82
Work in a cooperative, friendly atmosphere	76
Have stability in your life and work	54
Have adequate retirement, health insurance, and other company benefits	53
IV. MONETARY GOALS	
Receive better than average salary increases	54
Make more money than the average college graduate	42
Make a great deal of money	27
V. MANAGERIAL GOALS	
Learn how the business is set up and run	45
Become a first-line manager in your line of work	43
Be the technical leader of a group of less experienced professionals	33
Learn administrative methods and procedures	33
Advance to a policy-making position in management	32
VI. SCIENTIFIC GOALS	
Establish a reputation outside the company as an authority in your field	29
Receive patents on your technical ideas	24
Publish articles in technical journals	15
Communicate your ideas to others in your profession through papers delivered at professional meetings	14
Be evaluated only on the basis of your technical contributions	13
VII. ANXIETY AVOIDANCE GOALS	
Work in a well-ordered job situation where the requirements are clear	26
Have few worries, tensions, and troubles	24
Have little tension and stress on the job	19
Be given clear, detailed instructions as to how to proceed with the job	11

sions are derived from a factor analysis of the correlations among the importance ratings of some fifty personal goals included in this survey. Again, the statistical implication of such dimensions is that an engineer who rates one goal in the cluster as "very important" is also likely to rate the other goals in that cluster as important. These dimensions will help to structure further analysis of the goals of development engineers. For example, the dimension representing Scientific goals corresponds to the "cosmopolitan" orientation. For this population it is least frequently indicated as "very important." By comparison, the Business goals dimension—or "local" orientation—is frequently chosen.

One further note on the dimensions: though they represent concepts that are statistically homogeneous, they may be correlated. In particular, the Scientific goals are quite highly correlated as a concept with the Technical goals. An engineer who indicates that the Scientific goals are relatively important is more likely to indicate that the Technical goals are important. However, as can be seen from Table 3.1, this does not mean that the importance *levels* are alike.

Other dimensions showing appreciable positive intercorrelations are the Business goals with the Managerial goals, and the Monetary goals with the Managerial goals. There is almost no correlation between the related Business and Managerial goals on the one hand, and the related Scientific and Technical goals on the other. The net result of this is that, empirically, holding *relatively* high "local" aspirations does not preclude also having *relatively* high "cosmopolitan" aspirations.

But looking at the over-all importance levels for this population of engineers, the primary conclusion that can be derived is that engineers are predominantly "locals." Their goals are directed primarily inward, directed at achieving the goals of the company and advancing within the company. In contrast, goals directed outward, directed toward establishing a reputation among fellow professionals through publication and participation in society meetings—the "cosmopolitan" goals—are least important of all. Identification with professional goals is much weaker than identification with company goals.

OCCUPATIONAL VALUES OR INDIVIDUAL CHOICE

Two questions commonly arise concerning these data.

1. Are these work goals *really* important to engineers or do the choices simply reflect the ideals of the occupation? Is the pattern of choice this way because engineers think that this is how they *should* answer as good engineers?

2. How general is this pattern? Is it unique to Electromech, or is it in fact representative of the engineering occupation?

In arriving at an answer I want to tackle question 2 first, for if the results are unique to the group studied here, then obviously there is no pervasive occupational ideal.

The comparison we want is provided by results from a nationwide sample of engineers conducted through the American Society for Engineering Education.[11] And while the number of directly comparable goals is limited, the general sense of the results of the study is identical to ours. In particular, the professional or "cosmopolitan" orientation is given little importance.

Table 3.2 shows some direct comparisons of results from the two samples.[12] I constructed the table from items which at first seemed to me to mean about the same thing. And while many of the comparisons show striking similarity, a few comments are needed. Obviously, item 8 and its companion must be different. Apparently, "membership in an organization" is construed by the respondents to mean a professional organization rather than a company. The item was presented in the context of other items related to professionalism, and apparently the contextual effect set the meaning. Evidently this effect is responsible also for the discrepancy between item 7 and its companion. So I speculate that these differences actually reaffirm the existence of a broad "local" orientation among engineers.

[11] LeBold *et al.*, "The Engineer in Industry and Government," *American Society for Engineering Education Proceedings*, LXXIII (1966), 237–73.

[12] The study by LeBold *et al.* presented engineer respondents with a three-alternative response scale on which to rate importance. Table 3.2 shows the percentage choosing the top category labeled "very important" on that scale, and compares this to my own 8–10 aggregate rating.

Table 3.2

Work Goals of Nationwide Sample of Engineers Compared to Those of Electromech Development Engineers

	Per cent indicating "Very important"	
	National sample	Electromech
1. To have a position where people are interested in working together and not encouraging petty jealousies	77	
Work in a cooperative, friendly atmosphere		76
2. A large degree of freedom to manage my own work	62	
Have freedom to adopt your own approach to the job		67
3. To be able to advance and move ahead in my position	62	
Advance to a high-level staff technical position		57
4. To have the respect of my colleagues because of my technical achievement	42	
Be known in the company as an expert in your field of specialty		49
5. To have an opportunity to move into a management career	41	
Become a first-line manager in your line of work		43
6. To have a position where I know exactly what my work responsibilities are	40	
Work in a well-ordered job situation where the requirements are clear		26
7. Association with other engineers and scientists of recognized ability	35	
Work with others who are outstanding in their technical achievements		54
8. Membership in an organization that is highly regarded by people in my profession	19	
Work for a company whose reputation is respected by others in your field		64
9. To be free to publish nonconfidential scientific contributions	15	
Publish articles in technical journals		15

Now for the first question. Do engineers really mean it when they say, for example, that they want to work on problems that have practical applications important to their company? The problem is akin to that posed in the analysis of results from personality inventories; people give "socially desirable" answers instead of the "correct" answers. That is, people tend to describe ideal instead of real selves, how they would *like* to behave instead of how they *actually* behave.[13] In our context this implies that the cosmopolitan scientist would be likely to say that publication is an important goal for him even if, deep down inside, he really gets no satisfaction at all from publication. Publishing is what science is about and he is a scientist. Similarly, perhaps the local engineer is bored to death by company profit statements, yet he recognizes that profits are the reason-in-being for the engineering department. So he tends to check "helping the company increase its profit" as important, for that is what engineering is about.

The point is this: If you want to learn what the social norm is, if you want to learn the accepted behavioral values of society, you can see them in the aggregated results of the personality inventory. So the values of the engineering occupation are reflected in the work goals profiles of engineers. And therefore it seems to me not important whether or not engineers "really" feel this way. The important point is that they believe they *should* feel this way. Behavior should tend in the direction of consonance with these values.

"COSMOPOLITAN" RESEARCH SCIENTISTS

If engineers show primarily the "local" orientation, scientists represent the "cosmopolitan" dimension. As a comparison group, I took a sample of Ph.D. scientists from the Electromech research center.[14] I chose the population from which the sample was taken to represent my idea of the "cosmopolitan." Thus, all had Ph.D.'s, had been pursuing research in physics, chemistry, or mathematics, and had been at the research center for over one year. But no attempt was made to sort out pure and applied research. As it turned out, the majority

[13] See Edwards, *The Social Desirability Variable in Personality Assessment and Research.*

[14] The data reported here come from a one-third systematic sample of all Ph.D. scientists engaged in research activities at the research center. I interviewed these scientists and also gave them a brief anonymous questionnaire. While this survey was subsequent to earlier surveys of engineers, it preceded the development of the major survey reported here. Thus, some of the items are missing.

were working on projects that might be classified as applied, and some were working in disciplines other than those in which they received the Ph.D.

The comparison between the goals of engineers and the goals of research scientists shown in Table 3.3 supports the idea that research scientists will have a "cosmopolitan" outlook. The scientists, much more than the engineers, emphasize the goals of communication with the professional community outside the company. Auton-

Table 3.3

Comparison of Work Goals of Research Scientists, Development Scientists, and Development Engineers

Work goal	Per cent indicating goal is "very important"		
	Research scientists (N=33)	Development scientists (N=25)	Development engineers (N=4,582)
How important is it to you to—			
have the opportunity to explore new ideas in technology or systems	—[a]	85	61
have the opportunity to help the company increase its profit	28	44	69
gain knowledge of company management policies and practices	19	32	60
participate in decisions that affect the future business of the company	6	24	41
work on projects that have a direct impact on the business success of your company	—[a]	32	47
advance to a policy-making position in management	6	36	32
work on projects you yourself have originated	75	32	32
establish your reputation outside the company as an authority in your field	84	72	29
publish articles in technical journals	88	72	15
be evaluated *only* on the basis of your *technical* contributions	—[a]	28	13

[a] This item not included in survey of this group.

omy is also rated highly. In comparison, engineers rate the business goals and advancement in company management as much more important than do the scientists.

But the neatness of these results is due to a careful selection of the scientific population. The research scientists work in an atmosphere which, I can attest, emphasizes "cosmopolitan" values. What might happen to a scientist working in an environment demanding "local" values—working in the development laboratory? [15] Some indication is given by the responses from the development scientists shown in Table 3.3.[16] These scientists again have Ph.D.'s and are working in a scientific as opposed to an engineering discipline.

The interesting result is that they fall squarely between the research and the engineering groups. The development scientists maintain the "cosmopolitan" value system, but seem to have adopted some of the necessary "local" outlook as well. Thus, greater emphasis on involvement in company affairs goes along with less emphasis on autonomy in originating projects. The development scientists are "local-cosmopolitans." [17]

But what is the process involved? Is it self-selection or socialization? The data do support the notion that research scientists are more "professional" than engineers. But do we then draw the conclusion that engineers' professional values have been subverted by organizational pressures or enticements? The analysis that follows suggests not. Evidently the "local" or "cosmopolitan" orientation is rooted very much in the work activities characteristic of the specialties of engineering or science, and recruits into industry from the universities will already possess appropriate values. Most important among these is an outlook toward career development.

[15] Quite different patterns of activities for Ph.D.'s in development and in research are found by Pelz and Andrews, *Scientists in Organizations*.

[16] This sample of 25 development scientists was winnowed by the computer from the 1,315 engineers in the Darby and Ferndale survey groups. It is the total group having (1) a Ph.D. and (2) engaged in work self-described as "physics, math, or other science." Beyond this I have no idea how representative the group might be. Incidentally, the size of the group again points to the place of science in development engineering.

[17] The appellation "local-cosmopolitan" is taken from Glaser's usage in *Organizational Scientists*.

SUCCESS IN ENGINEERING

Once you get a good background in engineering you can go into anything. It's basic to everything. . . . It takes an engineer to be able to see what's practical. The function of management is to make decisions, that's your job. Good judgment comes from an engineering background. After all, a decision's a decision, engineering or personnel.[18]

This is the way the future looks to a recent M.S. in engineering. Differences in the personal goals held by engineers and those held by scientists reflect higher aspirations by engineers for moving ahead in their organizations. Most engineers initially aspire to positions in management, and these aspirations are not modest. As part of a larger research study following engineers' careers through time, a sample of thirty-two new recruits in Electromech were asked about their career expectations. In a confidential interview the recruits were asked to check their estimation of the maximum position they would achieve, the minimum position, and their estimate of the position they would most likely achieve if they stayed in the company. This was done on a chart showing the various organization levels. In their "most likely" estimates, over three quarters of the group expected to advance to third-level management or beyond! Even in their minimum estimates, 80 per cent counted on achieving at least first-level management positions. My first reaction was that these were completely unrealistic expectations. But even if the results are exaggerated because individuals want to look "good," these estimates point out the importance placed on advancement in the value system of engineering.[19]

And how unrealistic are these expectations? One way of checking them against reality is to examine the factual career achievements of

[18] Ritti, "Engineers and Managers," unpublished doctoral dissertation, p. 125.

[19] Beyond our own survey data and those in the national sample cited previously, there are some other studies pointing to the importance of advancement. See Barlow, "Discontent among Engineers," *Journal of College Placement*, xxv (1965), 24 ff.; Riegel, *Administration of Salaries and Intangible Rewards for Engineers and Scientists*, p. 31; Eugene Raudsepp and the Editors, "Why Engineers Change Jobs," *Machine Design*, xxxv (January 31, 1963), 70–74; Peter, "Human Factors in Research Administration," in Likert and Hayes, eds., *Some Applications of Behavioral Research*, pp. 136–37.

engineers who have been with Electromech for some period of time. The facts are that for a group with between eleven and fifteen years of service, about one half of those engineers in the development laboratories are in management positions. Another one third of this group are in staff positions supposed to be equal in salary and status to the management positions. Only 15 per cent of the engineers with degrees remain in nonmanagerial (or equivalent staff) positions.

The point is that career aspirations reflect the needs of the specialty. Engineering development in large industrial organizations is more bureaucratized than scientific research. And most engineers in industry are employed in large industrial organizations.[20] The complex division of labor with its attendant specialization means that individuals with different skills are required to perform complementary assignments. Complex engineering efforts can easily involve several years of work on the part of hundreds of engineers. There will be many engineers needed to perform coordinative or managerial assignments.

And so we find the attitudes of student engineers geared to the likelihood of a career in management. These attitudes are reflected in the responses shown in Table 3.4.[21] Student engineers see no conflict between management and engineering. To some, in fact, the two are synonymous.

These ideas are not exceptional among engineering students. Their "local" outlook has two major facets. First, students feel that their training provides them with skills that fit them for a wide range of work activities. These activities are general rather than specific, and involve the management of both material and human resources.

> I really didn't have a good idea of what an engineer does. And I still can't tell you. People asked me, "Well, what does a mechanical engineer do?" And I would give them examples, that's all. I could go on and on and on in the examples and that pertains to any engineer. All

[20] Over three fourths of the engineers in the national sample cited earlier are employed by organizations with over 1,000 employees. See LeBold *et al.*, "The Engineer in Industry and Government," *American Society for Engineering Education Proceedings*, LXXIII (1966), 243.

[21] These data are taken from a study of engineering seniors about to graduate. See Ritti, "The Purdue Engineering Graduate," unpublished master's thesis.

Table 3.4
Attitudes about Management Careers
Expressed by Engineering Seniors Graduating in 1956

Statement	Per cent agreeing (N=346)
More and more, industry is realizing that engineers make the best executives	69
The goal of most engineers is to become a member of management	60
Ability to deal with people is the most important factor in an engineer's success; technical knowledge rates a poor second	52
An engineer might be termed a failure if he does not eventually move above a slide rule and drafting board job	52
A staff engineer's important work is on his own technical projects; he leaves the organization of others' efforts to management	25
Since his highly specialized technical skills are so much in demand today, a trained engineer should not want to become a manager, but should work to develop his specialty further	19

> you have to do is just look at the placement records of engineers and they go into everything.[22]

As a result of this kind of background, we find that the typical student engineer is looking as much for answers in his job interviews with companies as he is looking for specific attributes that meet his expectations.

> I tried to interview a range of companies because I didn't know exactly what I wanted to do . . . so I tried to interview a wide range of companies and find out what they had to offer, kind of meet my requirements, something I might like to do. That was the big question that I was asking every one of them. Just what would I be doing? What type of work would I be doing?

Perhaps we should reflect for a moment on the contrast of this kind of statement with the picture of the independent "professional" offered by the literature. In fact, engineers must learn their craft on the job. This, I think, accounts for the emphasis on "training pro-

[22] This and the three quotations that follow are taken from an interview survey of engineering seniors in three eastern engineering schools conducted for Electromech by the Opinion Research Corporation.

grams" for engineers. These serve as an introductory period in industry in which the engineer can postpone a decision to enter a given area of endeavor, thus avoiding a potential hazard to his career as a result of unwise decisions made through a lack of experience.

> They are a good sized company and a successful company. The pay is very good. The climate out there, of course, is very nice too. I think it was mostly the training program and the graduate schools that influenced me . . . to me a training program is important because it will give me a broad view of the industry. I'll have four assignments in four different sections and I'll have a choice of one of them as my more or less permanent position. And I'll also have a broad background. That's what I'm searching for. . . . I'm not really sure what I want to do.

Second, while engineering students stress adaptability to different kinds of work activities, they expect to move into positions of influence in the management hierarchy. They expect to be in positions that allow them to contribute to the success of the business enterprise. Career considerations enter directly into the choice of position. No one wants to start off at a disadvantage. Engineers select companies nearly as much on the basis of potential for advancement as they do on the basis of interesting work.

> I tried to think of my future in these companies' plans. In each one they were good but in [company name] the electronics part is a small part of this big company which is basically a chemical company rather than electronics. While at [company name] it is more of an electronics-minded company so that if you did move ahead in management, you might be able to go further.

And so vagueness of expectations and emphasis on career development on the job characterize the outlook of recruits. This is functional, however, because much of engineering practice is specific to the kind of business the company is in. Engineering is a "local" pursuit.

The psychology of the student engineer is summed up in this way by Becker and Carper:

> Lacking any firm commitment to a particular task and armed with an ideology that stresses their universal ability [engineers stress advancement into positions of influence].

> [Engineers] find the field desirable because of the remarkable skills and abilities engineering training is supposed to produce in them, abilities implied in the occupation's name. With few exceptions, these men are agreed that, as one put it:
>
> "All our lives and all through our work we are being trained to think logically and to analyze. If you can do these two, I don't think anything can stop you."
>
> The ideology tells them that anyone called "engineer" has learned to reason so rationally and effectively . . . that the engineer is equipped to solve any kind of problem in any area quickly and effectively.[23]

SUCCESS IN SCIENCE

If success in engineering is largely a function of position on the management ladder, success in science is based on reputation in the community of science outside the company. Consequently, it is not so much that scientists are not interested in "getting ahead" as it is that definitions of success are very different from those in engineering.

The act of communicating the results of scientific investigation through journal articles serves a number of personal needs. Such publication is commonly understood as a personal satisfaction for the scientist, a personal desire to be highly regarded for his achievements, but it also represents much more. The flavor of this is caught well in the following tape-recorded interview from one of the research scientists in our sample.

> I also wrote another paper when I was at [the state university] which is probably the one that got me hired here. . . . It took a long time of hard work and gut grinding. And yet it was definitive, and if possible, that's the kind of papers that I would like to be able to publish. . . . The paper which I published when this laser business came out I quickly got out of the way. I got out of that business again because I just felt that it was going to get ganged up with a zillion people.
>
> [INTERVIEWER] You got out by choice?
>
> Yes I did. Well, the thing is I wasn't ever asked to get into it. I just went into it as a bootlegger. Everybody bootlegged at the beginning

23 Becker and Carper, "The Elements of Identification with an Occupation," *American Sociological Review*, XXI (1956), 341–48.

because Joe Paulsen came around and said, "Everybody goes to press." But it was published in a hurry and everybody knew it. . . . But coming back to papers, I see, I recognize that papers to some extent are the lifeblood of a guy. If I should decide to up and leave this company, and [with] the fact that I haven't any decent papers published in four years, it's going to make people wonder what the hell this guy's been doing. It's pretty obvious that this guy's been doing something awfully funny. So it is obvious that I missed the boat along that line somewhere.

The necessity of publishing clearly limits the nature of acceptable work assignments and leads both to the celebrated conflict between "cosmopolitans" and the management and to the necessity of autonomy in choosing work assignments. From this point of view, doing "applied research"—or better, research that seeks to produce a device or machine whose function is dictated by practical aims—can pose a threat to the career of a scientist. Another man had this to say in his interview:

Applied research, at least my definition of it, would be research that is performed with some very distinct and immediate practical goal in mind. It has been my experience that it is very exacting, very complicated, very technical. It is difficult to draw concrete and simple conclusions from the work.

[INTERVIEWER] Isn't that what science is supposed to be?

No, I don't regard science as necessarily very complicated and difficult. At least many of the basic projects often have rather simple and elegant explanations.

He went on to explain that by "technical" he meant involving technology, involving the making of something that was to operate to a designed purpose, and something that must be investigated under real conditions as opposed to the investigation of phenomena under ideal circumstances.

If your problem is essentially to produce a device, then you have trouble in that you immediately have to sit down and decide what the problems are that you have to solve. And sometimes you can't answer that. Because the device per se is a complicated thing—you have interaction from a number of different places . . . and there aren't always clear answers to this. So you can end up doing an awful lot of work and having almost nothing to show for it in terms of written results.

To summarize, then, the aspirations and career goals of engineers and scientists are very much related to the work activities that are typical of the pursuits of engineering or science. The conflict between the aims of the scientist and the aims of the businessman is primarily whether investigations should be motivated by the marketplace or motivated by the current status of a scientific discipline (i.e., the logical next step in unraveling a problem). The "cosmopolitan" scientist must be a "problem person" in a large *industrial* laboratory.[24]

But this does not mean that an engineer is a "good employee." There is plenty of room for conflict between "locals" and business—and conflict there is. It is over how best to achieve the goals of the business, over which systems and technologies will fare best in the marketplace, over the allocation of limited manpower and funds to competing technical alternatives. As with the scientists, careers are very much at stake, but over different issues. Since the development of a product or system spans many people and many projects, influence both technologically *and* organizationally is the key to success. And for most, influence in the organization is keyed to advancement into management positions.

I think it is this feature of engineering that accounts for the emphasis engineers place on "advancement" or "career development." An engineer wants to be in a position to test his ideas in a concrete product—"to see the lights flash." But his piece of the product must be big enough, important enough, to give him a sense of identification with the outcome. And as we have already seen, this probably takes place only at the level of project leader or project manager in systems development engineering.

So I think an engineer's emphasis on getting into management is not so much a desire to manage people—to *supervise* others—as it is to achieve an organizational status that permits him a wider latitude of technical involvement.

[24] This point is made in Shepard, "Nine Dilemmas in Industrial Research," *Administrative Science Quarterly*, I (1956), 298–99.

VALUES, WORK GOALS, AND THE REALITY OF THE LABORATORY

Engineers have "local" aspirations that match the kind of work assignment typical of the development engineering laboratory. Research scientists and scientists in the development laboratory each display a pattern of goals that seems appropriate for their own endeavors. And apparently these appropriate aspirations are produced by some accommodative mechanism that extends beyond Electromech, for our results are typical of those found in a nationwide survey. Furthermore, graduating seniors bring the "local" value system to the job. All this argues strongly for the existence of selection and socialization processes that operate to provide the engineer with suitable expectations prior to his initial work experience.

And yet we know that engineers are anything but well informed about the specifics of the jobs they will take. Interviews reveal that students have only vague and general notions concerning their future work activities as engineers. So the possibility exists that engineers may bring to a given work situation some aspirations that do not match possibilities. In particular, the realities of complex systems development engineering may not meet student expectations based on an occupational myth derived from engineering activities in smaller, less complex endeavors. Therefore, if systems development engineering is different from general expectations, we should find that the importance accorded to certain goals will be changed in the direction of their perceived likelihood of attainment. Put differently, if an engineer intends to remain in a given work situation, he will adjust the importance placed on a goal to be more in consonance with the possibilities afforded by that situation.[25]

As a first step in testing these ideas we can ask what differences exist between the average importance rating given a goal and its corresponding average likelihood of attainment. Our survey results provide the answer. In addition to checking off an importance rat-

[25] This statement is based on formulations from "balance theory" or "dissonance theory." See, for example, Festinger, *A Theory of Cognitive Dissonance.*

ing for each of his personal goals, each engineer was asked also to rate the likelihood of achieving that goal in a "full-term career with Electromech." This was done for about twenty goal statements, with the likelihood of achievement rated in a different section of the questionnaire. Now, if we compare this likelihood estimate to the importance rating for each goal over the set of twenty goals, we find a strong correspondence between the importance level and the likelihood of achievement.[26] The most important goals for Electromech engineers are also rated the most likely to be achieved. However, the relationship is not perfect and there are certain goals whose likelihood and importance do not match; the rating of likelihood of achievement is either much greater or much less than that which would be predicted from the aggregate importance rating. Now, if there are patterns in these deviations, they may suggest the kind of process taking place.

First, there are two goals that Electromech engineers rated much higher in likelihood of achievement than in importance of attainment: to "have published several important articles in technical journals" and to "be the technical leader of a group of less experienced professionals." This pattern is interesting if only to back up the ideas we have been developing about the lack of importance of the "cosmopolitan" goals. Obviously the low importance accorded these goals is not due to their perceived difficulty of attainment.

The second deviation in goal importance–likelihood pairs is more to the point. This concerns goals whose likelihood of achievement is relatively much less than the importance accorded them. Furthermore, a striking pattern emerges. All the goals in this group deal with influence within the organization:

—Be making decisions that set the direction of technical effort in the company.

—Be making decisions that affect the future business of the company.

[26] The rank order correlation is .80. The per cent of the total survey group indicating "very important" and the per cent indicating "very likely" were separately ranked and then compared over the twenty similar statements. Since the importance ratings were generally higher than the likelihood ratings, the deviations between importance and likelihood are taken from a best-fitting straight line drawn through the scatterplot.

—Be making *all* the decisions on matters directly concerning your technical responsibility.

—Hold a policy-making position in management.

One other pair showing a large difference deals with influence or reputation outside the company.

—Have established a reputation outside the company as an authority in your field.

All in all, these results suggest that the realities of the systems development environment differ most from engineers' aspirations in the area of opportunity to influence important decisions. An engineer wants to "make a difference," but I maintain that the anonymity of complex systems design thwarts this aspiration both inside the organization and outside. For how can he establish his reputation as an authority in his field outside his company if he has difficulty doing it within? My contention is that the values, work goals, and work environment of the laboratory match rather well except in the area of control or influence. A possible interpretation is that the process of socialization in the engineering occupation which emphasizes the importance of generalized decision-making skills—the myth of the engineer decision-maker—is inappropriate for the complex systems environment.

If this inference is correct, then we should be able to discern corresponding differences among the goal importance patterns of (*a*) graduating senior engineers (for whom the initial socialization process is complete), (*b*) short-service engineers who differ from the students primarily in having one or two years of full-time engineering employment, and (*c*) all engineers employed by Electromech.

Data for the senior student group are available from a series of Electromech recruiting surveys. During the period when the larger engineering study was being carried out, very brief questionnaires were sent to students to whom the company had made offers of employment. The return rate on these questionnaires was quite good, with approximately equal numbers being returned by both those who had accepted the offer and those who had rejected it. Several of the personal goals appearing in the larger survey were incorporated into these student questionnaires.

Now, if the reality of the laboratory has an impact on the importance accorded to the various work goals, this should become apparent as soon as the engineer has an opportunity to understand what the laboratory is all about. Thus, I will use for comparison a group of Electromech Junior Engineers. This is a category of engineer reserved for new recruits who are going through what is presumably a proving-out period. These are men without previous experience. Only in exceptional circumstances would they be in the Junior category for less than one year or more than two. Thus, the only real differences we should observe between the Junior Engineers and the student engineers are those that develop under the impact of the environment. That is, I recognize that long-term changes take place because of individual considerations (e.g., an engineer learns that he is not as capable as his competitors and readjusts his expectations). Therefore, while group responses might differ because the more capable or ambitious have selectively left the experienced group, there has been little time for such a process to take place with the Junior group of engineers.

Comparisons of the goal importance levels are shown in Table 3.5.[27] Percentages for the key influence goals are shown in italics. Over-all, there is a high degree of agreement among the profiles of goal importance for all development engineers, Junior Engineers, and engineering students. The ordering of the goals is very similar, with the "local" goals rated high in importance and the "cosmopolitan" goals much lower. But several large differences do exist between the pattern of goals of the employed development engineers and that of the engineering students. These are exactly in the areas revealed by the goal importance—likelihood analysis we carried out earlier. It is striking that all the "local" influence goals show the same pattern—the graduating seniors placing much greater importance on these goals than do the Junior Engineers, with the juniors quite similar to the entire development laboratory population. Since the importance profiles for the students and juniors look so alike on

[27] For computational convenience I have used only the Darby and Ferndale laboratories here. They contain the majority of Junior Engineers. Since the various laboratories differ somewhat in the importance accorded different goals, I offer only development engineers in Darby and Ferndale for comparison. However, reference to Table 3.5 will show that the differences from the entire group are on the order of but 2 to 3 percentage points.

Table 3.5

Comparison of Work Goals of Development Engineers, Junior Development Engineers, and Senior Engineering Students

Work goal	Per cent indicating goal is "Very important"		
	Development engineers[a] (N = 1,315)	Junior engineers only (N = 174)	Engineering students (N = 447)
How important is it to you to—			
have the opportunity to help the company build its reputation as a first-class organization	67	68	75
have the opportunity to help the company increase its profit	64	61	57
have the opportunity to explore new ideas in technology or systems	57	61	72
work on projects that have a direct impact on the business success of your company	42	39	48
participate in decisions that affect the future business of the company	*36*	*40*	*64*
participate in decisions that set the direction of technical effort in the company	*33*	*39*	*68*
advance to a policy-making position in management	*29*	*36*	*55*
establish your reputation outside the company as an authority in your field	*27*	*43*	*41*
publish articles in technical journals	14	17	20
be evaluated *only* on the basis of your *technical* contributions	12	12	14

[a] See footnote 27.

many other goals, I conclude that the differences are due to reevaluations in line with organizational reality.

On the other hand, the "cosmopolitan" influence goal—"establish your reputation outside the company"—shows a different pattern. While the difference is not very large, both juniors and students attach greater importance to this goal than does the group of all development engineers. Apparently, nothing in the first few years of employment blocks the attainment of this goal. Therefore, I speculate that individual factors rather than the work organization of the laboratory lead to the readjustment of importance observed in the older group. However, there is no way of telling whether this difference is due to maturation or simply to the selective removal of individuals through promotion or attrition.

Significantly this cannot be an explanation in the case of the "local" influence goals. Here we have strong evidence that some kind of secondary socialization is taking place. Engineers are learning that the opportunities afforded in a systems environment are not necessarily those they were led to expect by their university training.

SUMMARY

The occupational situation of the engineer seems to need some explaining. As well-paid "professional" employees, engineers show a pattern of dissatisfaction and underutilization that is puzzling. In the preceding chapter we found that utilization of skills and satisfaction go hand in hand. Jobs that afford high visibility of individual contributions, that are important to the business success of the company, and that are technically demanding are good jobs. Yet apparently they are not easy to find.

Our working explanation for this situation lies in the nature of the productive process characteristic of systems development engineering. Through detailed description I have tried to demonstrate the necessity that tasks for many will be inherently unsatisfactory. Put differently, I have tried to make plausible the idea that the mode of work organization appropriate to the business of big systems development implies an individual problem of underutilization of skills.

The task of this chapter has been to examine the work goals of engineers. And this inquiry has been conducted on the aggregate, social system level. We are interested here more in the shared outlooks and expectations, the value system of the occupation generally, than we are in the examination of the differences among individuals. Finding that the majority of engineers have a "local" outlook in no way denies the existence of "cosmopolitans." But it does suggest that we look for the explanation of the tension between expectations and environment in other than the language of thwarted professionalism.

Now, the point of view suggested by this chapter is that occupational socialization is appropriate to the endeavor. Thus development engineers show a pattern of goals and aspirations appropriate to an occupation whose aim is the development of useful technologies that will compete as products in the marketplace. Research scientists exhibit a pattern of goals that reflects what we know of the value system and work organization of science. But these goals and aspirations are to some extent flexible and reflect occupational ideals as much as individual interests. For this reason I interpret changes in the patterns of personal goals as reflections of differences between the occupational ideal envisaged in pre-employment socializing institutions (e.g., the university) and the reality of the work situation as the young engineer comes to understand it through the secondary socializing mechanisms of his fellow workers. And so I was told by a young engineer in another company, "I felt like quitting the first day I came to work here just from listening to the guys talk around the lunch table."

For these reasons it is significant that we find the greatest adjustment taking place in the goals which reflect desire for influence within the organization. This backs up our suspicion that the unsatisfactoriness of many systems development jobs stems from the combination of a desire for personal development and career advancement with the underutilization and lack of influence inherent in the productive process.

What we are confronted with, then, is a conflict between expectations and reality, and with some built-in organizational barriers to changing that reality. With this in mind, I want to devote the next chapter to an examination of the fact of this conflict in somewhat different terms and thus set a framework for our analysis in depth of the roots of underutilization and the constraints on organizational influence.

4

Work Goals and Organizational Roles

We now have the necessary background for understanding the problems inherent in large systems development organizations. Evidently the goals of engineers and the typical engineering work role are in some ways mismatched. And engineers appear to be dissatisfied with this condition. But more than that, they are unwilling to accept unsatisfactory work as a condition of employment. By way of contrast, production workers are less satisfied with their work than engineers, but they seem to accept the kind of work available to them and their status in the organization as an inevitable consequence of their lack of training.

The motivation to "do more" leads me to discuss the problems of engineers in terms of *conflict* rather than dissatisfaction. That is, both production workers and engineers are relatively dissatisfied when compared to other kinds of workers in Electromech. But the engineers experience a much greater gap between their aspirations and the reality of the work situation. Thus the conflict stems from frustrated attempts to increase goal satisfaction. Engineers seeking ways to meet their personal goals are blocked by the typical work organization of the laboratory. This is the reason why our discussion of conflict will be an examination of the ways in which the typical work role of the engineer is a block to goal satisfaction—a source of conflict.

RATIONALITY AND BUREAUCRACY

The development laboratory in a technology-based business is a production facility. The future of the business depends upon the ability of the development laboratory organization to "deliver the goods." The date of delivery and the specifications of the newly developed product are items that cannot be left to chance, cannot come into being as spontaneous creations of the free play of imagination. The technology-based business plans and manages its innovation, and most certainly cannot afford to innovate its own products off the marketplace before a reasonable return has been realized on the expense of development and manufacture. All this means that large development laboratories in technology-based organizations must be rational or bureaucratized organizations very much like the production plant.

The term *bureaucracy* carries for many people a connotation of waste and inefficiency. But bureaucracy was first used to refer to a kind of authority structure that was both more rational and more dependable than authority systems based on the personal attributes of a leader or, similarly, the right of inherited authority. In describing these systems of authority, Weber pointed to the rational, legal, and impersonal qualities of bureaucracy.[1] One of the primary characteristics of such rational organizations is, of course, that the rights and duties of positions in the organization are defined independently of the people in those positions. In theory, at least, if each one learns the "job description" for his position, the total organization should function smoothly and dependably regardless of the incumbent.

Alfred Krupp, the German industrialist, is reported to have said:

> What I shall attempt to bring about is that nothing shall be dependent upon the life or existence of any particular person; that nothing of any importance shall happen or be caused to happen without the foreknowl-

[1] This brief discussion is intended for those unfamiliar with the work of Weber. Serious practitioners of engineering administration might profit from Chapter 3, "The Types of Authority and Imperative Coordination," in Max Weber, *The Theory of Social and Economic Organization,* trans. A. M. Henderson and Talcott Parsons.

> edge and approval of the management; that the past and determinant future of the establishment can be learned in the files of the management without asking a question of any mortal.[2]

Social scientists who write about professionals in industrial organizations emphasize the inherent clash between professional values and the bureaucratic form of organization.[3] But as we have seen, the values implicit in the work goals of engineers are not "professional," and the conflict which certainly does exist is over very different issues. Yet, the description of a large systems development laboratory in terms of the bureaucratic model is reasonably accurate. When over-all goals and business strategies have been arrived at, it is a management task to allocate resources so as best to achieve these goals. Once schedules and commitments are firmed, the development laboratory becomes a production plant. Top management emphasizes reliability, not innovation. Accountability and predictability are uppermost—"nothing of any importance shall happen or be caused to happen without the foreknowledge and approval of the management."

The bureaucratic model implies a defined system of rights and responsibilities or duties that are attached to various positions in the organization. These positions, apart from their current occupants, carry with them sets of expectations about the performance of the occupants of each position. The set of expectations attached to a position is known as a role.

> The prescriptive expectations and demands of other members of an organization constitute a special class of environmental forces which are termed *role pressures.* For the most part, these pressures are exerted by other members in adjacent positions in the organizational structure, i.e., by superiors and subordinates in the authority structure, by those who have a functionally dependent relation in the work-flow structure requiring some co-ordination of activities, by close friends or respected "models" in the informal structure.[4]

[2] Nussbaum, *A History of the Economic Institutions of Modern Europe,* p. 379, quoted in Thompson, *Modern Organization,* p. 15.

[3] See, for example, the discussions in Kornhauser, *Scientists in Industry,* and Thompson, *Modern Organization.*

[4] Wolfe and Snoek, "A Study of Tensions and Adjustments under Role Conflict," *Journal of Social Issues,* XVIII (1962), 103. They use the term "role senders" to refer to those who communicate expectations about appropriate behavior to the incumbent of a given organizational role.

In a development laboratory the role of the engineer is communicated to him by others through the expectations they place upon him. In this case the engineer's manager and others with whom he must interact communicate to him the kind of work behavior that is expected from someone in his organizational role.

An obvious though important consequence of this is that role restricts performance. Unlike the research scientist whose role requirements place few external restrictions on his studies, the systems development engineer will generally be working under quite specific requirements. He will have competence in many areas that are defined as not being part of his job. In general, where there is a mismatch of individual to role, there will be increased emphasis on role requirements by responsible management or by peers who depend on the performance of that role. The inexperienced engineer who is relatively overqualified for a given work role will be subject to attempts to convince him that he doesn't understand what working in industry is all about—he doesn't understand his role. "Green" engineers are sometimes perplexed—"Why did you hire me if you don't need me!"

> Look, in college you get texts and work the problems. Here you never see anything like this—problem solving. I feel that there are problems like this somewhere; they existed before, they didn't dream them up out of the blue sky—they must exist now. I was led to believe that I would be doing the same sort of thing in industry.[5]

People who define the work role—role senders—will attempt both to make the role seem legitimate in the eyes of the incumbent and to ensure some kind of dependability in role performance. This attempt, of course, will be a function of the extent to which they depend upon the performance of that role for the achievement of their own personal goals.

But how are roles defined for these role senders? In the development laboratory work roles will be very much a function of the way the over-all task is broken up or "factored" into subprojects.[6] For a

[5] Ritti, "Engineers and Managers," unpublished doctoral dissertation, p. 97.

[6] Thompson, *Modern Organization*, p. 15. The factoring of a complex task is a specialist function, according to Thompson, p. 83. But in a development laboratory organization whose management hierarchy is made up of specialists this factoring is a management or hierarchical function. Our discussion differs from

given development objective, the shorter the lead time, the greater and more complex will be the factoring. The consequence is that work roles become increasingly specific and responsibilities more narrow as the organization grows in size and the factoring becomes more complex. In this kind of situation it is difficult to match individuals with different abilities and personal goals to the available work roles. Furthermore, the level at which the responsibility for a complete project or subproject resides in a single organizational position moves farther up the management hierarchy as the organization itself increases in size. In times of stress, uncertainty, or competitive pressure, anxieties over control and predictability are bound to develop and to result in the withdrawal of influence to even higher levels of the hierarchy. Under these conditions firsthand knowledge by responsible management of the details of development tasks will be limited. Decisions made under these conditions are bound to show little consideration for individual needs, or for the needs of subparts of the organization for that matter. The management is "throwing troops into the breach." More effort is wanted on Project X and therefore additional resources are added. That these resources (i.e., engineering bodies) may not find tasks waiting for them is not known to top management and is out of the control of first-line management. And this is the significance of bureaucratic organization for our inquiry. It is why aspirations for individual performance and individual influence are sources of conflict in the development laboratory.

JOB SATISFACTION AND CONFLICT

Job satisfaction will be greater when job-related personal goals are being met. I take this as a definition. Thompson, in his book *Modern Organization,* states that satisfaction is greater when jobs have the following characteristics:

1. The job requires a high level of skill.
2. The job requires the use of a number of different programs rather than one or a few.

---

that of Thompson at points because such specialists are the "line" organization in these specialist organizations.

> 3. The work role is compatible with employee's self-image and non-work role.
> 4. The job is considered to be a career.
> 5. There is considerable autonomy in decisions.
> 6. Work relations are predictable.
> 7. The organization has less control over the job (that is to say, the job is less organizationally defined).
>
> In other words, an occupation provides more satisfaction to the individual when it provides him with status and function and with some power or control over his destiny.[7]

By *program,* Thompson means "an organized and fairly complex set of activities of the goal-achieving kind . . . among other things, a profession is a number of interrelated programs." [8]

The organizational problems of the development laboratory show a correspondence to these dimensions. As we have discussed previously,

—utilization of skills
—influence
—career development

are focal points for the clash between the work role and personal goals of engineers. Simply the fact of working in a large systems-oriented development laboratory means that the job will be more organizationally defined than that in a field environment. The programs will have been factored to a more specialized level than the field programs. Now, if an increased level of satisfaction stems from the achievement of personal goals, then conflict develops when the work or work role does not provide the means for meeting these personal goals.

As March and Simon point out, the inability to make a decision is at the heart of conflict. It is, in fact, a way of defining conflict. "The term [conflict] is applied to a breakdown in the standard mechanisms of decision-making so that an individual or group experiences difficulty in selecting an action alternative." [9] In organizations, there are two levels of conflict—the conflict experienced by an individual over individual choices and the conflict that takes place between groups or factions in an organization.

[7] *Ibid.*, p. 31. [8] *Ibid.*, p. 33. [9] March and Simon, *Organizations*, p. 112.

> Decision problems may arise that at the outset are primarily intra-individual—inside the individual members. In this case, the organizational problem is that none (or very few) of the members has a known acceptable alternative in terms of his own goals and perceptions. The second type of organizational conflict arises not from the problems of individuals in making up their minds, but from the differences between the choices made by different individuals in the organization. In this case, the individual participants are not in conflict but the organization as a whole is.[10]

Now, the "motivation to produce stems from a present or anticipated state of discontent and a perception of a direct connection between individual production and a new state of satisfaction."[11] Motivation in these terms is the desire to perform tasks that the individual perceives to provide the means for—to be *instrumental* for—achieving his personal goals. On the other hand, much of the talk about "motivating" professional personnel is really talk of how to encourage an engineer to perform tasks he perceives not to be instrumental to his important personal goals. And these are generally tasks that result in underutilization. "Motivation" is provided by finding trade-offs in goals, by emphasizing the achievement of certain personal goals at the expense of others.

Following this line of reasoning we should make a distinction between a state of dissatisfaction and conflict. Conflict stems from blocked attempts to meet personal goals, from defeated attempts at instrumental behavior. Conflict will exist when an individual is unable to find an alternative that suitably removes the obstacle to goal attainment.[12] The decision problem is the unacceptability of available alternatives. It is dissatisfaction with the current state of affairs that leads to coping behavior, to attempts to resolve the unsatisfactory situation through a search for alternatives. A state of conflict is inherently unstable. The individual strives to resolve the problem through instrumental behavior that removes the block. "Doing more," getting a promotion, quitting, transferring, or convincing oneself that the situation will change and simply waiting it out: these are forms of behavior that resolve the conflict. Another way of meet-

[10] *Ibid.*, p. 118. [11] *Ibid.*, p. 51.

[12] This kind of conflict has been termed "person-role" conflict. Examples and a discussion appear in Kahn *et al.*, *Organizational Stress*, p. 59.

ing conflict is through "making your peace" with the situation. The individual can redefine the situation for himself, reevaluate certain goals and elements of his view of the situation, thereby reducing the gap between his personal goals and the work role, and thereby reducing the intensity of the conflict.[13] Organizations have ways of helping individuals do this. Salary increases for the disgruntled or promotions to special positions for ineffective managers are ways in which organizations help individuals reevaluate the situation and reduce the motivation to act directly.[14]

WHY STUDY CONFLICT?

Obviously there are a number of socially important reasons for the study of this kind of conflict. People interested in industrial mental health have been concerned. Problems of recruiting members into specialty occupations also lend importance to the study of conflict. Already it is clear that there are some difficulties in recruiting students into engineering. For our purpose, however, the study of conflict is important primarily as a symptom of organizational malfunction.

Conflict is the symptom not the disease. What we are concerned with here is diagnosing the underlying problems by examining the symptoms. For example, basic problems in matching individuals and work assignments, problems inherent in the nature of systems design, may erupt as difficulties in "man-manager" relations. Management would like to treat these symptoms directly rather than go to the root of the malady. The emphasis in the literature of industrial

[13] This kind of situation has been discussed by Festinger and his students in terms of relieving "cognitive dissonance." Festinger would postulate a motivation on the part of individuals to bring incompatible bits of "knowledge" or cognitions into line. This can come about in a number of ways, but, for example, when all elements of the situation except goals are relatively fixed we should expect the goals to change.

[14] The act of placing an individual in a situation in which it is "unreasonable" for him to make a complaint against offending individuals or agencies has been likened to the way in which "confidence men" set up their "mark" so that he is motivated not to report the incident to the police. See Goffman, "On Cooling the Mark Out: Some Adaptations to Failure," *Psychiatry*, xv (1952), 451–63.

human relations has been on interpersonal conflict, where the blocks to goal attainment may be ascribed directly to the inadequate behavior of individuals. There is conflict because individuals do not have the interpersonal skills required to understand the problems of others, or to help others see the situation in a different light, or to help another individual achieve his goals within the context of the situation. Effective leadership behavior has been a central topic in the study of human relations. A central concern is the modification (or at least the understanding) of individual behavior with the end in view of reducing conflict.[15]

In presenting the results of an attempt at leadership behavior modification, Fleishman states:

> Industrial organizations are becoming more deeply concerned with the interpersonal relations of their members. They seem increasingly anxious to reduce conflict and to promote harmonious working relationships. . . . These industries want their supervisors to understand and be able to use certain techniques which will develop and sustain mutually satisfying human relations in the industrial situation. Implicit in these programs is the assumption that such relationships will result in increased organizational effectiveness.[16]

The program of behavior modification produced something quite different from what the researchers anticipated, however. They discovered that the role relationships among members of a large organization constitute a behavioral system in the true sense, and that attempts to modify certain segments of the system without attention to compensating changes in the whole will not be very effective. Says Fleishman:

> The results lead to a view of leadership training as an attempt at social change. The purpose of such training is to produce a lasting change in behavior, but existing behavior patterns are part of, and are molded by, the culture of the work situation. The findings here seem to indicate

[15] Unfortunately, the term "conflict" has been used to refer to a number of different kinds of situation. Besides the March and Simon definition there are at least two other major uses in the literature on industrial problems. One comes from human relations and has its focus on interpersonal competence. Another is taken from labor relations and sees conflict primarily between economic factions.

[16] Fleishman, "Leadership Climate, Human Relations Training and Supervisory Behavior," *Personnel Psychology*, VI (1953), 205–22.

that the problem in such training is much more complex than the simple addition of little positive and negative values to certain attitudes and ways of doing things. In order to effectively produce change in individual behavior some reorganization of the social environment also seems necessary.[17]

We shall discuss the findings of this study in more detail later. The important conclusion here is that conflict flows from an entire organizational system that includes economic, technological, and behavioral elements. "Leadership" training acts on but a small part of the total system.

But we need not contend that this kind of activity is useless to put forward the point of view that such an emphasis on individual flaws is also a handy way of ignoring real problems in organization function. Putting the blame on an individual, replacing him with another, and the various moves that constitute "organizational musical chairs" are ways of denying flaws inherent in the system. As Thompson puts it:

[Emphasis on human relations] has performed the ideological function of diverting attention away from needs for institutional change by emphasizing the possibility of fitting the individual into the existing institutional structure. Keeping problems on the level of individuals protects the integrity of the institutional structure by presenting officials with a series of individual problems rather than with the need to revamp the whole structure and the possibly fatal admissions which that course of action implies.[18]

Perhaps the use of the word *ideology* suggests something more sinister than is intended. In this case, the term *ideology* is used to suggest a more or less coherent system of mutually held ideas, beliefs, or values that serves to make current practice legitimate or acceptable. It is for these reasons, then, that the symptoms of conflict are treated as the disease rather than as indications of some more basic malfunction.

Where conflict exists, it is officially denied, hidden by fictions and myths, or attributed to the individual. It is to be removed by analytical processes of discussion and counseling, reorientation and training, or by the removal of error and misconception through communication. . . . if

[17] *Ibid.*, pp. 205–6. [18] Thompson, *Modern Organization*, p. 122.

conflict persists, individuals must be remade or eliminated because conflict attacks the legitimacy of the organization.[19]

However, in recognizing this we must also recognize that changing an organizational system in any major way is a much more difficult operation than training, communication, etc., simply because it requires a vast consensus among individuals who have learned to cope more or less well with the existing situation. The following is the reflection of one engineer on this problem:

> My work assignment requires that I search for new solutions to problems, try to devise implementations for these solutions, and "sell" the solutions to middle- and top-level management. My reaction, after several years of this, is that there is no available route for instituting a major or gross change in our way of doing business. Little changes and trivia are easy, but a major change, in particular one which crosses department or divisional organization lines, is nearly impossible. Change and progress are looked on as something to be feared, and the roadblocks which prevent progress are far too numerous.

These arguments lead me to cast the analysis of the problems of systems development laboratories in terms of work organization. I take this approach because I feel that problems of work organization are more directly accessible to policy-level action than are interpersonal relations. I also feel that work organization is the heart of the problem. And while I certainly do not deny that a source of conflict exists at an interpersonal level, I would maintain, as does Thompson, that "interpersonal competence" is overemphasized partly to deny basic organizational malfunctions.

My point of view is that actions to correct the organizational malfunctions of which conflict is a symptom can best be achieved through modifying the organization as a system of interrelated work *roles*.[20] I would not deny that it may be necessary to remove a policy-level executive to make these modifications—but I emphasize that it is his *policies* that need removal. His "interpersonal competence" is another matter. In short, the perspective that is taken here

[19] *Ibid.*, p. 123. This use of conflict seems to apply more in terms of organization factions as represented by individuals in responsible roles. However, it applies directly to the more specific situation under discussion.

[20] This, of course, is the position taken by Kahn *et al.*, *Organizational Stress*, pp. 388 ff.

is that the task of organizational improvement is one of structuring a system of work roles as opposed to one of modifying the behavior of role incumbents. It is this perspective that motivates the research reported here.

SOURCES OF CONFLICT IN THE DEVELOPMENT LABORATORY

We have already described three conditions—underutilization, lack of influence, and lack of career mobility—that tend to prevent an engineer from reaching his personal goals of performance, responsibility, and advancement in the organization. These conditions are the product of bureaucratic phenomena and are primarily due to the way the engineering work force is impersonally matched to specialized tasks that are produced by a management factoring of over-all organizational objectives.

Reducing the discrepancy between engineers' personal goals and what is offered by the work role can be done in a number of ways. An engineer may reevaluate the desirability of certain goals. For example, it seems likely that junior engineers quickly reevaluate the desirability of the influence goals upon coming to understand the nature of work organization in the development laboratory. Other ways would include a reevaluation of your own abilities, or perhaps recognizing a mismatch between what you really can do and what is needed by the organization. And such reevaluations are not necessarily illusory. For example, the engineer may recognize that the exciting work in which he thought he would be engaged is nonexistent but, on the other hand, the salary he is paid for doing this work is good, and if he doesn't "fight it," he can relax and live the good life. In the same way, conflict stemming from career advancement problems can also be resolved. You simply focus your attention on the drawbacks of managerial responsibilities and the positive aspects of the alternative ladder of professional advancement.

Therefore, our discussion of conflict between the engineers' personal goals and the typical development laboratory work role will center on an analysis of the situations that tend to evoke conflict responses. The survey questionnaire contains several sections designed to measure various facets of situations that evoke conflict responses.

Table 4.1 shows the results of a factor analysis of this group of questions. The questions are placed in two different contexts. One set is introduced by the following statement: "All of us occasionally feel bothered by certain kinds of things in our work. Below is a list of things that sometimes happen on the job. How often do you feel bothered by the following situations?" This set is headed in Table 4.1 by the phrase "How often are you bothered by . . .

Table 4.1

Major Dimensions of Sources of Conflict

	Per cent indicating "Sometimes" or "Usually" a problem
I. INDIVIDUAL INFLUENCE	
How often are you bothered by:	
feeling you have an important job to do but not being able to carry it through because you lack the authority to make sure the right steps are taken	47
feeling unable to influence your manager's decisions and actions that affect you	41
knowing a better way to get the job done but not being able to get management to listen	37
feeling that management should be given the correct technical facts on an issue but having no way of communicating these facts personally	26
needing certain kinds of information to do your job but being in a job classification that makes it difficult for you to get the information	17
II. STATUS ANXIETY	
How often are you bothered by:	
not knowing what opportunities for advancement or promotion exist for you	69
knowing there is a difference between what you would like to be doing on the job and what you know pays off in terms of salary increases or promotions	55
not knowing what your manager thinks of you, how he evaluates your performance	52
thinking that someone else may get the job you want, the one you feel qualified for	26

	Per cent indicating "Sometimes" or "Usually" a problem
III. SPECIALIST ISOLATION	
If there are some important goals you feel you would *not* achieve, what would you say are the main reasons for this?	
People at my level have no "say" in larger matters	62
In my line of work there are very few important projects	46
The company makes no provisions for really giving recognition and status to "individual contributors"	36
Obtaining a transfer to another area seems to be impossible for me	36
The company has no need for sophisticated theoretical contributions from people like me	23
IV. SKILL OBSOLESCENCE	
If there are some important goals you feel you would *not* achieve, what would you say are the main reasons for this?	
I may not have the abilities required to achieve these goals	66
Opportunities to advance are becoming fewer for people like me	59
My technical training is becoming out of date	51
I feel I have become classified by management as a person who cannot handle broader responsibilities	42

A second set of items refers to a longer-range conflict perspective. These statements are introduced by the question: "If there are some important goals you feel you would *not* achieve, what would you say are the main reasons for this?" These statements come from a section on career expectations and deal with the reasons for not achieving certain personal goals in a full-term career with the company.

As in previous descriptions of this kind, I have included a per cent figure showing the relative "popularity" of the various items. Again, I would caution the reader strongly against interpretation of the absolute value of the numbers. They are intended primarily to show the relative relationships among the items.

The *Individual Influence* dimension describes a conflict situation in which the engineer is not able to carry through his technical ideas because he is unable to influence those above him in the management hierarchy. The source of conflict is concern about getting action on technical ideas. The second dimension, *Status Anxiety*, is a source of conflict dealing with concern about advancement for its own sake. However, we should expect these dimensions to be correlated and they are.

The two dimensions of conflict that stem from expectations of not achieving several important goals also relate to one another. The dimension labeled *Specialist Isolation* seems to be getting at a conflict situation where the engineer works in a specialty group in which he is basically an individual contributor. It has some elements of the Individual Influence dimension along with elements of the nature of the work given to nonmanagerial specialists in large development laboratories. It does not correlate, however, with length of service or occupational level on the staff professional ladder. On the other hand, the dimension labeled *Skill Obsolescence* is quite highly correlated with length of service ($r = .40-.50$) and for that reason is also correlated with the higher occupational level ($r = .25-.30$). Both of these dimensions relate to an inability to perform, one because of work role, the other from personal qualifications.

Role Influence and Individual Influence. In the chapters that follow I find it necessary to distinguish between two kinds of influence. One of these is influence endowed by an organization membership role, the other is a function of the entire work situation. *Role influence* is the more specific of the two. It reflects the set of expectations communicated by others concerning the technical role appropriate to a given position. For example, the manager who tells his engineering technician, "We're not paying you to think—just to get the job done," is defining that technician's role. Now, to the extent that higher organization members—management—share this view there exists a consensual role definition for the position of technician. On the other hand, if the situation is an individual one between a given manager and his technician, perhaps a departure from common practice, then the situation represents a loss of *individual influence.*

The difference between these two concepts as they will be operationally defined here lies also in the greater generality of individual influence. Nontechnical as well as technical content is included. Personal as well as organizational factors can limit individual influence. Looked at another way, role influence is more likely to reflect organizational system effects and to be sensitive primarily to perceived organizational definitions of the legitimacy with which technical influence may be exercised by given positions. Individual influence reflects a broad spectrum of individual situations and influence-mediating factors. It should not be as sensitive as role influence to organizational situations but should reflect them.

To measure role influence I used the question "During the past year do you feel that your position has allowed you to make the decisions you felt were necessary to ensure the best technical course of action for Electromech?" Individual influence was measured through a scale score on dimension 1 of Table 4.1. The reasons for doing this will become apparent later, for they lie not in a theoretical framework outlined before the data were collected, but rather in some clear and consistent differences in the patterns of association displayed by the two measures.

For the present it seems sufficient to point to a fact that continually surprises me, namely, motivated respondents to the best of their ability answer the exact question asked of them. I originally worded the role-influence question with the phrase "your position has allowed" in order to detect differences between responses of engineers in staff professional positions and those in equivalent managerial positions. Apparently the question was answered in terms of a perceived membership role. The individual-influence scale was defined through factor analysis and does include elements of role influence. Thus we find that the measures are correlated (.39 in Darby and .35 in Ferndale).

INSTRUMENTALITIES FOR CONFLICT RESOLUTION

There are two major ways of reducing conflict between personal goals and the work role:

1. Performance
2. Influence

There are, of course, hosts of small ways of reducing conflict through the instrumentalities of various minor adjustments within the job situation. There is also the possibility of getting a transfer to a new situation. But these do not directly work on the underlying problem. There is also the major step of quitting and joining another organization, but that is beyond the scope of our consideration here. There is also the instrumentality of readjusting goals the better to match the possibilities. And we have seen some evidence that this does take place. But what concerns us here is an analysis of the problems of the systems development organization through the study of problem situations that evoke conflict responses. Therefore, the major thrust of the chapters that follow will be toward gaining an understanding of the twin problems of underutilization and lack of influence. In particular, we want to understand why engineers say "I prefer to do more," and why they claim "my position did not allow me to make the decisions I felt were necessary."

The set of explanations we use will fall ultimately into one of two categories: technological—derived from the productive process; or administrative—a product of systematic management actions and procedures which derive from the prevailing management philosophy.

In consequence of this, the next two chapters are organized generally to deal first with the individual and technical factors contributing to feelings of underutilization—to understand underutilization—and then to examine the organizational, primarily nontechnical factors which appear to be responsible for the problem.

5 The Problem of Underutilization

> I don't think that they're using me to my full capacity here. One big thing I feel is that there is a shortage of people using engineers as engineers. The work I've done here in the past two years—any one of the technicians I've had helping me could have done the job. . . . Another thing, you go like hell one day and then do nothing on the next. It seems that there's a tendency to overhire to meet the peak loads that come up. . . . In our area a good wireman could do the job working with a couple of technicians. You could jump everybody up a step and get better work because everybody would be challenged. . . . You like to feel that you spent four years busting your ass and you should get something [a project] to use it [education] on. I feel that I've forgotten more in the two years I've been here than I've learned.[1]

Engineers who feel that their full skills and abilities are not being utilized in their job assignments are dissatisfied. Engineers who say "I prefer to do more" are echoing the frustration and disenchantment that stem from the conflict they perceive between their work role and their personal goals of performance and growth.

The skills of engineers are relatively underutilized. Compared to other kinds of workers, a significantly greater proportion of engineers indicate that they would like to be "doing more" than they are. Yet there are some unanswered questions. We have established only that engineers are more likely to respond "prefer to do more" on attitude surveys. We have seen also that utilization of skills is the major factor in accounting for satisfaction of personal goals. How-

[1] Ritti, "Engineers and Managers," unpublished doctoral dissertation, p. 75.

ever, it is still an assumption that these reports correspond in fact to a real work situation in the laboratory.

I have found a marked reluctance on the part of laboratory management in accepting the idea that the full abilities of so many professionals are underutilized. A number of ingenious hypotheses have been advanced to me as explanations. They have in common the comfortable assumption that there is no problem. So one purpose of this chapter is to investigate the likelihood of these alternative explanations for the "prefer more" response. A second purpose is to analyze the job conditions associated with reports of underutilization.

But it is only fair to point straight off to the general agreement in the literature that underutilization of engineering skills is a problem commonly cited in studies of "professionals." Kornhauser, reviewing studies of professional people in industry and government, concludes that managerial assignments may actually appear to be more challenging to the professional than technical work. He explains:

> The operations of an industrial work establishment typically limit the scope for creative work on the part of professional people. Work often tends to be of a routine character that technicians could and do perform; controls tend to be tight; opportunities to develop new ideas and skills are often limited; the chance to write and publish research findings usually is restricted; time to keep up on new developments in the field by reading and talking with colleagues is small; and so forth. In study after study, scientists and engineers in industry indicate that they think their special competence is not adequately utilized.[2]

Kornhauser goes on to cite a number of studies that lead him to this conclusion, but unfortunately he does not always differentiate engineers from scientists—though neither do the studies. One of the most interesting of these from our point of view is a 1946 Roper survey showing 18 per cent of the engineers in a refinery claiming that their present job uses their training "practically not at all."[3]

However, the problem with most of the studies cited in Kornhauser is not the conclusion that engineers feel they are underutilized, for the statistics reveal this, but rather the assumptions about what the problem is. Most of the studies assume that engineers—to the extent that they are professionals—have goals in common with sci-

[2] Kornhauser, *Scientists in Industry*, p. 139. [3] *Ibid.*, p. 140.

entists, and are frustrated at not being able to publish and at not being free from the practical affairs of the business and thus able to work on research that contributes to scientific knowledge. It is this kind of assumption, I believe, that leads Kornhauser to puzzle over the results of the Roper survey of refinery engineers: "The high dissatisfaction with professional utilization among production engineers does not accord with our previous analysis." [4]

As I read it, Kornhauser's line of analysis is that production engineers, being less "professional"—less cosmopolitan and more local—should not be dissatisfied with the conditions of industry. There should be less conflict over publication and autonomy. But as we have seen previously, it is not publication and autonomy that are likely to present problems. I think the point missed by the Kornhauser analysis is that the goals of engineers, goals of advancement and influence, are achieved through performance of tasks that allow them to demonstrate their capabilities.

Another report dealing with the utilization of scientists' skills needs some comment. Hirsch, Milwitt, and Oakes state that the creative output of scientists in industry could be increased by a factor of ten or more. But while their report talks of scientists, it is clear from the description of their sample that these people are, in fact, engineers by our definition. For example, they belong to aeronautical and electronic societies and have an average of 4.66 years of college education. This is comparable to the educational level of our development laboratory population. Therefore, it is of special interest that a statistical analysis of work activities conducted by the authors leads them to conclude that "there is a loss of from 20 per cent to 50 per cent of potential useful output due to time spent on activity beneath a scientist's abilities." [5]

Raudsepp, in his series of studies appearing in *Machine Design*, reports that 34 per cent of the nonsupervisory engineers in his sample feel that their present job does not utilize their training, skills, and abilities. These engineers indicate that while the job may require a background of engineering knowledge, it does not utilize

[4] *Ibid.*

[5] Hirsch *et al.*, "Increasing the Productivity of Scientists," *Harvard Business Review*, XXXVI (March–April, 1958), 66–76.

specific engineering skills, and technicians or intelligent high school graduates could do the job with little supervision.[6] When asked whether they handled assignments that could and should be done by technicians, 78 per cent of these engineers said "Yes." [7]

These figures are comparable to those obtained from our surveys. Sixty-five per cent of Electromech engineers answered yes to an almost identical question.

The literature on causes of engineering unionism gives underutilization as a significant source of dissatisfaction contributing to the drive for unionization. For example, Northrup cites a survey of over 1,100 engineers showing that 77 per cent felt they spent over 30 per cent of their time doing routine clerical, testing, or other work which a competent technician could handle.[8]

In summary, the theme continually running through studies reporting feelings of underutilization is that engineers are frequently assigned work that could be handled by people with less technical training than themselves. But what is not so clear from these studies is why engineers should dislike this. The assumption is made that underutilization blocks professional activity such as publication, though it is evident that no one has thought to ask why underutilization is an unsatisfactory state of affairs.

Perhaps part of the answer can be found in the reasons why engineers unionize. If we regard union activity as a response to an unsatisfactory situation, we find the following:

> Practically all of the unionized firms hire their engineers either by the hundreds or by the thousands . . . the engineer is frequently treated merely as one of the great mass of employees. . . . In short, he is treated much the same as the hourly worker is treated in many companies.
>
> . . .
>
> Engineering union leaders say that engineers unionized because they wanted to regain the professional status they felt they had lost with the mass employment of engineers.

[6] Raudsepp, "Improving Engineer Productivity," *Machine Design*, XXXVI (January 2, 1964), 83–86.

[7] Raudsepp, "How Well Are Engineers Utilized?" *Machine Design*, XXXV (December 19, 1963), 100–2.

[8] Northrup, *Unionization of Professional Engineers and Chemists*, p. 5.

> The engineering societies have examined the problem and likewise feel that there is genuine professional dissatisfaction among engineers.

The engineering societies point to these reasons:

> 1. Engineers want to be classified as part of the management, but many companies do not include them in this group.
>
> . . .
>
> 6. Engineers are frequently assigned to jobs which do not require a high degree of engineering ability. In short, engineers are hired to do draftsmen's work. This retards the engineer in his professional development and denies recognition of his skill.[9]

From these studies and from our own survey results, I am led to believe that saying "prefer to do more" does correspond to a condition of skill utilization that has its basis in fact. "Prefer to do more" is a response to career anxiety generated by the lack of opportunity to perform, together with a self-concept held by most engineers in which performance is central.

These sentiments show up in the following statement by a young engineer who was involved in work I would definitely class as nonprofessional:

> I feel that [my manager] expects you to show up better than the guy next to you, no matter what kind of work you are doing. You feel like you're competing with the draftsmen there—like he expects you to lay that lead on the paper better than the guy who has been doing it for fifteen years . . . what I ask is, "How can I be rated as an engineer when I don't do any engineering work?" [10]

UNDERUTILIZATION—FACT OR FICTION

Before getting into the examination of various hypotheses about the sources of feelings of underutilization, it seems worthwhile to establish the fact that there is a close relationship between saying "prefer to do more" and reporting underutilization on the first dimension of the work characteristics description—utilization of skills. So, for example, if the more than 800 engineers in our sample from

[9] Bambridge *et al.*, *Unionization among American Engineers*, pp. 6–7.

[10] Ritti, "Engineers and Managers," unpublished doctoral dissertation, p. 77.

the Darby laboratory are divided about equally into three groups, 60 per cent of the 261 in the low-utilization group respond "prefer more," while but 8 per cent of the 328 in the high-utilization group say the same.[11] The underutilized engineer is the one who says "I prefer to do more."

However, I realize this does not deal with the possibility that both reports are generated largely by the imagination of the individual who feels underutilized. Therefore, let me go on to deal with three classes of conjecture about the reasons people respond "prefer more." These conjectures all imply that no problem exists, and are therefore explanations rooted in individual psychology as opposed to organizational problems. They are as follows:

1. Saying "prefer more" is a socially desirable response and is thus prompted by a desire to look good on the questionnaire.[12]

2. People who say "prefer more" are simply malcontents. They cannot be trusted with more responsibility but do not realize that this is true. (Substituting "better people who cannot be given enough" creates the mirror-image explanation which has also been used.)

3. People with certain kinds of goals or ambitions say "prefer more" because their self-image demands it. They would not feel right if they did not want to do more.

To check on the validity of these ideas, we need more information about individual respondents than that afforded by the anonymous questionnaires. Therefore I asked a sample of engineers to fill in questionnaires that carried an identifying number. Each individual

[11] The category descriptions of low, average, and high utilization used to establish the functional relationship are relative descriptions. These categories are established by dividing the distribution of utilization scores into three approximately equal groups. This is done by computer program based on the expected sizes calculated from a normal distribution. This procedure will be used throughout where distributions are grouped into categories for descriptive purposes.

[12] The term "socially desirable" is used to describe subjects' tendency to check responses that describe an ideal self rather than the real self. The ideal self behaves in ways that closely conform to the norms of behavior that the subject believes to be positively valued by his social reference group or groups. See Edwards, *The Social Desirability Variable in Personality Assessment and Research.*

received a special letter from the Corporate Director of Engineering telling him that the identification number would allow the research director of the study (myself) to match the survey with "other kinds of data." The sample is representative of all the larger laboratories, though there is a slight overrepresentation of high-level nonsupervisory engineers. The per cent returning the questionnaire by mail was very close to that of the total population (about 70 per cent), and the per cent saying "prefer more" almost identical (30 per cent compared to 29 per cent in the total population).

The analyses that follow are based mostly on these data. They take up several of the popular hypotheses advanced to account for feelings of underutilization, all based on the initial assumption that there is no organizational problem.

Wanting to Look Good on the Survey. This explanation implies that we are looking at an organizationally random response, that somehow a certain proportion of individuals will respond this way because it "looks good." However, it is difficult to take this kind of explanation seriously in light of the differences we see between occupational groups. For in order to explain these differences we must resort to explanations that have engineers wanting to "look good" to a much greater degree than do salesmen or other engineers in the field. We must also assume that technicians want to "look good" to a greater degree than do the comparable field servicemen.

No, using this kind of hypothesis requires an additional assumption—that some kinds of people want to "look good" more than others. Perhaps the more able people respond this way, and there are differences in abilities among the populations. A way of testing this is to look at the results as a function of scholastic success and amount of education. Using Electromech personnel records of class standing at graduation as an indicator of scholastic success reveals a slight uniform tendency for more able engineers to say "prefer more"—32 per cent vs. 27 per cent. But this difference between those in the upper 15 per cent of their class and those in the lower half can hardly be said to explain feelings of underutilization. Furthermore, the level of education also explains little. In fact, the over-all difference between Darby and Ferndale, about 10 per cent, is considerably larger than the differences among educational levels,

3 per cent in Darby and 4 per cent in Ferndale among the advanced degree, bachelors, and no degree groups.

All in all, it seems quite unlikely that we are dealing simply with the human tendency to want to "look good" on a questionnaire survey.

The Malcontent Hypothesis. The second kind of explanation that is essentially a function of individual circumstances contends that those who say "prefer more" are malcontents—are people who have been assigned jobs commensurate with their abilities but whose self-estimate of those abilities is exaggerated. This form of explanation concedes that there are engineers assigned to marginal work, but that such work has been assigned accurately and the engineers are wrong in not realizing this. There is also the mirror image of this hypothesis which contends exactly the opposite. Those who say "prefer to do more" are the very best people. You simply cannot give them enough to do. This form of the explanation goes on to say that a high level of expressed underutilization is a good thing because it shows a high level of motivation in the population.

If these conjectures are useful in explaining feelings of underutilization, we should find some relationship between the following indicators of success in the organization and the "prefer more" response.

1. Performance rating most recently given before the date of the survey.

2. Salary level adjusted for length of service and degree level. That is, an engineer's current salary is partly a function of things that have nothing to do with how well he has performed in the organization, and these factors may obscure relationships or produce spurious ones. In this case, the correlation between salary level and a composite predictor made up of length of service, degree level, and time since most recent degree is .64. This indicates that there is a fairly high degree of association between these factors and salary level. Our measure of success is the difference between the salary we would predict from these factors and the actual salary the engineer is receiving. This difference should thus be a function primarily of success in the organization.

3. The last salary increase received by the engineer before the time of the survey, adjusted for his over-all salary level. This indica-

tor is thus the percentage of increase received by the engineer in his last raise. Presumably a better job is rewarded with a bigger increase.

The primary conclusion I draw after performing these analyses is that there is no relationship between success in the organization and claims of underutilization. Those saying "prefer more" are neither malcontents nor top performers—at least as far as the company is concerned. The tiny relationships between the "prefer more" response and both performance rating and adjusted salary rate lead, in fact, in contradictory directions.

However, the remaining indicator—percentage of salary increase —shows a small but probably real relationship. The data show those receiving the largest increases less likely to feel underutilized, 22 per cent compared with 32 per cent for the smallest increase group. But the interpretation of this is ambiguous. For if we assume that above-average increases are given for above-average performance, we must take into account the fact that a prerequisite for performance is the opportunity to perform. As we have seen previously, this is not always present, and that is what "prefer to do more" is all about. It is what this engineer is talking about when he writes:

> I believe an employee should know exactly what his status is at all times in relation to pay raises and promotions. On some projects a man can do his job and because of the job itself be tagged as a nonperformer and thereby hurt his chances for raises and promotions.

To summarize, the malcontent hypothesis and the various corollaries thereof seem to offer little toward increasing our understanding of the underutilization problem.

The Motivational Hypothesis. Perhaps engineers with high levels of motivation say "prefer more" simply because this is the characteristic way in which they approach everything. This is the malcontents–best people hypothesis without the connotation of ability. It considers only motivation, and suggests that those who are eager to get ahead will be the ones saying "prefer more." This explanation further implies that, in reality, such individuals are just as well utilized as the next engineer.

The major weakness in this motivational hypothesis is, of course, the same as that of the other individual explanations—it does not account for the differences we see in populations. But it is certainly reasonable to expect that highly motivated individuals will be more susceptible to frustrations stemming from work organization than those with lower levels of motivation, or perhaps different types of motivation. For this reason we should examine the relationships between the various dimensions of personal goals and feelings of underutilization.

The personal goal statements fall roughly into two classes; one—managerial and business goals—deals with achievement, the other—anxiety avoidance and security goals—does not. Engineers' reports of underutilization do show a consistent but small positive relationship to the goals in the achievement class, and a similar but negative relationship to the others. That is, those who give *low* importance to the anxiety avoidance and security goals tend to show *higher* levels of the "prefer more" response. Yet assuming that the importance ascribed to goals is parallel to the levels of motivation to achieve, we find no more than a 10 per cent difference in reports of underutilization between the high- and low-motivated groups on any of the goals' dimensions. However, certain of the goals show more relationship than others.

The business goals (e.g., participate in decisions that affect the future business of the company) show a somewhat greater than expected correspondence to the "prefer more" response, while the scientific goals show a somewhat less than expected correspondence. This greater correspondence is true also of the managerial goals (e.g., move into a policy-making position in management).

Over-all, the relationship between the various personal goals and feelings of underutilization is rather weak. Thus, while the results are consistent with earlier analyses (i.e., those holding goals of influence and of gaining responsibility in the affairs of the business are more affected by the work organization of the development laboratory), it is clear that differential motivation is not a major source of reports of underutilization.

A summary of our net findings about explanations of the "prefer more" response stemming from individual as opposed to organizational factors is brief. Individual attributes are of little value. While some motivational factors measured by questionnaire responses do show some slight relationship, it is obvious that we now must seriously consider organizational conditions as the primary factor.

ASSIGNMENT TO UNDERUTILIZATION

The Junior Engineers in Electromech show uniformly higher levels of underutilization than more experienced hands. Table 5.1 shows the frequency of the "prefer more" response arrayed by level in the organization, Staff-2 being the highest nonsupervisory category and Junior the lowest. Now, the only thing these Junior Engineers have in common is the fact that they are all recent college graduates, having worked at their trade for less than two years. Yet their feelings are understandable in light of their situation. They expected engineering to be something different from what it is. They thought it would be more challenging, use more fully their technical training. Combine this with the manager's reluctance to trust a new man with important work until he learns more about that man, and you have a natural situation for frustration. The young engineer enters industry impatient to make his mark and show what he can do, but finds himself memorizing books of company specifications. His manager is a busy man and knows that he will not have to waste too much time on his junior subordinate if the subordinate is busy

Table 5.1

Preference for More Work by Professional Level; Two Laboratories and "Identified Sample" Compared

Professional level	Per cent saying "I would prefer to do more"		
	Ferndale	Darby	Identified sample
Staff–2	17 (35)	33 (63)	33 (49)
Staff–1	11 (88)	28 (231)	26 (84)
Engineer–1, 2	22 (249)	30 (745)	26 (158)
Junior Engineer	37 (82)	38 (159)	44 (34)

Note: Sample sizes are indicated in parentheses.

grubbing through books of specifications. In fairness to the manager, this is probably necessary—but how disillusioning.

> Due to being a new employee fresh from college, I am quite disturbed that I have been left to "entertain" myself and have been assigned very little work. I realize that a new employee cannot expect to be assigned to a project of which he knows nothing, but I do feel that it is at this point in his career with the company that he is forming his first real opinions about the company. I have had days in which the only relief from boredom was to spend time in the library, which is informative, but does nothing to introduce me to my job.

With these facts in mind, then, let us take a look at the manager's view of the situation. I asked each supervisor of an engineer in the identified sample to rate the time demands and the intellectual demands of his subordinate's job. These questions are identical to those in the general survey and were given in an eight-item questionnaire bearing on possible sources of underutilization. The managers were assured that the questionnaires were to be used only for research purposes and would in no way affect the careers of themselves or their subordinates. I suppose such reassurances are needed, but I also expect that some bias creeps into the manager's responses in favor of having his subordinates appear well occupied. In any event, the manager's reports of the time and intellectual demands of the job are shifted quite a bit to the heavy side in comparison with the reports of subordinates. Table 5.2 shows the percentage of engineers who reply "prefer to do more" as a function of both their own and their supervisor's rating of the demands of the job. For example, 54 per cent of the engineers whose *supervisors* rated their job as having light time demands responded "prefer more" on their own questionnaire. However, 70 per cent of the engineers who reported *themselves* to be in jobs with light time demands responded "prefer more." The discrepancy is due partly to the fact that fewer supervisors completed the survey form and partly to the bias on the heavy demands side noted previously. However, there is evidently a substantial degree of correspondence between the manager's perception and the subordinate's perception. Even given the possible double source of error in filling out the questionnaires, the relationship persists.

Table 5.2
Preference for More Work as a Function of Time and Intellectual Demands of Work as Reported by Engineers and Their Supervisors

Type of work demands	Per cent saying "I would prefer to do more"		
	Level of work demands		
	Light	Slightly heavy	Quite or very heavy
1. TIME DEMANDS			
Engineers' report	70 (67)	21 (140)	17 (125)
Supervisors' report	54 (37)	29 (108)	23 (124)
2. INTELLECTUAL DEMANDS			
Engineers' report	54 (108)	21 (118)	14 (107)
Supervisors' report	42 (48)	26 (89)	27 (132)

Note: Sample sizes are indicated in parentheses.

Another interesting feature of the supervisory judgments is that lower-level engineers are underrepresented in the light time-demands category, while the staff-level engineers are overrepresented. Eighteen per cent of the Staff-1 and Staff-2 engineers were rated as having light time demands by their supervisors, while only 9 per cent of both the Engineer-2 and Junior Engineers received similar ratings. Thus, these results are not due to an overrepresentation of a high "prefer more" group—the Junior Engineers—in the light time-demands category. The results suggest also that managers tend to overestimate the demands placed on their junior people.

The relationship between judgments is not as strong for the intellectual demands, but still shows reasonable agreement. For one thing, it seems likely that it is more difficult for a manager to judge the intellectual demands of the job, and that to some extent he is rating the absolute, not the relative, demands of the job. That is, he tries to assign advanced work to the more senior people, and thus sees their jobs as more demanding intellectually. But an experienced engineer may actually see the demands of the job relative to his skills as being light. This, of course, cannot happen in ratings of time demands. And so the Junior Engineers are somewhat overrepresented in the light intellectual-demands category of the manager's rating.

All in all, then, there is a substantial degree of relationship between what is objectively true (if we grant the manager that God-given grace of being completely objective) and the attitudes expressed by subordinates concerning the extent to which their skills and abilities are being utilized. Furthermore, this degree of relationship is much greater than any we could achieve using analyses that seek to explain feelings of underutilization on the basis of individual psychology. Underutilization is not a collective hallucination.

"PREFER MORE" AS AN INSTRUMENTAL RESPONSE TO UNDERUTILIZATION

Work that meets the personal goals of engineers is work that is important in achieving the business aims of the company and work that gives an engineer the opportunity to demonstrate his ability to handle difficult assignments, and we have seen that there is a very close relationship between the response "prefer to do more" and ratings given by an engineer of the extent to which his skills and abilities are being utilized.

The underutilized engineer is in a conflict situation. The work role in which he is cast is blocking attainment of his personal goals. Behavior that will be instrumental in reducing this conflict is behavior that leads to increased performance. Hence the expressed desire to "do more"—an expression of the underutilized engineer's desire to perform, to achieve his goals by gaining an opportunity to show what he can do.

Questions naturally arise about the remedy for this situation. Such remedies include raising the work load, hiring more technicians, increasing the technical content of the work, and the like. But the basic issue for engineering managment is whether this response means that engineers simply do not have enough to do, or whether it means that they want increased theoretical or intellectual content in their work. When this question first came up in Electromech as a result of earlier surveys, I believed that engineers saying "prefer to do more" were referring to the quality or intellectual content of the job. Management certainly preferred this explanation and was certainly just as unwilling to take the response literally.

But it is not that simple. Figure 5.1 shows an analysis of the "prefer more" response as a function of both the time demands and the intellectual demands of the job. The three curves represent different levels of intellectual demands, with time demands increasing along the base of the graph. The results for both Darby and Ferndale are shown as an unweighted average.[13] The configurations of the curves are so similar that combining the data results in no loss of information. Also shown in brackets is the per cent in each group who gave the highest rating on the work satisfaction question used earlier ("How do you like your job—the kind of work you do?").

Several points stand out immediately. In the group reporting both heavy time demands and heavy intellectual demands, the per cent responding "prefer more" is the least, and the per cent indicating satisfaction with the job is the greatest. Conversely, the group reporting both light time demands and light intellectual demands shows highest underutilization and lowest satisfaction. And this is about what we would expect. A second feature of these data is that the group representing light time demands but heavy intellectual demands is missing.[14] The significance of this is that heavy intellectual demands imply heavy time demands as well.

But heavy time demands do not necessarily imply heavy intellectual demands, and that is the next point. The group reporting heavy time demands but light intellectual demands is not empty. Significantly, data not shown in Figure 5.1 reveal that 36 per cent of this group indicate they had *too much* to do. And this figure takes on additional interest when compared with the 27 per cent responding "too much" in the group reporting both heavy time

[13] In this instance an unweighted average is used to give the two laboratories equal representation in the results. Since the patterns within the laboratories are identical for the results shown, this procedure prevents the overrepresentation of the larger laboratory in results that are supposed to be generalized across a population of laboratories.

[14] In addition to being small, these groups in the two laboratories are inconsistent in reports of underutilization. In Ferndale, 1 out of 7 said "prefer more"; in Darby, 5 out of 7.

Figure 5.1
Preference for More Work
as a Function of the Time Demands of the Job
for Three Levels of Intellectual Demands

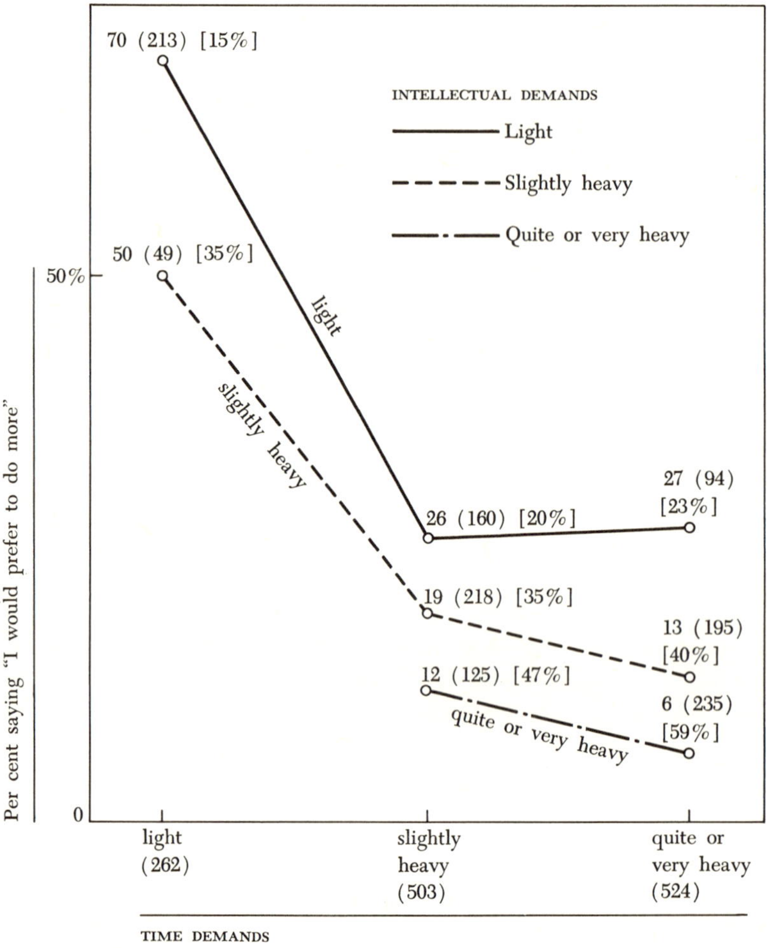

Note: Sample sizes are indicated in parentheses. The per cent rating the job "very good" is indicated in brackets.

and heavy intellectual demands. The paradoxical conclusion is that moving the intellectual demands from light to quite heavy or very heavy reduces the perceived work overload! It seems that when heavy time demands are combined with intellectual interest, motivation or willingness to do the task increases and makes the task seem less onerous. The figures on work satisfaction reenforce this line of reasoning. For a given level of time demands, satisfaction with the job increases greatly with increasing intellectual demands. This can be seen in each of the three vertical arrays of bracketed numbers in Figure 5.1. Thus the primary aspect of utilization that determines job satisfaction is intellectual content. However, for given levels of intellectual demands, small increases in job satisfaction also accompany increases in time demands.

UNDERUTILIZATION AND MISUTILIZATION

The data suggest yet another line of inquiry. The skill utilization condition in the group with both light intellectual demands and *light time* demands seems to be different from that in the group with light intellectual demands but *heavy time* demands. This suggests different work situations in which engineers say "prefer to do more." One group seems to have little of any kind of work, the other seems to have a heavy work load but little intellectual challenge. One group is underutilized, the other is misutilized.[15] The pattern of misutilization as a function of the time and intellectual demands of the job is shown in Figure 5.2. The curves are constructed in the same manner as those in the preceding figure on underutilization. The measure of misutilization used in constructing Figure 5.2 is the following: "Would you agree that there is considerable malutilization of people in your kind of work—too many professional people working on details that others could handle?" Respondents could check either "Agree Fully," "Agree Partly," or "Disagree." In our sample 22 per cent agreed fully and 17 per cent disagreed.

[15] Shepard differentiates between "misemployment" and "underemployment" in his discussion of types of R&D organization. The distinction is related to, but somewhat different from, my terms "misutilization" and "underutilization." See Shepard, "Patterns of Organization for Applied Research and Development," *Journal of Business*, XXIX (1956), 52–58.

Figure 5.2
Feelings of Misutilization
as a Function of the Time Demands of the Job
for Three Levels of Intellectual Demands

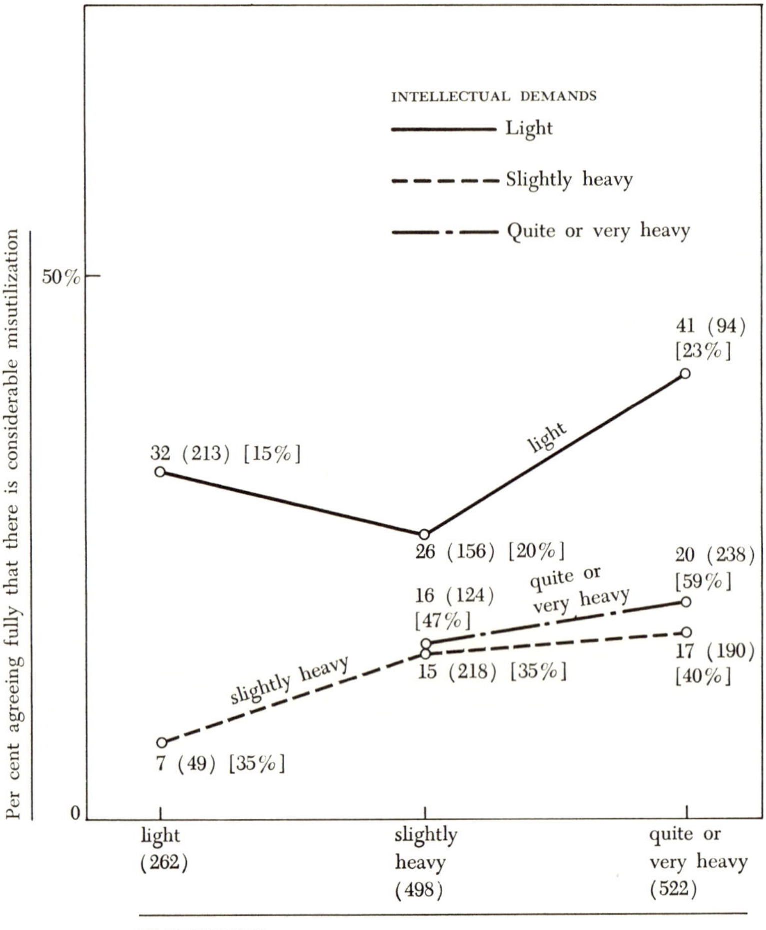

Note: Sample sizes are indicated in parentheses. The per cent rating the job "very good" is indicated in brackets.

The pattern of misutilization is quite different from that of underutilization. The group reporting highest misutilization is the one with heavy time demands but light intellectual demands. The group reporting lowest misutilization—with light time demands and slightly heavy intellectual demands—showed the second highest feelings of underutilization in Figure 5.1.[16] The work satisfaction ratings show less correspondence to the misutilization figures than to those on underutilization, though they are clearly related to the intellectual demands.

All in all, what emerges from this analysis is that misutilization increases somewhat with increasing time demands, though it shows the opposite relation with intellectual demands. Feelings of misutilization actually increase as jobs become *more* satisfactory due to increased total demands. Looking at a given level of intellectual demands, we find that assignments producing the *least* underutilization tend to show *higher* levels of misutilization. And so it is not misutilization that leads to saying "prefer to do more." If anything, the increased time demands that lead to increased misutilization tend to decrease the instrumental "prefer to do more" response.

Some comments from our survey make these last points more plausible. These two engineers plainly have enough to do, but not as engineers.

> Engineering is required to do too many mundane, trivial details. At times I feel like an IBM printer pushing out paper work. Is this really necessary? Why pay someone an engineer's salary to do something a robot could do? All in all I would say that my attitude toward Electromech would improve 100 per cent if top-level management (the boys who decide schedules) realized that people are not machines and can't be worked 24 hours a day 7 days a week.
>
> Now many people are *expected* to work 52 or more hours a week!!! In my department there are three engineers and two nonexempt technicians doing identical work. If the engineers try to get the technicians to do any routine paper work there is a major battle.

This is misutilization!

[16] In this case the groups with light time demands and heavy intellectual demands showed identical results on misutilization, 0 out of 7 in both laboratories. Perhaps for this reason the point should be plotted, but for consistency it is again omitted as in Figure 5.1.

The other conclusion—that a number of engineers literally have nothing to do—is illustrated by these comments.

> Too often I have the feeling that my talents and those of other [specialists] are not being fully utilized. Presently management (first line) seems more interested in assigning a project number to a [specialist] than in actually assigning him a work task. Once the project number has been assigned the manager feels his responsibility has been fulfilled, even though actual work on the project may not be scheduled to begin for months. This is not merely my opinion but has also been expressed by other [specialists].

This comment comes from the same laboratory in the same general work function:

> Several groups near our area have been on scheduled overtime for months. These same people, on the whole, waste time, etc., all day long and most of their overtime period (twice a week at four hours). It seems to me that Electromech would benefit by working these people 40 hours and not putting them on O.T., as most of them complain about O.T. anyway.

And finally, a comment from an engineer at a different location:

> Since I have been here I have seen fantastic amounts of time thrown out the window. There are many people around here doing *nothing* for eight hours a day.

And so we have reports that engineers are doing little or nothing, together with reports from them that they would like to be doing more! The explanation must be that in fact there is nothing for them to do. But why should this be so? I think that here again we find the answer in the typical work organization of a large development laboratory. And this is pointed out in one of the comments. Functions are established, projects formed, and bodies allocated on the anticipation, rather than the presence, of a work load. In fact, it seems likely that the more successful managers are most at fault in this respect. They are not going to be caught shorthanded when the work arrives. But less dramatically and more generally, the problem lies also in the interdependence of design functions and the division of labor among design specialities. In a simple instance, if Stage 1 must be complete before Stages 2 and 3 can begin, there must be some reallocation of manpower after Stage 1. This is where the problems are generated. Add to this indecision, cancellation, and revision, and multiply a hundredfold in complexity; toss in some inevitable confusion and incompetence, and underutilization seems all but unavoidable. And so it is plausible—given the production-plant work organization of the development laboratory—that substantial numbers of "professionals" will at times have no work assignment to ease their boredom.

DESCRIBING THE ENGINEER WHO SAYS "PREFER MORE"

Thus far we have been concerned with establishing the credibility of various ideas about why engineers say "prefer to do more" and with elaborating some of those ideas through more intensive analyses. But now I think we should ask a slightly different kind of question. It is this: If we knew the way an engineer feels about other issues, if we knew his "scores" on the other attitude dimensions, how well (on the average) would we be able to classify him as being an engineer who says "I would prefer to do more"? The reason for undertaking this kind of analysis is that it will provide some idea of how much we know about underutilization. A number of attitude dimensions are associated with the "prefer more" response, but these in turn are related to one another. Therefore, a technique that allows us to put all our information together for the purpose of describing who says "prefer to do more" will give some insight into the extent of our understanding of the problem. We shall use a statistical classification procedure to do this. The aim of this procedure is to derive a single "new" score for each individual based on a "best" combination of his scores on the original dimensions. If the classification procedure works perfectly, we could divide the new scores at some point and find that all those above this point are, say, in Group A, and all those below the score are in Group B. If the procedure works less than perfectly, some will be misclassified, some engineers whose scores put them in the A group will actually be B's, and vice versa. If the procedure does not work at all, we would expect to have about 50 per cent classified correctly and 50 per cent incorrectly—chance level. In order now to interpret the results of this analysis we determine the degree of association of each original score with the single new score. This kind of analysis not only tells us how much we know about feelings of underutilization if we use all our information, but will also help us identify new dimensions that are associated with the problem.

Table 5.3 presents the results of the classification procedure for our Ferndale and Darby Development Laboratories. The classification procedure is based on thirty-six original scores comprising the work characteristics, personal goals, and eleven conflict dimensions. Several other items on decision-making, as well as on time and intellectual demands, are also included.[17] (See Appendix B for details of the dimensions included.) For the purpose of generalization, I have included in Table 5.3 only those dimensions that show correlations of greater than .20 in both laboratories. I would say that there is a high degree of agreement between the two analyses.

This procedure shows that we have correctly classified 77 per cent of the Ferndale population and 80 per cent of the Darby population, thus indicating that we have quite a bit of information about the reasons why engineers feel underutilized. Beyond this, the analysis shows us, in part, what we already know; the time and intellectual demands of the job are by far the most highly associated with the "prefer more" response. Other dimensions already identified as relating to feelings of underutilization are *Visibility of individual contributions* and *Importance to the business*, as well as the *Business goals*.

The profile of the underutilized engineer conveyed by this analysis agrees with our earlier findings on the goals of engineers and our conclusions about how the typical work role in the development laboratory comes into conflict with these goals. The engineers saying "prefer to do more" feel that the demands of their job are low, and

[17] It should be noted that a difference in this analysis from the previous ones is that a composite scale of time demands is used. This was my original procedure. Later, for the sake of comparability with the intellectual-demands item, I used the single time-demands question in all analyses. However, since the patterns of correlation are so similar I decided to save myself the effort of redoing this analysis.

Table 5.3

Classification Analysis of "Prefer More" Group Compared to All Others; Correlations of Original Variables with Classification Score

Variable	Correlation coefficient	
	Ferndale laboratory (F1) (N=457)	Darby laboratory (D1) (N=858)
Time demands	74	79
Intellectual demands	66	61
Satisfaction with participation in setting goals of department	33	47
Self-rating of productivity	25	48
Visibility of individual contributions	28	32
Importance to the business	22	32
Status anxiety	−20	−34
Business goals	22	24

Note: Negative correlation means a high score on the variable is associated with the "prefer more" group.

consequently rate their own productivity below what they feel it should be. Their work tends to be less important to the business affairs of the company and they feel their contributions are lost in the over-all effort. This in turn produces an anxiety over status in the organization. Lack of opportunity to perform creates anxiety about opportunities for gaining increased responsibility and influence.

One new dimension to the underutilization problem emerges from this analysis—participation in goal setting. Apparently the underutilized engineer is one who also feels he has little to say about correcting the work situation in which he finds himself. However, as we shall see in the chapters that follow, the relationship between influence on technical programs and underutilization is complex. Therefore, I will avoid a detailed discussion now and simply point out what the analysis shows.

The influence dimensions not shown in Table 5.3 bear relatively weak and inconsistent relationships to underutilization within the two laboratories. Thus, the *individual influence* scale correlates .26

in Darby and .04 in Ferndale with the "prefer more" classification score; the *role influence* variable correlates .36 in Darby and .18 in Ferndale. All in all, influence does *not* seem to be a factor that consistently helps to explain why, *within* a given laboratory, one engineer rather than another feels underutilized. However, we must keep in mind that our analyses have been confined to intraorganizational factors. This is important because the data show that Darby and Ferndale differ considerably in over-all levels of underutilization. The probability of an engineer saying "prefer more" is about one in three for Darby, compared to one in five for Ferndale. These observations suggest the presence of another set of interorganizational factors that will account for the differences between the two laboratories. For this reason it makes sense to summarize now our findings on the factors affecting underutilization within a laboratory, and to hold for the next chapter an analysis of the differences among laboratories.

SUMMARY

Engineers saying "I would prefer to do more work" are apparently responding to a real work situation, and the primary factor in this situation must be the work organization of the development laboratory. The laboratory work force is allocated to meet over-all laboratory objectives rather than individual needs. Major development programs within the laboratory are factored down into smaller projects. Problems of coordination and articulation of the work in these various projects means that there will be times when individuals or entire groups will have little productive work to do—underutilization. Problems of matching men and tasks within the constraints of "headcount" and time lead to individual work assignments whose only justification is that "someone has to do it"—misutilization.

The consequent conflict that arises between engineers' personal goals and the engineering work role leads to the expressed desire to do more. Engineers regard performance as the instrumentality through which they can achieve their goals of more interesting work, increased responsibility, and advancement. But the job must first give them the opportunity to perform. Thus, the primary factors involved in underutilization within a given laboratory environment are the time and intellectual demands of the job.

Misutilization and underutilization are quite different problems, producing different effects and calling for different remedies. Indeed, the more satisfactory jobs show somewhat higher levels of misutilization. From my own point of view misutilization is a far less interesting situation than underutilization. This is so for two reasons:

1. Misutilization is probably not related to the evolving systems development organizations of interest here. It could easily occur in a small shop where an engineer is required—often happily—to be a jack-of-all-trades.

2. The problem is recognized and even fairly well understood. The solution is known, if seldom implemented completely—technical support to handle the "grunt" part of the job.

For these reasons I will spend little additional space on misutilization and delve further into the organizational conditions that promote underutilization.

To review the information we bring to the next chapter, we know that occupational groups differ in characteristic levels of underutilization, and we know also that these occupations reflect different organizational situations. Engineers in the laboratories claim three times the underutilization of engineers in the field. What we shall find in the next chapter is that similar kinds of differences exist as well among the laboratory locations. Engineers at Avondale are about two to three times more likely to report "I would prefer to do more" than their colleagues at Foster. The reasons for this, somewhat surprisingly, appear not to lie so much in the technical content of the work as they do in the organizational environment of the laboratory. Thus, we now turn our attention to the laboratories themselves as our unit of analysis, to an investigation of the environment of underutilization.

6 The Environment of Underutilization: Some Differences in Organizations

At the completion of the project we were transferred arbitrarily to a new organization of menial tasks, breaking our performance record and postponing indefinitely a choice of new work. Besides being shoved around, we are kept in the dark about other opportunities in Electromech. Transfers are discouraged and stymied by management.

Engineers who work in development laboratories are more likely to express feelings of underutilization than are engineers who work out of the smaller field offices. Earlier we conjectured that this difference could be explained by the kind of work organization in the field as opposed to that of the development laboratory. In the previous chapter we were looking at the factors directly associated with the job. Now our problem will be to understand the organizational context of the job and the reasons why underutilization should exist. Is size a factor? Or perhaps the problem is overqualified personnel.

Our inquiry will be based on a point that we have neglected in previous analyses, that the various laboratory locations differ considerably in the levels of utilization expressed by their engineering populations. Table 6.1 shows these data as well as the comparable figures for field salesmen and service engineers.

INTERPRETING LOCATION DIFFERENCES

Simply the fact that locations differ in their over-all response to some survey item is of little meaning in itself. While there are some complex questions of statistical inference involved, let me try to

Table 6.1
Level of Underutilization for Twelve Major Laboratory Locations (Engineers only)

Laboratory	Per cent saying "I would prefer to do more"
Centerville	42
Avondale (A1)	41
Easton	35
Beverly	35
Hammond	32
Darby (D1)	32
Danville (D2)	31
Garwood	29
Fargo (F3)	23
Ferndale (F1)	21
Aurora (A2)	20
Foster (F2)	17
Service Engineers	12
Salesmen	9

make clear the meaning of an analysis of differences among locations as opposed to an analysis of differences among individuals within a location.

Obviously, we should be very surprised to find all the laboratory locations identical on a given measure. That is, we do not expect each laboratory location to show 29 per cent of its professionals saying "prefer to do more." "Chance" fluctuation would lead us to expect a certain range of values. The question is how large these variations must be before we start inferring that they are not simply due to chance but represent some real differences in the way the laboratories are managed, or in the nature of laboratory development missions. We are interested in factors that affect an entire laboratory location. Such factors produce more variability among the locations than we would expect to see simply because of the variability among individuals we have observed within a given laboratory.

Techniques of statistical inference allow us to say that the differences we observe among these laboratory locations are without much doubt greater than those due simply to variability among individuals. The conclusion is that there are differences in the management climate or the work environment of the various laboratories that are responsible for the results we see. This chapter presents an analysis of the reasons for these differences and a further inquiry into the problem of underutilization.

CHARACTERIZING THE LOCATIONS

People in Electromech management make several interesting observations about Table 6.1. They suggest that the laboratories with the older and more experienced laboratory managers are lower in feelings of underutilization. This is a characteristic response; as pointed out earlier, managers feel comfortable thinking in terms of individuals. But a complete inspection shows too many exceptions to the idea that experienced managers have the better laboratories. Another observation (made partly in jest) is that underutilization decreases with increasing distance from the corporate management staff. There are stories about visits from officials that disrupt program activity and create turmoil. The nearer locations are accessible by car, others require an overnight stay. More distance, less turmoil and underutilization.

Now this kind of conjecture can be checked. We can rank the locations in order of their level of underutilization and also rank their degree of accessibility. The measure of association between these ranks corresponds to the correlation coefficient we have used before. When the ranks match perfectly the degree of association is indicated by a value of 1.00, and no match at all by a value of .00. However, working with only 12 data points means a high probability of observing a rather large correlation. A correlation of .50 has a probability of 1 in 10 of occurring by chance. This does not of itself mean that smaller correlations are not "real," simply that the possibility of chance should be taken into account in interpreting the results.

Back to the effect of distance. In fact, there is a very high degree of correspondence between level of underutilization and proximity to the corporate staff ($r = .78$).[1] While we are not yet at the point where we can discuss the implications of this, the probability of chance occurrence of a correlation coefficient this large is negligible, pretty close to 1 in 1000!

Other conjectures can be examined in this manner. Most of these are relatively direct ideas about two-variable relationships between underutilization and certain characteristics of the laboratory and its work force. For the level of underutilization may be simply the result of size, or perhaps the level of education or age.

Size. Administrative problems may increase as a function of the size of an organization. If larger numbers of people lead to increased problems of coordination and a variable work load we might expect some relationship to underutilization. But our data show no relationship of this kind. I think the reason for this is that even the smallest laboratory in the Electromech Corporation is part of the planning and administration of a much larger organization. My guess is that the administrative benefits of small size accrue only to independent organizations.

Education. While we have already established that there is no relationship between education and underutilization within a given laboratory, we have not ruled out the possibility that organizations having large numbers of advanced degree personnel will not be able to utilize these people as well as those with smaller numbers. But again no relationship is apparent. There is no correlation between the percentage holding master's and Ph.D. degrees and levels of utilization. Similarly, no relationship shows up between utilization and length of service or percentage in the higher job classifications.

Keep in mind that this does not mean the variables are unrelated for individuals. It does mean that they do not account for the differences we see among the laboratories in level of underutilization.

Technical Support. Engineers may be assigned a technician (i.e., technical support) to help them in the routine phases of their work.

[1] Data on which the rank order correlations are based can be found in Appendix A. Ranking of distances from headquarters is based on convenience of travel rather than absolute distances. For example, the two most remote laboratories are Aurora and Fargo. While they are equal in distance, the trip to Aurora entails sufficiently greater inconvenience and auto travel to warrant the difference in rankings.

Technicians build engineering models, do routine design, or wire "breadboard" circuits. The idea is, of course, that relieving the engineer of these chores will free him for jobs that better utilize his skills. Engineering administrators use the ratio of technical support to professional personnel as a guideline, and often argue about the "proper" ratio. Our data suggest that these arguments are meaningless. The correlations diagrammed in Figure 6.1 clearly indicate that lack of technical support is not the reason for underutilization. The key to this interpretation is that engineers in laboratories with the

Figure 6.1
Diagram of Relationships Between Underutilization, Misutilization, and Technical Support; Rank Order Correlations Based on Twelve Laboratory Locations

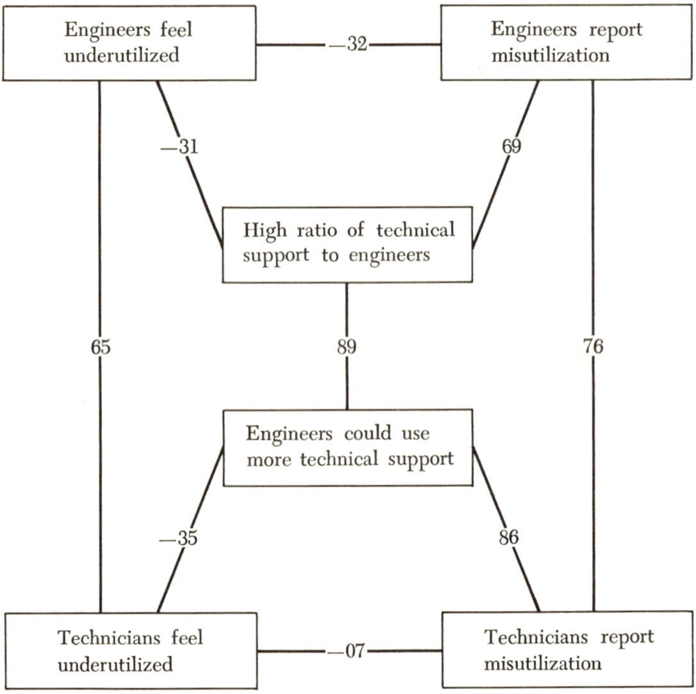

Note: Decimals omitted from correlations.

most technical support are also the *most* likely to say that they could use additional technical support. There is almost a one-to-one correspondence. However, in the laboratories where engineers are *most* likely to say they could use additional support, they are *least* likely to feel underutilized (i.e., there is a negative correlation).

Not so for misutilization. As we saw in Chapter 5, misutilization is quite a different state of affairs from underutilization. And here our data suggest that technical support may in fact help. Apparently the laboratories with more need for support get more—but less than they could use. The result is increasing misutilization. Note that reports by technicians are very similar to those of the professionals with whom they work.

The conclusion to be drawn is that the technical development mission assigned to a laboratory determines the need for technical support. It also determines to a great extent the amount of routine "grunt" work that must be done, and hence the level of misutilization. But we are still unable to account for underutilization.

The problem, then, is to find a way of sifting through the mass of attitudinal variables in search of clues to help explain the observed differences. An approach is suggested by the data as shown in Table 6.1.

ALIKE IN WORK, UNLIKE IN UTILIZATION

The divisional groups of laboratories are relatively alike in levels of underutilization. Darby and Danville look similar, and Ferndale, Foster, and Fargo form a relatively homogeneous group. The outstanding exception is the large difference between Avondale and Aurora. These laboratories have relatively similar missions in the development effort and are engaged in relatively similar types of work activities. To substantiate this the over-all ratings given by both laboratory populations to the time and intellectual demands of their work are nearly identical. Both division management and development mission are alike. And, interestingly, Aurora is the least accessible to the corporate staff while Avondale is the most accessible.

One procedure for understanding the differences among the laboratories is the classification analysis used in Chapter 5. There we examined the differences between the "prefer more" group and others. The logic of analysis will be the same as before. In addition, we shall run a similar analysis on differences between the Avondale and Foster locations. These laboratories represent extremes in feelings of underutilization but have different development missions. As in the previous classification analysis, we shall enter some thirty-seven predictor variables, including work characteristics, personal goals, and conflict dimensions, as well as dimensions of time and intellectual demands of the job, satisfaction with participation, decision-making, and productivity.

In examining the results of the analysis, keep in mind these features of the locations involved:

1. Aurora and Avondale are both in "Division A" of Electromech. Their mission is the development of prototype systems that will penetrate new areas of the market. Applied research and market feasibility are key aspects of this mission.

2. Division A has a history of mission change. Executive management has in the recent past redefined the emphasis of the division several times. This, of course, involves concomitant birth and death of projects.

3. Foster is involved in the development of standard Electromech systems. Generally these are less complex than those developed at the other locations. The Foster mission has been relatively stable over the past few years.

The results of the analysis are shown in Table 6.2. These are the dimensions that serve best to separate Avondale from the other two locations and appear in *both* the Aurora and the Foster analysis.

Several other dimensions entering into the analysis separated the locations well in one analysis but not in the other. They do not appear in Table 6.2 but will be discussed later. These dimensions are unique to the particular comparison being made and thus cannot generally account for the observed levels of underutilization. A high correlation means that the dimension involved is highly associated with the composite classification score that serves best to classify an engineer as belonging to one or the other of the laboratories

Table 6.2

Results of Classification Analysis for Dimensions Common to Both Analyses; Correlations Between Original Predictor Scores and Composite Classification Score (Engineers only)

Dimensions	Correlations	
	Aurora vs. Avondale	Foster vs. Avondale
Role influence	49	53
Satisfied with participation in goal-setting	40	38
Unpredictability of management (scale)	−37	−34
Help to take problem up with manager	37	30
Status insecurity (scale)	−32	−28
Visibility of contributions (scale)	28	22
Manager emphasizes commitments (scale)	23	48
Individual influence (scale)	20	32

Note: The (−) sign indicates that Avondale has a higher score on that dimension. Decimals are omitted.

involved. Negative values mean that Avondale has more of the attribute, and values under .20 are not shown.

The success of the Foster-Avondale classification (77 per cent correctly classified) is somewhat better than that for Aurora-Avondale (72 per cent correct). Beyond this, one feature of the analyses is immediately clear: the variables related to organizational influence consistently discriminate between the extreme laboratories. That is, role influence—"During the past year do you feel that your position has allowed you to make the decisions you felt were necessary to ensure the best technical course of action for Electromech?"—and satisfaction with participation in goal setting—"How well satisfied are you with your present degree of participation in setting the objectives of your department?"—strongly differentiate both Foster and Aurora from Avondale. Furthermore, other dimensions that relate to influence in the organization are common to both the analyses. A dimension of problems in decision-making termed *Unpredictability of management* also figures in both analyses. That is, "not being able to predict the reactions of people above you" and "having to anticipate the preconceptions of higher management" are cited as obstacles in arriving at the best decisions for Electromech. Similarly, the dimension labeled *Status insecurity* reflects influence problems—"having your authority undercut by someone above you."

Another variable that differentiates both Aurora and Foster from Avondale and falls into the influence category is the following:

> Suppose someone in your kind of work was dissatisfied with something in your department—such as the amount or kind of work he was expected to do, pay, opportunities for a transfer, etc. Listed below are several things such a person might do in this situation. For each of these, indicate if you think doing this might help.
>
> —take it up with his manager.

While this statement is framed in terms of individual, first-line managers, it differentiates between entire laboratory locations—a good illustration, I think, of the impact of laboratory environment on the individual "man-manager" relationship. It also suggests a reason for the association between levels of underutilization and lack of influence.

Points of difference between the two analyses first show up in the different size of the correlation with the *Manager emphasizes commitments* dimension. Compared to Avondale, Foster presents a picture of a laboratory where project objectives are relatively well defined and where there is emphasis on meeting the commitments of budget, time, and system performance—"Manager Emphasizes Commitments." This is further supported by the fact that the *Uncertainty of objectives* dimension of the work characteristics appears strongly in the Foster-Avondale comparison (.44). Education (−.39) and the Business and Scientific goals (.30) also appear, completing the picture. The Avondale mission is more of an applied research *and* marketing mission, and a different type of engineer is employed to pursue it. Finally, note for future reference that neither the time nor the intellectual demands differentiate the laboratories in a consistent way.

All in all, an analysis of locations that differ greatly in levels of underutilization suggests that opportunity for an engineer to influence the technical course of action is the primary factor associated with the environment of underutilization. The favorable situation in Foster seems also to be associated with a more clearly defined organizational mission. But this is not true of Aurora, and suggests that uncertainty is not as general a factor in underutilization as is influence.

But the fact that locations with different levels of underutilization differ on these dimensions does not prove of itself that there is a direct association between influence or uncertainty and underutilization. So now we narrow our search and examine the relationship among these dimensions for all the laboratory locations included in this study.

ROLE INFLUENCE AND UNDERUTILIZATION

Since the role influence variable seems to differentiate best between extreme locations, this is the first relationship we should examine for all twelve laboratories. The scatter diagram in Figure 6.2 shows the per cent at each location saying "prefer to do more" as a function of the per cent who report they could *seldom* or *never* make necessary technical decisions. Also shown are data from salesmen and field service engineers.[2] And Figure 6.2 leaves no doubt that there is a strong over-all relationship between role influence and the over-all level of underutilization in a laboratory.

The rank order correlation for the data shown is .83. Perhaps even more interesting is the way in which the data representing the field sales force and the field service engineers conform to this relationship. In accord with the ideas we have been developing about the difference between the field environment and the laboratory environment, we see a considerably more favorable situation in the field.

[2] Underutilization data for the salesmen and field service engineers come from a later survey and thus are different from, though very similar to, those presented earlier. The reason for this is that while the earlier survey is closer in time to our development survey, it did not have the role influence question. To adapt this question to the field situation, the word "technical" was omitted from the wording. The rank correlation for these data does not include the field observations and is based on the mean levels of the variables for the twelve laboratory locations.

Figure 6.2

Level of Underutilization as a Function of Role Influence for Twelve Laboratory Locations and Two Field Groups (Engineers only)

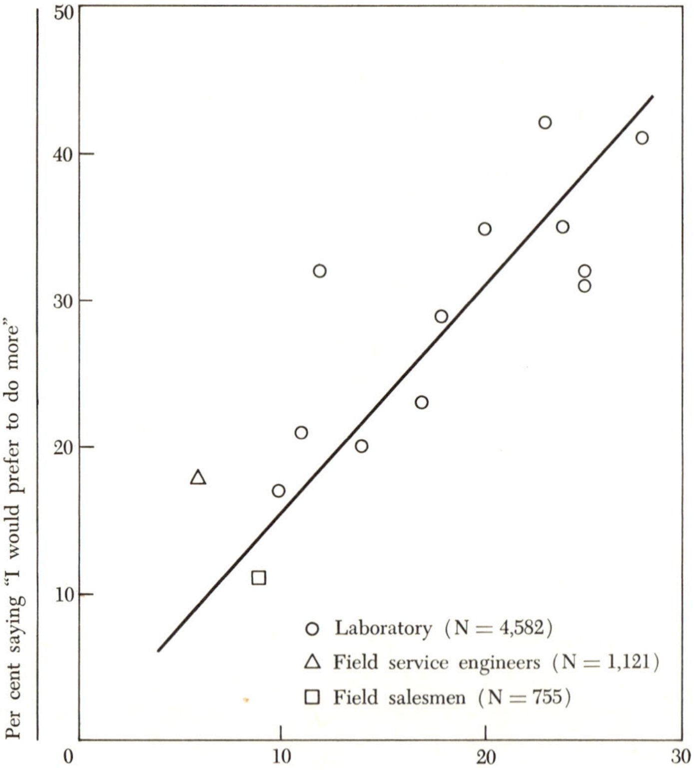

Per cent saying "I was seldom or never able to make the decisions I felt were necessary to ensure the best technical course of action for Electromech"

These data suggest at least two major questions for our consideration:

1. Why should level of underutilization and level of role influence be related?

2. Why should two dimensions that are only slightly related at the level of individual analysis be so highly correlated when we examine the data for entire laboratory locations?

Before attempting to answer these questions let me define two terms that will be used frequently in the discussion that follows. The first of these is "management environment." I shall use this term to refer to a set of social or organizational expectations that are mutually held by organization members. These are not expectations concerning individuals *as individuals*, but as members of organizational classes—nonsupervisory, supervisory, top management, and the like. They are expectations about the way tasks will be done and about who will do them. In particular they reflect a shared understanding of who has a legitimate right to determine the course of technical programs, who should be consulted. Reflected as well is the prevailing outlook of management concerning the necessity for, and the desirability of, formal control and review procedures.[3] The relationship between role influence and management environment should be obvious.

As it has been described, I can see at least two factors which contribute to the establishment of a management environment. One of these is the belief of management in "best" ways to manage. The second is the set of technological factors that constrain management to act in limited ways. I have termed this set of factors the "technical mission" or the "laboratory mission." And this is the second term that must be defined. By "technical mission" I mean the total package of technical program activities assigned to a given laboratory by division or corporate management. The technical mission fits into the over-all corporate strategy and is very much a product of the long-range planning processes discussed in Chapter 1. The mission may or may not be homogeneous throughout a given laboratory. In the case of the Danville laboratory which appears later in this chapter, the mission is that of support for major technical programs based at Darby. Various kinds of tasks are involved, but they do flow from a stated mission. The point is that different kinds of technical activity are characteristic of different missions. And while it seems reasonable to assume that limitations on the technical mission will limit influence, this remains to be seen.

[3] In this respect our use of the term "management environment" is similar to the typology used by Burns and Stalker in their description of the management practices of British electronics firms. We shall deal with this in detail in Chapter 9. See Burns and Stalker, *The Management of Innovation.*

Now to return to our first question about the relationship between role influence and underutilization. One conjecture to explain the relationship (and incidentally to take care of question 2 as well) is that an over-all attitude "halo" exists at the locations. High morale locations will be relatively favorable on all dimensions. And this does seem to be true to some extent. A management environment that affords engineers the opportunity to pursue work that meets personal goals will affect many facets of job satisfaction. But if some over-all halo does exist, satisfaction with salary should be affected though salary is *not* tied in to the work environment. Like most large companies, Electromech has a uniform wage and salary administration for all its locations. Therefore, the relationship (or lack of it) shown in Figure 6.3 is evidence of at least one negative instance, and points to a need for further explanation of the utilization-influence relationship. The halo theory does not suffice.

In briefly reviewing our findings, then, I think we can see that low satisfaction derives from blocked opportunities for goal achievement. The management environment of the systems development laboratory resembles that of the factory, but the expectations of the development laboratory workers—engineers—are unlike those of the typical blue-collar worker. "Prefer to do more" is the expression of the resulting person-role conflict, the conflict between expectations and opportunities. Work assignments are dictated by over-all laboratory objectives with a view toward "getting the product out the door." Engineers are assigned to these projects as a work force, not as individuals. Taking the problem up with his manager is not going to do an engineer much good where the over-all level of underutilization is high. Under these conditions the amount of influence an individual can bring to bear on technical programs is limited. If his work assignment is blocking performance, blocking goal achievement, the engineer will feel both underutilized and relatively powerless to do anything about it. I think the wording of the role influence question is important, ". . . do you feel that your *position* has allowed you to make the decisions . . ." The wording suggests that the nonmanagerial positions carry more influence at some locations than at others. Technical ability and experience that might be brought to bear in resolving technical issues are left untapped.

Figure 6.3
Level of Underutilization as a Function or Rating of Salary "Considering Duties and Responsibilities" for Twelve Laboratory Locations (Engineers only)

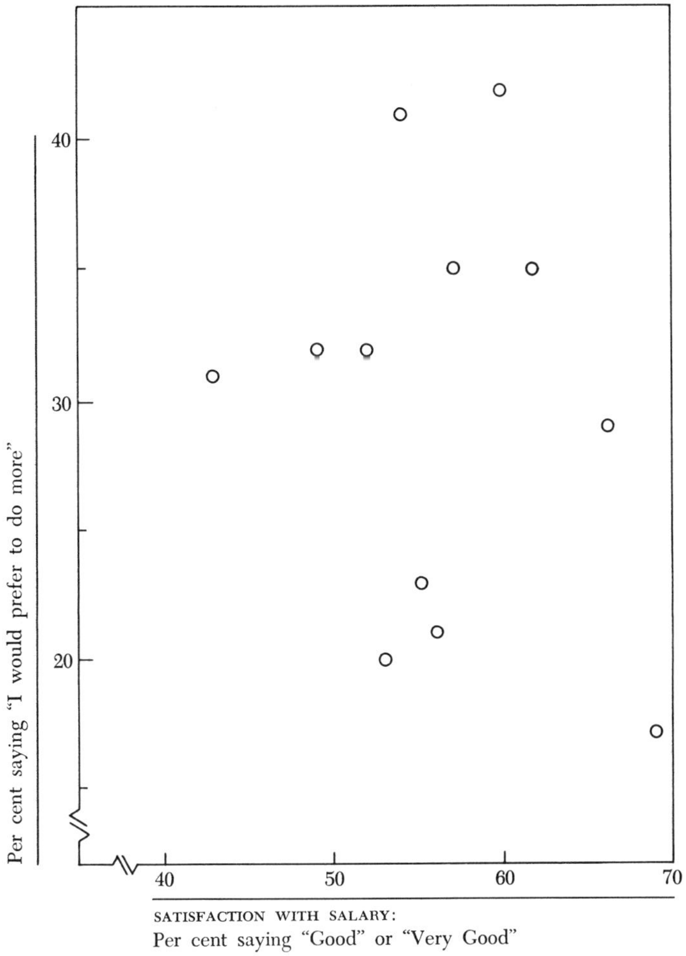

Therefore, the most plausible explanation for different over-all levels of underutilization should be found in some set of situational factors which have the effect of removing influence and responsibility from lower-level positions. As already noted, these may be simply inherent in the technical mission—the productive process—or they may flow from the more complex management environment, a product as well of the planning and control philosophy of management.

One evidence of the differential effects of organizational situations we have seen already in the relatively low underutilization and high influence of the field groups. My explanation for this has been that in the field, where local offices are small and autonomous, where there are fewer levels in the management hierarchy, there are fewer obstacles. Organization goals are clear, tasks less specialized, and measures of performance more tangible. The field positions necessarily include a broader range of discretionary decision powers—influence. The decision to increase performance and satisfaction is a decision that can be acted upon directly in the field by going out and doing more.

Still, I have some uneasiness about this explanation. There are plausible alternatives. Perhaps the field engineers *are* different, having been attracted to this kind of work and having a different outlook to begin with. Or perhaps their far greater exposure to the problems of other organizations has broadened their viewpoint, made them better appreciate what they have at Electromech. And so, while we cannot conclusively establish one or the other explanation, I think it necessary to review what data we have bearing on this issue.

In addition to previously shown data on satisfaction and underutilization for field salesmen and development laboratory engineers we have data on two special groups, engineers recruited especially into the field sales force and salesmen who have been assigned to a bureaucratized field environment in many ways like that of the development laboratory. Now, the comparisons I want to make are between four groups whose organizational situations will shortly be described in detail.

1. Engineers recruited directly into the field who currently have about two years of service.

2. Engineers recruited directly into the Darby and Ferndale laboratories with no more than two years of current service—the Junior Engineers.

3. Salesmen in a unique, bureaucratized situation whom I term "office salesmen."

4. All field salesmen.

In addition to these groups, for reference comparisons I have included other technical and nontechnical employees recruited for the same field jobs during the same period as the engineers, as well as the group of all development laboratory engineers.[4]

If the situational explanation is reasonable we should find that the engineers recruited into the field are far more satisfied and better utilized than their counterparts in the laboratories. We should also find that their responses resemble those of others recruited into this situation more than they do those of fellow engineers in the laboratory setting. As for the office salesmen, we would expect the heightened frustration of the bureaucratized environment to increase the level of conflict responses and concomitantly to lower satisfaction to a level below that of their field colleagues. This would imply that greater exposure to outside organizations makes little difference.

The reader will probably not be surprised to find that this is exactly the picture shown in Table 6.3. Now let me try to make this picture reasonable by a better description of two of these groups, the office salesmen and the engineers recruited into field sales.

Bureaucratized Salesmen. One group of Electromech salesmen work in an environment that is considerably different from the usual field situation and that has some characteristics in common with the development laboratory. They work with agencies of the United States government. They are not on commission and they are not

[4] Unfortunately, the role influence data are missing for the key group of "office salesmen" because that survey was conducted before the development of the question. The survey of sales recruits dates from a period three years subsequent to the other surveys. The unpublished Electromech report from which the recruits data are taken does not give the individual sample sizes. However, the three groups total around 1,000 with approximately 500 being engineers.

Table 6.3

Attitude Toward Job and Reports of Underutilization by Engineers and Salesmen Working in Field and Laboratory Situations

	Attitude toward job (Per cent saying "It's very good")	Underutilization (Per cent saying "I prefer to do more")
All field salesmen (508)	63	9
Engineers two years in field[a]	62	12
Other technical personnel two years in field[a]	57	12
Nontechnical personnel two years in field[a]	64	14
All office salesmen (82)	44	23
All development laboratory engineers (4,582)	37	29
Engineers two years in development laboratory (174)	34	38

[a] Group sizes not given in report. Total of two-year field group is approximately 1,000 respondents.

measured directly. This means, of course, that the link between performance and goal attainment is less direct than for the field or commission salesmen. Furthermore, the job is more specialized. The salesmen function more as order takers. They are assigned to an agency and work with the people in that agency. They are called in when the agency decides on the need for certain kinds of equipment. Then the salesman is asked to study the problem and make a proposal. In fact, often it appears that the agency already knows exactly what it wants and is looking simply for a price quotation. Finally, orders are sometimes placed on an "irrational" basis. The federal government, for reasons of its own, may want to spread the business among a number of suppliers. Consequently, the most acceptable bid may be "best" for reasons other than the merit of the individual proposal.[5] Add to this the long time span required as the

[5] It seems apparent that at least one consideration in letting government contracts is maintaining multiple sources of supply. Where there are only a limited number of suppliers to start with, the result of the policy may be that contracts are let in part to maintain the economic viability of a supplier. For an instance

proposal filters through the various federal agencies involved, legal considerations, and proposal reviews and the situation becomes quite like that of the development laboratory.

Engineers in the Field. Several years ago Electromech for the first time systematically recruited engineering graduates for its sales force. That is, company representatives went to the campus and tried to interest engineering students in a field sales or service career. The reasoning behind this decision was that the sales function was becoming more technical while the service function obviously had many elements of selling. Management reasoned that it might be easier to train engineers to sell than to give nontechnical people the necessary technical training. The upshot of this decision was the hiring of large numbers of engineering graduates who had not specifically sought out sales as a career.[6] It must be said, though, that management did not do this without some trepidation. Management was familiar with notions about engineers preferring things to people. So it was decided to keep track of the job attitudes of this group. The data shown in Table 6.3 should allay any fears—at least about the field group. These engineer-salesmen are more satisfied with their situation and feel considerably *less* underutilization than the directly comparable laboratory group. And this is all the more significant in view of the fact that other data show only 12 per cent of this sales group of engineers willing to admit using their technical training to a "considerable extent." The similarity of the profiles for the "other technical" and "nontechnical" groups reinforces the situational explanation.

What it boils down to is this: Engineers bring to their work some rather vague expectations which emphasize broad capabilities in the logical analysis and systematic solution of problems. This is the pattern we saw in Chapter 3. They are interested more in achieving re-

---

of this in the aircraft industry see Mecklin, "The C-5: The Ordeal of the Plane Makers," *Fortune*, LXXII (December, 1965), 158 ff.

[6] It should be pointed out that these engineers were recruited for the "field" as opposed to either sales or service. This decision is made later. As it turns out, about half go to sales and half to service. But the difference between these types of position is not so great as it might seem. In fact, because they are so similar in most respects Electromech management is seriously considering doing away with the distinction altogether.

sults than in weaving abstractions. They want to contribute, to make a difference. The likelihood of doing this in the field is greater than it is in the laboratory. But this is not because the work is technically more sophisticated; it is because there are crucial differences in the situationally determined work roles of development engineer and sales engineer. The division of labor and the consequent fragmentation of responsibility typical of systems development constrain performance and restrict influence. Place salesmen in a corresponding environment and they exhibit the same attitudes. And if engineers in the field situation have the same pattern of attitudes as nontechnically trained salesmen, it is because the opportunity to perform and the accompanying role definitions are more consistent with the description "management" than with the description "worker."

LABORATORY ENVIRONMENTS AND INDIVIDUAL CIRCUMSTANCES

We come now to the second question. Effects that are associated with differences in laboratory levels of underutilization are different from those that lead one engineer rather than another to say "I would prefer to do more work." We are faced with the problem of understanding why dimensions of organization that can generally be labeled influence dimensions seem to differentiate well among laboratory locations, but do not seem to help much in predicting underutilization at the individual level. Figure 6.4 shows in different form what we learned about the relationship between influence and underutilization in the previous chapter—that the degree of association is fairly strong in Darby (almost a group of laboratories in itself) but weak and inconsistent in other laboratories.

Two important features of this family of curves should be noted:

1. The spread among the midpoints of the four curves is greater than, or about equal to, the range of extremes in three of the four. Foster and Ferndale show about a 10 per cent range compared to the 17 per cent spread.

2. As seen in the group sizes, there is a strong shift in the decisions question among the per cent responding "usually or always," ranging from 39 per cent in Avondale to 64 per cent in Foster.

Figure 6.4
Preference for More Work as a Function of Role Influence Within Four Laboratory Locations (Engineers only)

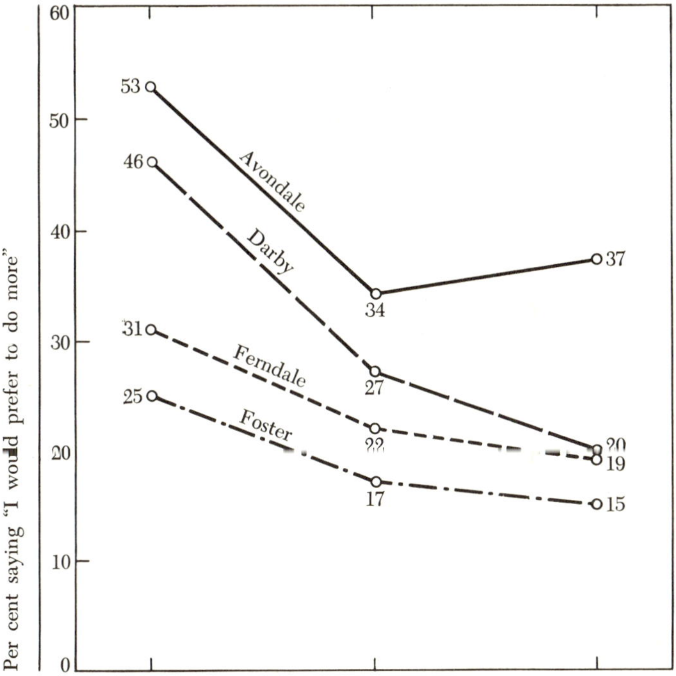

seldom or never	sometimes	usually or always	
(45)	(51)	(62)	Avondale
(219)	(259)	(260)	Darby
(54)	(134)	(243)	Ferndale
(17)	(52)	(123)	Foster

"During the past year do you feel that your position has allowed you to make decisions you felt were necessary to ensure the best technical course of action for Electromech?"

These facts suggest that there are large differences in the laboratory levels of both underutilization and influence, and that these dimensions characterize management environments that are relatively homogeneous. The explanation that is most consistent with the facts is that the management environment defines the extent of influence that can be exerted by those occupying the nonmanagerial *role*. The data suggest that the laboratory level of underutilization is the result of relatively broad program decisions that are a product of top management unwillingness or inability to allocate effectively resources for maximum *individual* utilization. It is likely also that this type of decision is out of the hands of local laboratory management who can modify, but not directly reject or ignore, ordered program changes. Remember that there is a strong correlation between the level of underutilization and the distance from corporate (as well as division) staff. An even stronger correlation between the role influence variable and distance (r=.87) suggests that the more accessible locations do get more of top management's attention than do the less accessible locations.

This distance effect apparently stems from the success of local management in disguising activities proscribed by executive management. Resistance is more possible when local management has a day or two of alert concerning a forthcoming visit. In this respect one manager is legendary. Stories about program changes run like this: "When you get out there and go through the lab you realize that all [the laboratory manager] has done is to rename the old project. Same people working on the same projects—nothing changed but the number and title." Whether this kind of behavior is productive from the over-all company point of view is another question, but in this case it was clearly associated with a better influence environment. Such strategies seem unlikely in more accessible locations.

I think these facts help explain why the laboratories differ so much in levels of underutilization. For while the time and intellectual demands of the job explain underutilization at the individual level of analysis, neither of these factors shows up strongly in the classification analysis. The correlations between level of underutilization and the levels of time and intellectual demands are .44 and .43 respectively for the group of twelve laboratories. The correlation with role influence is much stronger. Furthermore, Aurora and Avondale show similar levels of job demands, having the lowest levels of time demands and relatively high intellectual demands. Despite this, Avondale shows twice the level of underutilization—41 per cent to 19 per cent. Quite clearly, the laboratory level of underutilization reflects other factors which tend to modify the relationship between job demands and underutilization.

The first of these is the relative homogeneity of the environment. The aim of the classification analysis has been to uncover attributes that best differentiate between the perceptions of engineers in high and low "prefer more" laboratories. If important differences in the laboratory environments exist, then these differences should be perceived by all engineers, whether or not they are underutilized on their own assignments. In fact, our data give remarkable evidence that this is true. Table 6.4, for example, illustrates the consistency in levels of underutilization and perceived role influence by project group within the Foster and Avondale laboratories. Each project group is made up of several smaller departments working on related tasks, while the projects may or may not be related in function.[7] Notice that even though the groups are small and the figures thus inherently unstable, there is almost no overlap for either variable between the locations. Notice also, as with the individual data, that there is no correlation between project levels of role influence and underutilization. And this condition extends to the management environment of all the laboratories, though less dramatically. For those readers more computationally inclined, the variance (F) ratio for the role influence variable over the 12 locations is 8.28 with 11 and 3,388 d.f. By contrast, the variance ratio for time demands is 3.12. Thus it seems that engineers do perceive the management environment uniformly and independently of the demands of their own tasks. To put it another way, the probability of underutilization is a parameter of the management environment, but within a laboratory those saying "prefer to do more" are those whose tasks exhibit low time and intellectual demands relative to their co-workers.

[7] As can be seen from Table 6.4, the projects shown here constitute about three fourths of the total laboratory group surveyed. When the survey was conducted the project groups at each location were coded on the basis of similar task responsibility and administrative grouping. The results for each of these groups were then reported back to the responsible managers. However, in a number of cases individual departments did not meet these criteria and were too small (under eight) to guarantee the anonymity of individuals in the feedback process. These departments were grouped as miscellaneous and are not shown here.

Table 6.4

Level of Underutilization and Level of Role Influence by Project for Two Laboratories Extremely Different in These Aspects (Engineers only)

Foster (F2)			*Avondale (A1)*		
Per cent saying "I would prefer to do more"	Decisions[a] (in per cent)	(N)	Per cent saying "I would prefer to do more"	Decisions (in per cent)	(N)
00	08	(11)	25	29	(13)
09	06	(11)	27	35	(15)
15	00	(13)	36	17	(11)
15	00	(13)	40	27	(15)
17	09	(24)	41	44	(17)
17	00	(12)	45	29	(22)
18	09	(11)	60	13	(15)
18	00	(17)	67	20	(9)
25	21	(20)			
25	08	(20)			
Total[b] 17	10	(152)	41	28	(118)

[a] Per cent saying they could seldom or never make decisions they felt were necessary.
[b] Percentages are for the entire location. N = 199 and N = 164.

A second factor explaining the relative lack of correspondence between levels of job demands and perceived underutilization is that "prefer more" is a conflict response, a response to blocked achievement. Within a uniform environment we have convincing evidence that goal achievement is related to over-all job demands. But it does not necessarily follow that entire organizations characterized by relatively low demands must experience conflict. Low time demands resulting from disorganization due to the complexity of systems design or to interference from top management seem certain to produce feelings of underutilization. But if the activity level results from a technical mission generated locally, seen as well advised and desirable, conflict should be reduced. These it seems to me are the reasons why the low time demands at Aurora—the most remote of the laboratories with the highest-rated top local management—are associated with far less person-role conflict than at Avondale—the most accessible with the next-to-lowest-rated top local management.

To review, top management decisions that impose programs in which underutilization is inherent or that disrupt current program activity are responsible for the observed association between the level of underutilization and role influence. When an unpopular program is imposed, and in particular where the program does not provide challenging assignments, local management is expected to "explain" the necessity of the new program to both nonmanagerial engineers and lower-level managerial personnel. This usually means telling them that there is no chance of changing the situation. Under these conditions technical influence is withdrawn up the management hierarchy. By way of illustration, such a situation exists when, for various reasons, the development mission assigned an entire laboratory is one of secondary importance in the total company development effort. This is the situation in the Danville laboratory. Many of the Danville-based functions are support activities for the major technical thrust at Darby. That the Danville people are aware of this is best illustrated by the following comments, the first from an engineering manager:

> Give the Danville Laboratory a real mission in the form of a vital product responsibility. The working organizations need this—so do the people. There is no project challenge. . . . Danville is now the spillover real estate from Darby with many Darby-based functions getting only care and feeding from the Danville lab.

> Danville's technical assignments or responsibilities seem to be the dog work for projects or products out of other areas. In general a question, "Is Danville Darby's stepchild or are we brothers?"

A second kind of situation giving rise both to underutilization and to influence problems is uncertainty. Program uncertainty results from the inability of management to formulate or maintain program activity and thus effectively to allocate resources at its disposal. When there is no set objective to work toward, an engineer is likely to be doing nothing—waiting for his management to "make a decision." He is also likely to have his own idea of what should be done, and impatient with having to wait. Influence problems and underutilization thus tend to coexist at locations beset by program uncertainty.

Our analysis, therefore, leads to the conclusion that environmental factors at the laboratory locations are responsible both for influence problems and for underutilization. That is, we must reject the notion that lack of influence causes underutilization.[8] For if this were the case low-influence engineers within the laboratories would show far greater underutilization than their high-influence colleagues. Stated in its most simple terms, underutilization is not the result of engineers not being able to have their own way; it is related to the way engineers are treated as a class. The relative invariance of the management environment within locations points to this. What I am saying is that low influence and underutilization are symptoms of the same problem, a problem we have yet to identify clearly. But what we do see is that locations differ in levels of underutilization to the extent that local management—whether by choice or by directive—adopts a plant or factory approach to the management of its engineering work-force.

The argument can be summarized in this way:

1. Laboratories differ in size and in level of education and average length of service of their employees, but these factors do not account for observed differences in underutilization.

2. The amount of technical support available to engineers also varies considerably. Misutilization of people is definitely tied to insufficient technical support. It is a product of working on tasks beneath one's abilities. But lack of technical support has nothing to do with underutilization.

3. The one organizational dimension that is consistently associated with utilization is influence, particularly role influence. This relationship appears to exist because conditions at a location give rise jointly to underutilization and lack of influence. That is, the association between these two factors exists because they are both related to some third factor.

The importance of this last statement will become evident when we turn our attention to the task of identifying the explicit source of the problems we have been describing—in our analysis of the meaning and sources of organizational influence. For the present, it seems

[8] Technically this means that the correlation between role influence and underutilization is spurious. I resist using the spurious description, however, because it might be interpreted to mean "incorrect" or "of no value for interpretation." Neither of these is the case.

sufficient to point out that appropriate organizational therapies flow from correct problem identification. If lack of influence and underutilization were related at the individual level, the appropriate action might be managerial training in the art of allowing increased discretionary influence to engineers. But this seems not to be the case. The problem is one of the entire organization. Put somewhat differently, the shared role definition of engineers within a given laboratory is to a great extent a product of management's understanding of how the technical mission is to be organized. Low-influence role definitions and a high probability of underutilization flow together from the management environment.

Engineers in field sales experience greater role influence and less underutilization in consequence of their environment, not, it seems evident, in consequence of some better system of allocation of individuals to tasks. The point is this: *Within* a given organizational situation the manipulation of *individual* influence probably will not have much effect on the over-all level of underutilization characterizing that situation. An engineer can be given greater freedom and discretion in the pursuit of his given task, in his hours, his coffee breaks, but the definition of the technical mission and the management environment are both beyond his control. Yet it is the mission and the environment that establish the character of individual tasks generally and determine the probability of underutilization for laboratory members.

Our pursuit of the roots of dissatisfaction and underutilization then leads directly to the necessity of understanding influence and control in organizations. For it seems to me that the conclusion to be drawn from our various analyses is that the way to attack these dual problems is through the development of a high role-influence management environment. How this might be done hinges on an analysis of the organizational limits on influence and the description of the control mechanisms applied to the management of systems development engineering. Our next two chapters are devoted to this purpose.

7 Influence

> In recent years our members have learned the bitter truth that attempts to influence the employer's policies in *any* area constitute an almost impossible task. The principal reason is that, in the field of industrial employment of professionals, there are more levels of supervisory and managerial authority than in any other segment of industrial employment. The lines of communication between the salaried professional and the management level at which effective influence can be exerted on the employer's policy are so long, so inefficient, and so fluid as to be useless.[1]

So writes the executive secretary of the Association of Scientists and Professional Engineering Personnel—an engineering union. He points to one of the special problems of large development laboratory organizations—lack of influence.

The anonymity of membership in large organizations clashes with the desire of highly educated personnel to influence the policies of those organizations—the desire to "make a difference." And especially personnel trained in technical fields expect to have some voice in formulating technical plans.

Perhaps it is this kind of expectation that makes the initial experience of working in the development laboratory an almost universal disappointment. For, as I have tried to show, the problems of the Electromech development organization are not unique in the indus-

[1] Andreas, "Cooperation among Professional, Technical and Non-professional Organizations in the Electrical Industry," in "Collective Bargaining for Professional and Technical Employees," Conference Report of the Institute of Labor and Industrial Relations, University of Illinois, May 20–21, 1965, pp. 2–7.

try. Witness these comments from engineers working for other organizations.

> It's not a profession in which people are in general happy. It gets back to the fact that engineers get used as a means to an end. I've seen an engineer shift five times in a year, and if you're on a job, you want to get it finished before management rips it away from you. This is more so where projects are large. But at Company C they're in a unique position . . . when product volume is small, everybody can be his own entrepreneur—a person can finish something. [Ph.D. in E.E.]
>
> Most of us feel our work is inconsequential. [B.S. in M.E.]
>
> You want to have an identity with your surroundings, to be an essential part of the group you work with . . . but then you're in a group of 250 people and you find yourself falling into an abyss. You feel at times detached; you feel you're slipping into something you don't want to slip into. But you don't know what to do about it . . . it seems to be a consequence of the size of the organization. It has to be a team effort, and each member can only make a small contribution . . . we're nothings . . . when a slack period comes, I think, "Look, what have I done, it's so small." [M.S. in E.E.] [2]

These comments illustrate the relation between work activities and the feeling of having some influence over things that matter. Top management reserves for itself the prerogative to factor the over-all development task as it sees fit. The logic and complexity of this factoring create roles to be filled by subordinate members of the organization—both engineers and managers.

This chapter is concerned with the meaning of influence in the development laboratory and aims to arrive at a better understanding of what is involved in making technical decisions. A special concern is illustrated by the opening quotation—how is it possible to exercise a significant amount of influence in a large bureaucratic organization with many levels of supervisory management? How much influence can a member of any work force expect to exert on "things that matter"?

Participation in "decisions that set the direction of technical effort in the company" is an important goal for many nonsupervisory engi-

[2] The preceding three quotations come from an unpublished report cited previously: Percy Black, "The Engineer's Self-Image and His Image of [Electromech]."

neers, and engineering students give even greater importance to this goal. Expectations concerning influence on technical decisions set the stage. We see also that having high role influence is very much a function of the type of organization. Engineers in the less bureaucratic field organizations are more favorably situated than engineers in the development laboratories. And within the system of development laboratories some environments are more favorable than others. It follows that any discussion of influence as a source of conflict must consider the total environment of the laboratory.

THE CONCEPT OF INFLUENCE

Power, control, and influence in organizations have been the subject of considerable attention in the literature of the social sciences. At this point I would like to review a few of the studies that use various concepts of influence in organizations.

A question that comes to mind immediately in a discussion of influence is: Influence on what? Studies discuss influence over other members of the group, over organizational policies, over work pace and methods of work. But the kind of influence we are interested in is influence over work assignments—what is it we are to work on?—and influence over technical decisions—how is this end to be accomplished? I also want to emphasize the organizational, impersonal aspects of influence rather than the interpersonal ones. Thus, for example, an engineer may find it impossible to influence his manager because his manager has no freedom to innovate within the given technological mission. This relationship is not the result of managerial style, does not occur because the manager refuses to listen, and is probably not the considered choice of the manager. Though I admit that influence must be exercised through others as agents of communication, it seems to me that the impersonal, structural factors that constrain the actions of others have been too often neglected in discussions of organizational influence. Thus, explanations of the results of systematic research tend to be presented in interpersonal terms.

Let me try to put this in more concrete form. Later in this chapter we will discuss an important characteristic of the distribution of influence over the various levels of organizational hierarchy. We will find that in some organizations all levels seem to have more influence than their counterparts in other organizations. Why should this be so? Explanations by other authors tend to be couched in interpersonal terms. In analyzing the results of their work in another development organization, Dalton and Barnes conclude that an organization member experiences greater influence or power when the dependence of others on him is increased.[3] Conversely, if he makes himself similarly dependent on others, then their influence as well will be increased. This seems reasonable as far as it goes. But to explain low influence is another matter. Tannenbaum suggests that the low-influence organization is characterized by laissez-faire relationships.[4] Leaders choose not to exert influence nor do they respond to attempts at influence by subordinates. The language of the accompanying discussion is that of interpersonal relations and leadership style. The explanation that seems to have been neglected, and which is particularly relevant for the systems development organization, is that the level of influence is determined by factors which transcend individual influence-dependence transactions. These factors are inherent in the development mission and in the management policies that govern the control of funding for technology programs.

I suspect an example is needed. In a project subsequent to, and largely unrelated to, this research I was facing the task of explaining to management some pretty grim-looking data. A continuing trend toward lower job satisfaction ratings was accompanied by a precipitous drop in the ratings of the performance of top management of the division. My interpretation was that this management had preempted control of technological programs and was generally fouling things up. Control was being exercised from "outside" and the situation was deteriorating. Unfortunately, the data did not fully support my explanation. For all levels, including division, were seen by the unhappy professionals as having little control over setting the general technical objectives for a department. I frankly told the management committee involved that I could not explain the data,

[3] Dalton *et al., The Distribution of Authority*, ch. 7.

[4] Tannenbaum, *Control in Organizations*, p. 20.

that the pattern was not what I had expected. I did not understand.

At this point one of the managers in the group spoke up. "Maybe you can't explain it," he said, "but I can. We're not running this division, we're being run by [Memo M]!" As it turns out, the division manager had introduced a detailed set of quantitative, formal procedures governing the funding and evaluating of development projects and the division was being run in accordance with those procedures. Now, the point of the example is this: to some extent there was no one running the division in the sense of exercising discretionary judgment. Highly specific procedures and criteria existed for initiating, evaluating, and refunding projects. Everyone lost a measure of control. Even the division executive who first promulgated these procedures had lost, for he could not afford to ignore completely his own directives in pursuit of his personal convictions.

At this point I can almost hear the engineer-reader saying, "Wait a minute, we have rules too, but we always find a way." Yes, and I am not maintaining that the engineers of this division followed those rules like so many mindless sheep. They did not. In fact, there seems to be an increase in the amount of scheming and misrepresentation present in all such organizations. Yet some measure of control had been lost, and it had been lost to something—not to someone. Increased effort was required to achieve even this lower level of influence, and this took its toll in job satisfaction. As a very disgruntled engineer put it, "We work our ass off just for the privilege of doing something."

To summarize, the aim of this and the following chapter is to learn the extent to which large systems development organizations can provide the opportunity for those in certain organizational roles—those in the work force as opposed to those in "responsible" management—to exercise technical initiative. The immediate concern of this chapter will be to understand the concept of influence in the laboratory context and to review ways in which the notion of influence has been treated in studies relevant to this research. Two points will be made. First, we will verify empirically that a pervasive management environment exists. Second, we will see that influence on technical programs is an organizational as opposed to an individual proposition. Influence is a parameter of the organizational system. Put differently, influence accruing to the role "engineer" is not subtracted from the role "manager"; rather it is only when managers as an organizational class have relatively high influence that engineers will experience high influence themselves.

LEADERSHIP STYLE, PARTICIPATION, AND CONTROL IN ORGANIZATIONS

The factors affecting the opportunities for individuals to exert influence on organizational matters that concern them may be partitioned into three separate, though related, clusters. They are:

1. The leadership styles of supervisors
2. Group dynamics and group participation in decision-making
3. The ways in which control is distributed over various levels of the organization

Studies in these areas have in common consideration of the extent to which subordinates are free to do things as they see fit. The studies consider outcomes related both to the productivity of the group and to the morale of its members. I will try to sort out and examine only the evidence related to organizational factors or leadership styles that tend to encourage or discourage influence attempts by nonsupervisory members.

Close vs. General Supervision. Managers who specify the work behavior of their subordinates in great detail are said to be exercising close supervision. In development engineering this style of supervision implies that all decisions about a technical design, large and small, are made by the engineer's manager. The following is what one engineer had to say of his close-supervising manager.

> His biggest detrimental quality is his mother-henness over the job, he won't delegate responsibility. . . . [My old manager] always said that you've got to pick up the ball and run with it. Here it's hard to find out if the ball's been put down by the referee. . . . He has the habit of making small changes on the drawings himself.[5]

Under these conditions we might expect an engineer to feel he lacks influence. Studies from the University of Michigan describe close su-

[5] Ritti, "Engineers and Managers," unpublished doctoral dissertation, p. 167.

pervision in this way: "The supervisor checks up on his employees frequently, gives them detailed and frequent instructions and, in general limits the employees' freedom to do the work in their own way." [6] In these studies, the closeness of the supervision is taken to be an individual attribute of leadership behavior rather than a manifestation of the management environment. The results of these studies show generally that close supervision results in lower job satisfaction but not necessarily in lower productivity. The conclusion regarding productivity is that close supervision of highly routine or unskilled work is likely to result in higher productivity. Little relationship is found for the highly skilled jobs.[7]

The notion of close supervision has been derived primarily from studies of nonprofessional workers, and therefore it is not surprising that it has more to do with the supervision of tasks already assigned than it does with the choice of tasks or the setting of work objectives. From this viewpoint we can examine the impact of close supervision in restricting influence related to decisions about a task already assigned, as opposed to decisions about which projects to work on.

The index of close supervision we shall use is a composite of the following five items taken from the supervisory behavior description: [8]

—He insists that you follow his instructions to the letter.
—He supervises your jobs very closely.
—He decides in detail what you should do and how you should do it.
—He insists that you follow standard procedures and practices.
—He handles details of your work that you would normally expect to handle yourself.

Our data show that this index of close supervision is not related to

[6] Katz *et al., Productivity, Supervision and Morale in an Office Situation,* p. 17.

[7] Morse, *Satisfactions in the White Collar Job,* pp. 137–38. See also the general conclusions by Dubin regarding the small effect of supervisory styles on productivity in Dubin *et al., Leadership and Productivity.*

[8] This dimension is derived from a factor analysis of several earlier surveys. See Ritti, "Control of Halo in Factor Analysis of a Supervisory Behavior Inventory," *Personnel Psychology,* XVII (1964), 305–18.

engineers' perceptions of lack of role influence (correlations average .12 for the Darby and Ferndale groups). And this is consistent with the model we have been developing. However, there is a somewhat higher degree of association between the dimension we call individual influence and reports of close supervision (.23), suggesting that there is some restriction of the engineer's freedom to carry out the job as he sees fit. By way of comparison, the dimension that seems to be most affected by closeness of supervision of work is *Visibility of Individual Contributions* (.36); those under closest supervision feel that their contributions to be least visible. The over-all conclusion from these data is that influence over technical program decisions is not related to individual styles in handling the work of subordinates. I think the reason for this is that such leadership styles relate to the way tasks already assigned are to be carried out, not to how those tasks are to be chosen or what the best allocation of departmental resources would be. Role influence involves broader organizational processes.

Group Participation in Decision-making. One organizational mechanism for allowing workers to exert influence on work objectives or policies is known as *participative management.* While this term has come to have many meanings, its origin lies in the studies of the dynamics of group processes carried on at the University of Michigan. One experimental study by Coch and French has had a great deal to do with the general interest in participative management.[9]

The basic formulation that led to the experiment in participation was the observation that the work group held standards of production that were not necessarily those set by management. Part of the problem that management faced when trying to increase production by a change in methods was that the standard of productivity the group felt to be fair was likely to be lower than that desired by management. The group applied social pressure to individuals to keep them in line with the group informal standard. From earlier work in group dynamics the Michigan researchers had become convinced that when group members are allowed to participate in set-

[9] Coch and French, "Overcoming Resistance to Change," *Human Relations*, XI (1948), 512–32.

ting standards or group goals they will become committed to achieving those goals. The role of management is to communicate the need for establishing certain goals. Group pressures are then applied toward meeting the new goals set in the participative process. Thus, the primary dynamic of participation is group consensus and commitment to newly set goals, as well as social pressure brought to bear on group members to achieve the new standard.

The message that the Coch and French experiment held for management was this:

> It is possible for management to modify greatly or to remove completely group resistance to changes in methods of work and the ensuing piece rates. This change can be accomplished by the use of group meetings in which management effectively communicates the need for change and stimulates group participation in planning the changes.[10]

Is the notion of participation in goal-setting as originally formulated applicable to engineering groups? Obviously, there is anything but restriction of production in development engineering. The full rationale of participative management needs some modification to be relevant to the problem of influence we have been examining.

Influence and Organizational Patterns of Control. More to the point is a concept of participation in the influence processes of the organization that currently appears in the literature. This concept appears to have little to do with restriction of productivity per se and more to do with the process by which effective coordination of productive activities is achieved.

> Significant influence exercised by persons at all levels, the leaders as well as the rank and file, provides the basis for the effective coordination of organizational activity. Such coordination is derived, in part, from the shared goals and agreement on the means to these goals which this pattern of control promotes. Similarly, the exercise of control by lower echelons is likely to bring with it greater acceptance of jointly-made decisions as well as an increased sense of responsibility and motivation to further the goals of the organization.[11]

[10] *Ibid.*, p. 532.

[11] Smith and Ari, "Organizational Control Structure and Member Consensus," *American Journal of Sociology*, LXIX (1964), 623.

Research based on these ideas has shown that both morale and productivity are related to certain patterns of control within some kinds of organization. One study of thirty-two stations in a company engaged in the delivery of packages shows that both productivity of the stations and the morale of station members are highly related to the amount of influence or "say" that the various levels of the organization felt they had in determining what went on in their station. That is, in stations where the several levels of station management and the workers all felt they had more "say," both station productivity and morale were higher. While the beneficial effects are presumably derived from a shared, acceptable system of work standards, it is not clear from the study whether or not the larger degree of control is arrived at through group processes. It does suggest that the increased effectiveness and higher morale result because organization members "have a part in determining organizational norms and consequently may be expected to be more motivated to accept them." [12] So again the link between higher productivity and influence on policies is seen to come through group standards of productivity that are mutually acceptable to all members because all members feel they have had some influence in establishing the standards.

The study just described is one of a growing number that deal with the way in which influence on plans and policies that affect organization members is distributed over the several levels of the organization. An important aspect of influence is that it is not a fixed quantity that must be divided somehow among the members within a given organization. Likert and others have pointed out that the total amount of control or influence exercised by organizational members at various levels can be greater or less at all levels.[13] In some organizations, all members feel they can exert greater influence than do members of other organizations. And if influence is related to both morale and the effectiveness of the organization, some means of achieving higher levels of influence seems desirable.

One study is particularly relevant to the concept of control or in-

[12] *Ibid.*, p. 636.

[13] Likert, *The Human Organization*. See also Tannenbaum, *Control in Organizations*.

fluence and its effects on the morale of engineers. It deals with the effects of a cooperative program at the TVA in which representatives of the employees and management engage in a continuing series of meetings to discuss work methods and other company policies. Management takes the recommendations of employees into consideration but retains the final responsibility for accepting and executing decisions. A research evaluation of the impact of this policy shows that there is a high degree of association between participation in work decisions and favorable attitudes toward the organization on the part of the professional groups involved. The author concludes:

> It seems likely that professionals like engineers have an image of their ideal work roles which includes an active role in planning of projects and selection among alternative methods. It seems likely also that professionals are more apt than skilled workers to view such participation as legitimate and for such participation to be important to their self images as first-rate members of their occupations. If this is so, then the extent to which professionals (and those with similar work needs) value their organizational roles would be expected to depend fairly strongly on the extent on which the organization gives them the chance to participate in work decisions.[14]

This is closer to the kind of participative management that might apply to the development laboratory situation. A formal organizational arrangement exists for the discussion of policies and programs that affect the engineers' day-to-day work activities. To some extent this kind of setup seems more related to company operating procedures than to design development. But there is no question that higher levels of personal commitment to the job and satisfaction with the engineering work role were achieved in this instance through generally increased influence on organizational affairs that are of importance to professionals.

To summarize, we have looked at a sample of studies that deal with the relationship between the extent to which an individual can influence various facets of his work situation and his job satisfaction or productivity. Almost none of these relate directly to the develop-

[14] Patchen, "Labor-Management Consultation at TVA: Its Impact on Employees," *Administrative Science Quarterly*, x (1965), 167.

ment population in which we are interested. Obviously, the work expectations of development laboratory engineers and those of production workers are different. The engineer, with certain "professional" expectations, will feel that it is reasonable for him to have more say in allocating company resources than would the production worker. And yet the jobs of engineers and production workers are in some respects similar. Therefore, we can sketch out some of the broad ideas in which the literature is in consistent agreement.

1. Organizations in which all members—both management and nonmanagement—feel they can exert more influence on policies and practices that affect them seem to show higher job satisfaction and productivity than similar organizations whose members feel they can exert less influence.

2. Organizations in which nonsupervisory employees are provided with some arrangement through which they can get action on their ideas through a cooperative effort with management will show higher levels of employee commitment to the organization and commitment to accomplish the task at hand.

Our task now is to take a look at the Electromech organization to see how these ideas of influence sharing might apply, and how the management environment corresponds to the distribution of control over the various levels of management.

MANAGEMENT ENVIRONMENT AND SUPERVISORY BEHAVIOR

I suspect that higher-level management in most organizations regards the management environment as a product of the supervisory styles of lower-level management. It follows from this viewpoint that interpersonally competent supervisors will create a positive environment. On the other hand, it may be that the behavior of supervisors is more the product than the source of the management environment. As pointed out by the human relations training study cited earlier, first-line managers tend to supervise much in the manner they are supervised themselves.[15] But subordinates will not necessarily perceive that their manager is not master of his own actions. The

[15] Fleishman *et al.*, *Leadership and Supervision in Industry*.

higher up the management ladder you go, the more the manager is looked upon as being "responsible" as opposed to simply carrying out instructions from above. Managers do little to discourage this view.

Managerial authority vested in the organization hierarchy is made legitimate or acceptable to subordinates through privileged information and technical expertise. Managers are reluctant to admit that they do not know an answer, or that they cannot solve a problem, because this tends to undermine the legitimacy of their authority in the eyes of their subordinates. It is understandable, then, that they sometimes attempt to hide their weaknesses under the guise of authoritarian practice. But the point is that an important part of their behavior is determined by an entire system of management as opposed to personal "leadership styles."

I witnessed a vivid demonstration of this in an earlier depth study of a group of engineering departments.[16] It was quite obvious that most of the engineers in the mechanical engineering department were engaged in "grunt" work, and were quite unhappy about it. Interviews with the engineers, their manager, and the manager of the entire function of which they were a part provide an interesting contrast in perceptions.

From the point of view of his engineers, the manager was not standing up for their interests.

> It seems that [my manager] isn't firm enough in the defense of his own interests—that he doesn't stand up for his own men. He takes on jobs for the men that he shouldn't. We do all the drawing for the people in [our function] including the E.E.'s. . . . During the last project when we were swamped with work he would take on these little extra jobs that he didn't have to; I've gotten this from others when he has made these little concessions.

Later on I had an interview with the manager and we discussed the work situation in his department. I also questioned him about the relationship he had with his own manager. He had this to say:

> [My manager] is a strong leader, an authoritarian leader. There is no questioning his rule. By that I mean that our policies wouldn't be con-

[16] The next three quotations are taken from Ritti, "Engineers and Managers," unpublished doctoral dissertation.

> trary to his very long. He has the strongest personality of anyone in the organization. I feel that this is good for us, though, for if the organization gets ahead, I will too. . . . There will be times when he will commit himself for the department . . . so he will ask me to help get it out. Knowing [my manager] from past experience, I know that if he has made a commitment there is no way that *I* am going to talk him out of it.

It seems at this point as though the engineers' perception of the situation is in focus. Their manager does in fact appear to be lacking in influence, and somewhat overwhelmed by his own very strong manager. Taking the matter a step further, I had a talk with the manager's manager. We discussed the work assignment of the department and how the tasks had been assigned. Here is part of the resulting conversation:

> I select the work for them—they don't select it. The work that they do has evolved from a contractual obligation that I have. The group was assigned to complete the work on the [project]. I feel that they were not happy with it, but someone had to do it and they were familiar with the work. It was a production job but production didn't want to handle it. I got saddled with it because we had the know-how. *I didn't want it either.*

My pursuit of the matter ended at his level, but these discussions, as well as further observation, brought home several conclusions to me. It is clear that the personalities of the primary individuals involved are quite different. The second-level manager is the stronger personality of the two. The people at lower levels tended to take their own manager's weakness as the explanation of their situation, but it seems to me that the immediate situation of this work group was much more a function of an impersonal factoring of the over-all development mission by top management. The group had the know-how and the job had to be done. Whether it was Group X or Group Y that finally wound up with the job is not the crucial issue from the viewpoint of the entire development laboratory organization. Perhaps different managers would have sloughed off the undesirable work on some other less politically astute manager. But the work is there and someone is inevitably assigned to do it.

From this point of view there is no question but that the interpersonal influence of managers *does* account for different levels of satisfaction among work groups. But there is a question as to whether or not the manipulation of these attributes can have any impact on the basic problems of the *total* development organization. The point of view that I shall try to make plausible here is that both supervisory behavior and engineers' influence over technical programs are jointly affected by some over-all factors that I call the management environment. The remainder of this chapter will be devoted to an example of such an environment and some conjectures as to its origin.

Figure 7.1 illustrates our first important point, that levels of influence tend to be alike for both supervisory and nonsupervising engineers. In the laboratories where first-line managers are relatively satisfied with their participation in setting the technical goals of their departments, engineers also feel greater role influence.[17]

Managers in an organizational situation that allows more flexibility can, and apparently do, pass on some of their power to subordinates. On the other hand, restrictions on managerial influence directly curtail the influence of subordinates.

In the previous chapter we saw that levels of influence are quite similar within locations. Projects within a given location do not show much variability. The data on engineering managers just related reinforce and amplify this observation. For if there is a homogeneous management environment, and if there is a one-to-one correspondence between the perceptions of both supervisors and subordinates, it seems unlikely that differences in supervisory style can be responsible for these data. This suggests that Likert and his associates are quite correct in focusing their attention on over-all patterns of organizational control.

Organizational Control Curves. One way of examining the influence patterns of organizations is through the use of "control curves." [18] I asked engineers this question: "How much 'say' or influence do you think each of the following actually has in setting the

[17] The rank order correlation for these two variables based on the mean values for the location is .87. The smallest laboratory location has 15 managers in the group, the next smallest 25. The largest group of managers is about 200. Thus, the regularity of the data is impressive despite the fact that the smaller managerial groups have inherently greater variability.

[18] Examples and a further description of this method can be found in Tannenbaum, *Control in Organizations.*

Figure 7.1
Level of Role Influence Perceived by Engineers as a Function of Managers' Satisfaction with Participation in Setting Goals for Department for Twelve Laboratory Locations

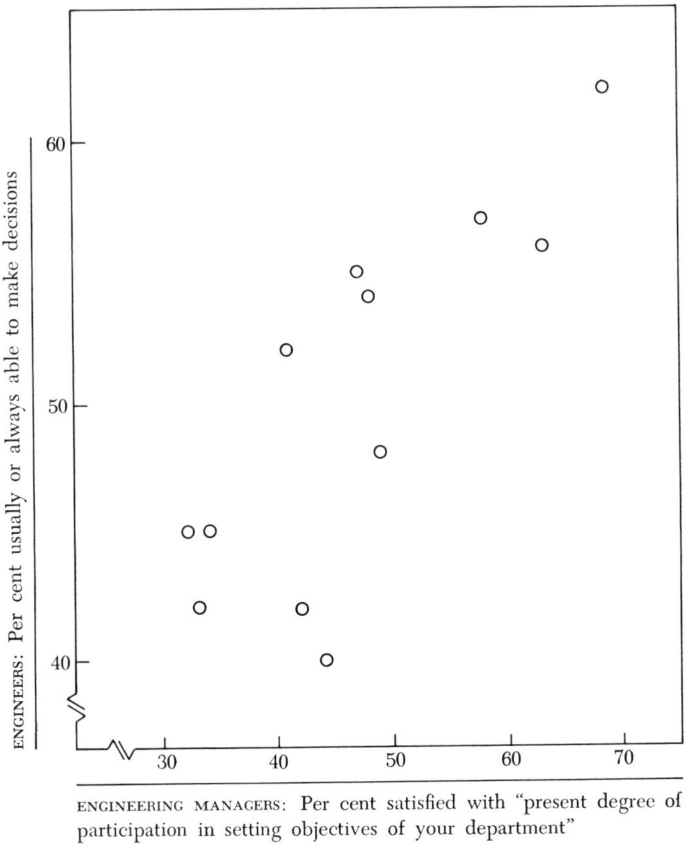

general technical objectives for your department?" Various levels of the organization ranging from "You yourself" up to "Division management" were then rated against this question. The results can now be plotted as a graph. The amount of control each level is perceived as having is shown as a function of organizational level. Levels are arrayed along the X axis from lowest to highest.

In this case I had to draw on data from a later sample survey of

Electromech engineers, and so there is no direct correspondence to the groups used earlier.[19] Ten major laboratories participated in the study.

To illustrate the idea of control curves as a reflection of the management environment I have shown in Figure 7.2 the patterns for two locations that represent extremes. The striking thing about these curves is their similarity in shape. Thus, if the curve for Belleville were shifted up one level of organization it would be almost identical to that of Avondale. While control is centered on second-level management in Belleville, it is seen to rest with top management in Avondale. The conclusion is obvious: the factors that determine the amount of influence that can be exerted by lower levels are seen as determining also the influence of higher levels of management. Factors that shift the over-all level of influence up the management hierarchy weaken the influence of supervisor and subordinate alike. But who is "responsible?"

Figure 7.3 provides one answer. When asked a question about how well each of the levels of management is doing its job, engineers at both locations apparently thought that top local management is primarily responsible for their situation. While all levels of Belleville local management are seen as doing a better job, the greatest difference in the ratings occurs at the top management level. Apparently division management is too remote from the nonsupervisory level to receive either blame or credit for the situation. In fact, roughly half of the engineers at both locations feel that they cannot rate the job being done by the divisional level of management.

How correct are these perceptions? What is the factual situation at the two laboratories? First let me take up the case of Belleville. I would say the perceptions here are quite accurate. The group has been hand-picked by management to work on their project. They are currently engaged in the development of a special system whose specifications they are free to set. Their only limitations are time,

[19] In fact, neither of these laboratory organizations was in existence at the time of the major survey three years earlier. While the Avondale location is the same as that cited previously, this organization is attached to a different division of the company and has entirely different personnel and mission.

Figure 7.2
Rating of Influence of Six Levels of Organization by Nonsupervisory Professionals at Two Locations

QUESTION: "HOW MUCH 'SAY' OR INFLUENCE DO YOU THINK EACH OF THE FOLLOWING ACTUALLY HAS IN SETTING THE GENERAL TECHNICAL OBJECTIVES FOR YOUR DEPARTMENT?"

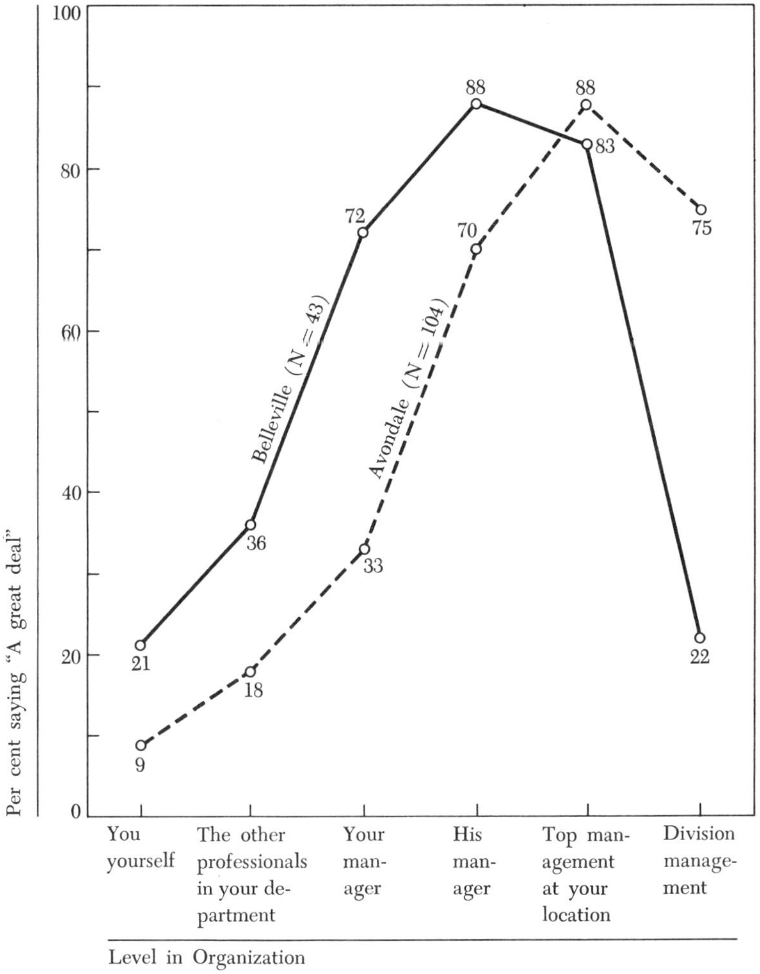

Figure 7.3

Rating of Job Being Done by Four Levels of Management by Nonsupervisory Professionals at Two Locations

QUESTION: "HOW GOOD A JOB DO YOU THINK IS BEING DONE BY EACH OF THE FOLLOWING LEVELS OF MANAGEMENT?"

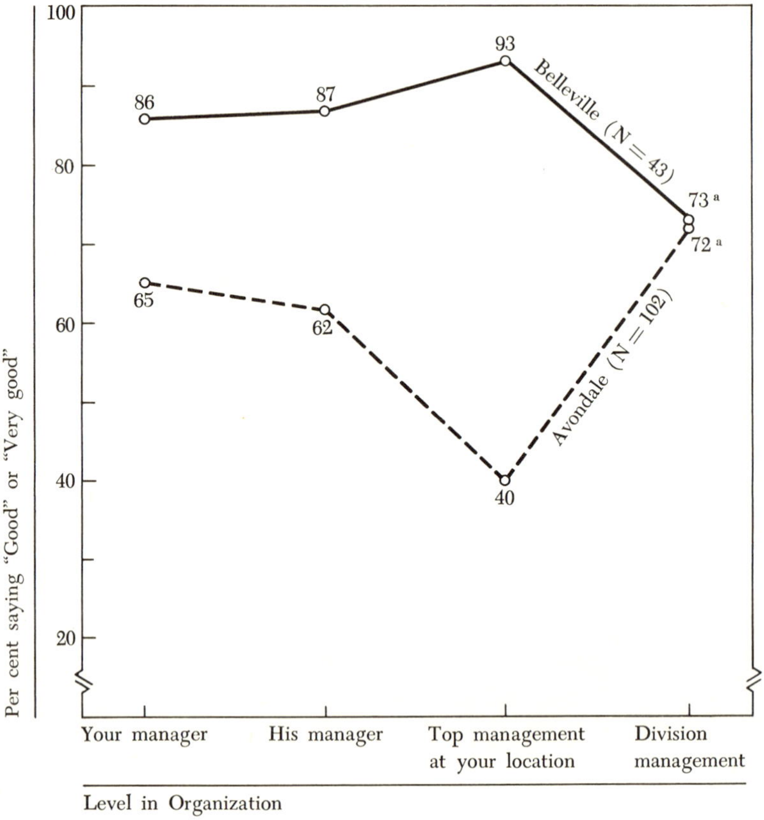

[a] Approximately 50 per cent of sample replied they knew nothing about the job being done at this level.

budget, and the "state of the art." The laboratory manager is one of the bright young men in Electromech engineering. He has been responsible for some notable past successes and was chosen directly by corporate management to head this project. His major strengths are on the administrative and political levels. He was given a free hand in choosing his geographical location, and picked one as remote as possible from corporate and division management.

Avondale is in the same division of Electromech. While the group here is about twice the size of Belleville's, it is also concerned with but one project. Beyond this, there is little similarity. Where I sensed a feeling of elitism at Belleville, the feeling is one of defeatism at Avondale. A member of top division management put it this way:

> Avondale was at the lowest point at that time. At that point the boys walked out of the hole and said we are not going to make it. They were up against the gun of having just missed their commitments. They were receiving a lot of grinding management attention. . . . The commitments they were trying to meet were made by others who met top management pressures and promised things that [those remaining] felt could not be met. They were left holding the bag.

At this point I asked why those who had made the promises were not now involved. He said:

> There are a number of top guys who had some skin in this thing. There were a number of violent arguments about it. [Later] the guys who said yes mostly went on to other things. The net result was that the guys who were on this thing lost the confidence of top management.

By this he meant that top company management no longer felt confident that local management could handle the project.

This is the situation from which the management environment developed. The key elements are: commitment to unrealistic specifications set by others, failure, and the consequent "grinding attention" from divisional management. To me it seems that the perception of the situation by the engineers at Avondale is correct except perhaps for the harsh judgment of top local management. For Avondale is closest of all the laboratories to division headquarters and Electromech is committed as a company to the project. There is probably very little that local people can do. Nevertheless, from the engineer's point of view, if local management is not looking out for his welfare, then who is?

The point of all this is that the management environment is the product of several factors, some of which are out of the control of local management. And this environment has an impact on all levels of the organization. The perception of the situation by the engineers themselves is but one indication of a total organizational situation. And what is the impact of this situation in terms of some of the other dimensions we have studied? Table 7.1 shows once again that the influence and utilization levels of a laboratory can be expected to be related—low influence, low utilization. And now it is clear

Table 7.1

Levels of Influence, Utilization, and Supervisory Descriptions for Two Laboratories with Different Control Levels (Nonsupervisory Engineers only)

	Per cent of favorable responses	
	Belleville (N=43)	Avondale (N=104)
1. During the past year do you feel that your position has allowed you to make the decisions *you felt were necessary* to ensure the best technical course of action for Electromech? (per cent responding "usually")	60	28
2. Do you ever feel that management is preventing your group from working in the directions that you should be? (per cent responding "seldom")	81	34
3. You participate in decisions that affect the future business of the company (per cent responding "sometimes," or "usually")	55	19
4. Your part of the project seems trivial or routine (per cent responding "seldom")	86	40
5. Your project offers you a real chance to show what you can do (per cent responding "usually")	71	32
6. You are free to choose the project on which you want to work (per cent responding "sometimes" or "usually")	62	32
7. Your manager asks for your assistance in establishing goals and schedules for your work (per cent responding "usually")	60	52
8. Your manager gets the opinion of his men before he commits the department to a goal or schedule (per cent responding "usually")	45	37
9. Your manager handles details of your work that you would normally expect to handle yourself (per cent responding "almost never")	40	56

that this situation stems from a pervasive management environment. Apparently the "management" that is seen as preventing the group from pursuing the proper course of action (item 2) is top local management. The more a laboratory is run like a factory and engineers are viewed as a work force to be applied impersonally to meet top management needs, the greater the likelihood that first-line managers will be merely ciphers in the system. In fact, as illustrated by Table 7.1, there is little correspondence between some indicators of "supervisory style" and the environment we know to exist. The niceties recommended by managers' training manuals—setting goals together, getting opinions, general supervision—seem to be followed by managers at both locations. Interestingly the largest difference (item 9) runs counter to the influence factors. Apparently the Belleville managers are *more* likely to be close rather than general supervisors.[20] But the impact of the management environment is felt through the first-line manager in other ways. When asked,

> Suppose someone in your kind of work was dissatisfied with something in your department—such as the amount or kind of work he was expected to do, pay, opportunities for transfer, etc. Do you think it would help him to take it up with his manager?

33 per cent of the Avondale engineers replied that it probably or definitely would *not* help. Only 5 per cent of the Belleville engineers replied in the same way.

THE DEVELOPMENT ENGINEERING FACTORY

I have tried to describe the management environment in terms of contrasting extremes. At best we can have a situation like the one at Belleville. While Belleville still functions as a systems engineering proposition—38 per cent say they are seldom or never free to choose the projects on which they want to work—there is yet an environment where all organizational levels are relatively influential.

[20] An interesting sidelight that helps to explain this observation is that the Belleville managers are also rated considerably higher on several indicators of technical ability and judgment. In this case it seems that the tendency toward close supervision of the work of subordinates stems from the inability of technically oriented supervisors to "keep their hands off" the work of subordinates.

In the worst situation it seems to me that the engineer is not much better off than the factory hand. He is the executor of technical tasks supplied by management. His own manager is reduced to the status of a transmission link, with little influence over the technical management of his group. The result is that engineers in this situation have about the same opinion of their jobs as do factory workers. Using the same job satisfaction question and the comparative data appearing in Chapter 1, we find that only 21 per cent of the Avondale engineers rate their jobs as "very good." When we recall that the comparable figure for Electromech blue-collar workers is an almost identical 18 per cent, the comparison is telling. Similarly, Belleville engineers resemble the field, with 47 per cent giving the "very good" rating to their own jobs.

In summary, I think we have seen evidence of the existence of the management environment in the fact that all levels of the organization share in increased or decreased levels of influence. I think also the case has been made that the results we observe are not a function of individual supervisory competence. Rather, it seems that the differences in supervisory behavior that do exist are the product, not the source, of the management environment. Finally, it seems to me that the outcomes observed at the lowest (engineer) level of the organization are in many respects beyond the control of local people, are in fact the long-range outcomes of division and corporate level policy decisions.

This last point provides the basis of a number of discussions I have had with Electromech management, discussions dealing with the "what can we do about it" problem. The basic management point, I think, is twofold:

1. If things aren't going well at a location it's top local management that's to blame.

2. We know that there are locations where engineers aren't making the decisions they want. That's just the way it is. The development mission of the laboratories has been assigned by us to meet the needs of Electromech. If that mission is one that implies a number of constraints on influence, well, there's not much that we can do about it.

While my summary of these arguments is rather stark, I think it poses the next problem well. To what extent is the development mission of the laboratories responsible for the observed management environment? For I do not mean to imply that Electromech management is not concerned about its engineers. Rather management thinks that things are not in such bad shape after all, and it firmly believes that the nature of the work itself rather than management policy is responsible for the observed differences. Therefore, before we can start to think about ways of improving the situation we must investigate the impact of the development mission itself on the management environment.

To rephrase the problem, we recognize that the development mission may affect the management environment as we have defined it. Certainly it seems reasonable to believe that technological constraints generally restrict influence and lower satisfaction. Technology and underutilization seem to be intimately related. So the question becomes this: If all laboratories were pursuing an identical mission, would the management environment then have any effect on satisfaction, influence, and utilization? That is, granting that systems development has a higher characteristic level of problem characteristics than other types of engineering, are there factors within the system that can be identified as mitigating these problems but that are unrelated to variations in technology? This is an important question, for if the management environment does have an effect independent of mission, then management is to some extent free to manipulate the situation to obtain more favorable outcomes.

8

Influence and Technology: The Impact of the Development Mission

> In my opinion, the [laboratory] suffers more from problems related to organization and procedure than any other kind. Problems which manifest themselves in the factors of morale, job satisfaction and general technical apathy seem to have their origin in the way we conduct our business. . . . There appears to be a general respect for [laboratory] management, but at the same time a general frustration with its performance. What else can we expect when it takes longer to follow administrative procedures than it does to make the product? Ideas for improvement are legion, but decision-making capability that will allow the facility to act responsively and competitively is scarce.

Advanced planning is the backbone of a technology-based organization. This is one of our first premises. A crucial part of this planning is programmed innovation. This means that new products are developed to a timetable. The larger the organization and the more complex the systems it develops, the more likely it is that entire suborganizations or laboratories will be solely devoted to the development of one or two complex systems. Under this kind of circumstance I have heard management talk of being "locked-in" by technical requirements. To meet schedules within the budget management must apply all its resources to the projected system.

On the other hand, the complaints of engineers themselves and of first-level management often center on management practices. The opening quotation in this chapter is a good illustration of these sentiments. Engineers talk of playing politics and of administrative confusion. They talk of decisions made by people who are in no position to know the facts.

Since the task of this chapter is to sort out the technological or mission constraints from the administrative or political ones, I think the first step must be to provide a more realistic view of what enters into the making of a technical decision. If we are to talk about influence in "setting general technical objectives" or in making "the decisions you feel are necessary to ensure the best technical course of action," we need some additional material concerning the manner in which technical decisions are made in the development laboratory.

WHO MAKES THE DECISIONS: SOME LIMITS ON INDIVIDUAL INFLUENCE

Decisions involve uncertainty. If the next step in an evolving project is completely clear, is dictated purely by the facts, then there is no decision to be made. At least there is no decision in the sense of a choice among alternatives. But it is rarely if ever that all of the facts point in the same direction and that all decision-makers elect the same course of action. Those who would choose other alternatives seem also to place emphasis on different sets of facts. Under these conditions charges of politics and personality are brought to bear by those who champion the other approaches. People say that decisions are made on the basis of personal opinion rather than on the basis of fact. And of course this is true to some extent. For in the face of uncertainty, decisions must be made on the basis of opinion. The "state of the art" in engineering is a dynamic thing. Not so much because of dramatic scientific advances, such as the discovery of solid-state devices, but because of the steady development of better ways of doing what is already known. Improvements in manufacturing methods make new alternatives economically feasible. The market also changes with continuing economic development. All this means that a certain amount of guesswork or "forecasting" is necessary in arriving at most engineering decisions. There are times when one course of action seems equally as good as another and it is necessary to make a decision simply to keep things moving. One engineer put it this way:

> Decisions have to be made by edict very often because you can't make a good engineering judgment. Two years from now you don't know how

> things may have changed so you'll never know whether you did the right or wrong thing . . . we make a lot of assumptions that are good to about ± 50 per cent. You have to include all of the dimensions, all of the variables, and you have to guess three to five years early in the game. You're going to get a lot of overlap in your alternatives because of this, and you can't make a solid engineering judgment. You need an edicted answer.

But, as I have tried to point out, "edicted" answers will leave some people unhappy. There are bound to be some engineers who are convinced that their alternative, their particular group of facts, is correct. Frustration is inevitable since the achievement of personal goals is highly dependent upon the opportunity to carry out what you believe to be the appropriate course of action.

To compound the problem, decisions about technical programs ("edicted" and otherwise) that most affect an engineer are commonly made at an organizational level quite remote from him or his immediate supervisor. Important technical decisions relating to systems designs are resolved at a level of management where all the lines of project authority come together. If important business considerations are also involved, the decision may move up another echelon.

A good example of this kind of decision involves the choice of technologies to use for system components. It is illustrative of how far decisions that are apparently purely technical are removed from the nonsupervisory level.

My first contact with the systems technology program came through a series of group interviews with development engineers responsible for various solid-state and competing technologies. One of these groups had responsibility for the development of one of the newer technologies. At the time the members of this group were quite dissatisfied, claiming that the top-level management of their function had a bias in favor of the old technology, and that the personal opinion of one member of top management was blocking them. They had developed a considerable involvement in "their" technology, and labeled as politics the efforts they saw to promote the old technology.

Perhaps a year later I witnessed a presentation of how a corporate-level decision was made on which technology to use in a proposed group of systems. This particular presentation was, as a matter of fact, given to a gathering of top engineering managers as a model of how planned, rational decisions should be made on choices of technology. An interesting sidelight of this presentation was that it advocated the use of the new technology described earlier by my group of engineers, and that it was made by the top-level manager whom they had accused of having an anti-new technology bias!

But who made the decision? The original presentation was made to a corporate committee which concurred with the recommendations. That was the decision in one sense. For such review boards do not necessarily concur, and they may ask for more facts or different kinds of facts. They can reject the argument as being inadequate. In another sense the decision is already made when the facts are gathered and put together in such a way as to point in a particular direction. People who work with facts understand that emphasis on one set of data as opposed to another can make one alternative look considerably better than another.

The types of fact presented are also significant. These are some of the kinds of data used:

1. The ratios of cost-to-performance estimated for system components made with each of the technologies under consideration.

2. Estimates of the improvement potential in these cost-to-performance ratios as a function of the improvement of manufacturing techniques. Presumably the older technologies are closer to minimum production costs.

3. Graphical comparisons of trends in cost-to-performance ratios over a period of time of both Electromech's and its competitors' system components. These include extrapolations (guesses) as to the ratios of future system components to be developed by competitors.

These and other kinds of data are then used to choose a technology that will provide a competitive edge in the marketplace perhaps three to four years in the future.

They form the basis of a decision for allocating resources to the main thrust of technological development over the next several years.

I have chosen this decision because it seems to be a good example of how a technical decision is made, and it shows why a decision is "made" at the top levels of the corporation. A decision like this is very important to the business success of the company. But it is full of uncertainty and subjective estimates. It contains many nontechnical elements. Much of the information required is normally not in the possession of the nonsupervisory engineer, but primarily such a decision is simply felt to be too important to be trusted to lower-level people. It is a decision that must be made by "responsible" management.

And what is the impact of this decision? For one thing, it means that resources are now allocated in much greater proportion to the chosen technology. This in turn means that many engineers must be reassigned. Not only is this a frustrating experience, but careers are involved. As one engineer put it:

> When the project gets killed, more often than not your group gets split up. You haven't proven yourself and you have to start all over again. You can't go back and point out what you've accomplished. This is going to hurt your career.

In addition to these directly foreseeable implications, there is a more remote impact that flows from the nature of systems design. Other engineering workers now find themselves with new or additional constraints that stem from system-compatibility considerations. It can easily happen that system plans and designs that were previously satisfactory are now seriously deficient in some aspect. Pet projects and bright ideas of one sort or another often fall victim to the far-reaching implications of broad systems decisions.

A second example of a decision made about a systems configuration concerns a much less important situation. But again it illustrates that technical issues are generally resolved by people other than those directly involved in the technical design. This case involves two groups working on similar designs at different laboratories. These groups were specialists in heat transfer, and the problem concerned methods of carrying off excess heat in order to maintain the system within an appropriate operating temperature range. The engineer with whom I discussed the problem pointed out that in the past the method of cooling had simply been one of forcing enough air through the system to carry off excess heat. The more cooling required, the more air required. He termed this parallel cooling. The group in the other laboratory was using this type of design. His group had come up with a different approach to the problem. In this case the solution was to use but a single air stream and to space heat transfer points at given intervals to reduce the temperature. He termed this series cooling. Each group championed its particular approach, pointing out the strong points of its own design.

In this case the design was finally chosen by the "systems people" who are responsible for the over-all systems configuration. The series design was chosen because of the advantages in requiring less duct work and being somewhat cheaper. The need for "systems compatibility" usually dictates the choice of one alternative that will be used by all.

But again, it is another group that chooses the final design—the "systems people"—a group of engineers set up to follow through on the design of a given system, and in a sense to do the "bookkeeping" of engineering. Decisions about technical design features are resolved in this group as a part of the design coordination function. The more important decisions are the responsibility of management. So when you are told that the "systems people" made the decision, it means that someone with managerial responsibility in this group has ratified the choice of a technical alternative.

The point of this example is that decisions are made by a fairly complex process. In one sense the decision is made by those who come up with the alternatives. As in the previous example, a limited range of alternatives is presented, and the choice is made by those responsible for the systems area or technology in question.

TECHNICAL DECISIONS IN SYSTEMS DESIGN

Two sets of constraints limit the influence of the systems development engineer. The first of these is economics, the second systems compatibility. More often than not the design problem is economic feasibility. The thing is technically possible but cannot be justified in the marketplace. Competitors are there to make sure of that. Quite often it is systems compatibility or uniformity that brings economic justification. And it is quite possible that within the over-all systems configuration *not one* of the proposed individual designs is best. That is, the design engineer knows technical approaches to make System A perform better within a given cost constraint, but this implies noncompatibility with systems B, C, and D. Unfortunately it is this compatibility upon which the ultimate economic success of the entire series of systems rests. To the individual engineer this usually means that for obscure reasons better solutions are ignored or rejected. When you add "lead time" problems—better solutions come too late—and the natural reluctance of coordinators to change design configurations when consensus has been attained, you begin to get some feeling for the decision potential of the individual engineer. And these factors derive primarily from technical considerations.

But there is something else that seems to be unavoidable in systems management, namely, the desire for explicit, rational decision rules for allocating resources. Because of the degree of complexity and functional interdependence characteristic of complex systems, there must be individuals whose prime responsibility is the coordination and compromise of proposed designs. This is a management responsibility at several levels, and the skills are those of politics—negotiation, mediation, compromise, and arbitration.[1] And yet I think engineers are uneasy with this kind of management. Certainly higher-level management in Electromech feels uneasy about this approach. Higher management of the company wants some assurance that the situation is under control, that decisions are being made on a rational basis, and that there is some way of *knowing* this. I think it is this impulse that leads to the development of rational, quantitative decision rules to guide systems development. Without getting into a discussion of the merits of this approach, certain outcomes should be apparent. Here is one reaction:

> Division, laboratory, and area management of [Division A] have informed me by word and action that the requirement, now, for either establishing or continuing any project in the [Division] laboratories is definite proof of the existence of a significant market for the products or product capabilities which are proposed for development.

[1] This characteristic of technical systems management is well described in Sayles, *Managerial Behavior.*

> I interpret this to mean that one must prove that the solution to a proposed problem has much greater value than its cost before one can be permitted to even begin to invest time and money in trying to solve the problem.
>
> . . . It is my view, however, that now, as well as in the past, so much of [the Division's] time and money have been invested in attempting to justify actions we or others might take, that little [time and money] remains for *taking action.*
>
> I believe that a total reliance on the test of *predicted expense* to *predicted revenue* by a management reluctant to trust its own judgment or other pertinent data has frequently led to the sterilization of the creative, the frustration of the productive, the stultification of the enterprising, and the loss of the competent.
>
> Prediction of a solution's value is recognized by most to be uncertain even when one has developed a solution to a problem and has applied it successfully to a limited set of experimental applications. Prediction of a solution's value when one is just beginning to comprehend the problem can be no better than random selection.
>
> When management sees its responsibility to be the maximization of success, rather than the minimization of failure, the morale of laboratory staff is usually high. When management gambles on the talents of its people, enough people succeed to more than compensate for those who fail.

The constraints that vex the writer of this letter are not technical, are not due to the development mission of his laboratory. They are imposed by management for the purpose of control. The situation is an illustration of a management environment produced by top management's unwillingness to rely on the judgment of lower levels. Since this kind of thing is within the control of management, while in most respects the development mission is not, we proceed now to examine the impact of the development mission on the management environment. For if we find that the development mission accounts for most of the problems we have examined, there may be little that can be done to improve the systems development organization.

CHARACTERIZING THE DEVELOPMENT MISSION

Some laboratories are more engaged in big systems work than are others; they are also more involved in "getting the product out the door" than they are in exploring new technical solutions. Other laboratories are working in new technologies or developing prototypes for future product designs.

This differentiation of development missions suggests one possible method of ordering the laboratories along a dimension that runs from exploratory or advanced development engineering to final design or product development engineering. While the laboratories are not totally homogeneous in this respect, Electromech management does attempt to assign similar development projects within a laboratory.

To characterize the typical development mission of a laboratory, engineers were asked how much emphasis they felt their managers placed on several kinds of project activity. Two of these,

—Building a backlog of technical discoveries toward future product developments

—Meeting schedules

are combined to form an index of mission (see Appendix C for the details of this index). Of these two kinds of activity, meeting schedules is emphasized more. The per cent responding "utmost" or "quite a bit" in indicating emphasis on meeting schedules ranges from 85 per cent at Danville to 58 per cent at Avondale. The corresponding range for the technical discoveries activity is 39 per cent at Garwood to 19 per cent at Hammond, with Darby showing an almost identical figure with the latter. The reason for using a combined index of the two activities is that they are related. That is, laboratory managements placing greatest emphasis on schedules also place the least emphasis on building a backlog of technology, and vice versa. Thus it does seem reasonable to order the development mission of the various laboratories along a continuum that runs from high emphasis on schedules *and* low emphasis on technology at one extreme, to lower emphasis on schedules *and* higher emphasis on technology at the other extreme.

I want to emphasize, however, that we are now talking about a more general construct than whether or not the laboratory is under time pressures. In fact, the laboratory ranking first in schedule emphasis ranks below the median—seventh—in perceived time demands of the job. Thus, while I will use "schedule emphasis" and "technology emphasis" to indicate which end of the mission continuum I am referring to, the reader should remember that the underlying mission concept is a complex set of attributes for which these "emphasis" variables are but one set of indicators.

The next step is to relate this development mission dimension to other attributes of the laboratory and its management environment. Specifically, I have computed rank-order correlations between mission and various attributes of supervisory behavior, influence, and utilization. These are summarized in Table 8.1. The supervisory attributes are grouped according to clusters derived from a factor

Table 8.1

Association of Certain Leadership and Organizational Attributes with Laboratory Development Mission for Twelve Laboratory Locations

Organizational attribute	Level of association
Manager consults with men: He makes you feel that you and the others in your department are members of a team (90)[a] He gets the opinion of his men before he commits the department to a goal or schedule (87)	High with technology emphasis
Manager shows consideration: He is friendly in his dealings with you (80) He encourages you when you are in a difficult situation (76) He tries to give reasonable answers to your questions (71) Manager is doing a good job (72)	Moderately high with technology emphasis
Individual influence (49)	Moderate with technology emphasis
Manager gives close supervision: He handles details of your work that you would normally expect to handle yourself (50) He insists that you follow his instructions to the letter (25) He supervises your jobs very closely (12)	Low with schedule emphasis
Level of underutilization and role influence: Prefer to do more (09) Position allowed you to make the decisions you felt were necessary (08)	No association

[a] Rank order correlations shown in parentheses; decimals omitted.

analysis of these attributes. The table also shows whether the behavior or attribute is *more* often present where the emphasis on technology is high, or where the emphasis on schedules is high. (Since these are opposite ends of a single continuum, of course, one implies the converse of the other.)

Now, the striking thing about these relationships is the fact that laboratory mission *does* affect the behavior of managers as seen by their subordinates. Those dimensions of leadership behavior that imply greater concern with good "man-manager relations" are quite highly associated with the laboratory development mission. Where relative emphasis on technology is high and relative emphasis on meeting schedules low, managers apparently are able to build more satisfactory interpersonal relations. Simply the fact of managing in a laboratory with strong emphasis on technology increases the likelihood that your subordinates will feel that you are performing your managerial duties well. This is especially interesting since very similar findings are reported by Fleishman and his co-workers with regard to the supervisory behavior of foremen in blue-collar work. Equating the demandingness of the work to the urgency of the division's time schedules, they found a "fairly marked tendency for the foremen in the most demanding divisions to operate with the least consideration." [2] The measures of consideration used in the Fleishman study are very like the measures ueed here.

However, another dimension of leadership behavior—close supervision—does not correspond so directly to the laboratory mission. There is also more variation in the degree of this association. Managers do appear to handle more of the detail work themselves, but they do not necessarily supervise the work of subordinates more closely. So while you might expect more detailed supervision in a schedule-emphasis climate, two factors seem to be at work that cancel each other. There probably is more pressure on managers to "follow the book" in laboratories emphasizing schedule, but there is also less time available for giving subordinates individual attention —and for "nitpicking."

Most important for our investigation is the fact that the role influ-

[2] Fleishman *et al.*, *Leadership and Supervision in Industry*, p. 99.

ence dimension—"Did your position allow you to make the decisions you felt to be necessary?"—is not at all associated with the development mission. The low role influence that is associated with underutilization evidently stems not from endemic technological constraints but from management policies—top management policies. For we must keep in mind the evidence that the characteristic behavior of lower-level management is the *result* of the total situation. Supervisory behavior is but one indicator of an organizational state of affairs which establishes mutual sets of expectations that constitute the engineer's role.

MISSION, ROLE DEFINITION, AND PARTICIPATIVE MANAGEMENT

Some of the supervisory behavior patterns most highly associated with laboratory mission (e.g., "he gets the opinion of his men before he commits the department to a goal or schedule") are usually thought of as indicators of high-influence management systems. The fact that they are not here related to a participative management environment needs additional investigation. Therefore I have shown in Figure 8.1 a most interesting set of interrelations among several indicators of influence, supervisory behavior, and goal satisfaction. These are correlations among ranks of over-all levels of the variables for twelve laboratory locations. (The full set of data is shown in Appendix D.) The data include a supervisory behavior variable not previously used—"When he receives new information he holds departmental conferences to discuss the course of future activities." This is the only item of twenty-one behavior description items to show any appreciable association with the role influence variable.[3] I shall now attempt to make this fact plausible.

The relationships found show an almost perfect two-factor structure. There is only one exception to the perfect ordering of magni-

[3] I recognize the possibility that this is a chance occurrence even though the correlation is quite large. However, the consistent pattern of correlations between this "holds conferences" item and the others persuades me that the association is meaningful.

Figure 8.1

Diagram of Degree of Association among Five Measures of Influence and Goal Satisfaction

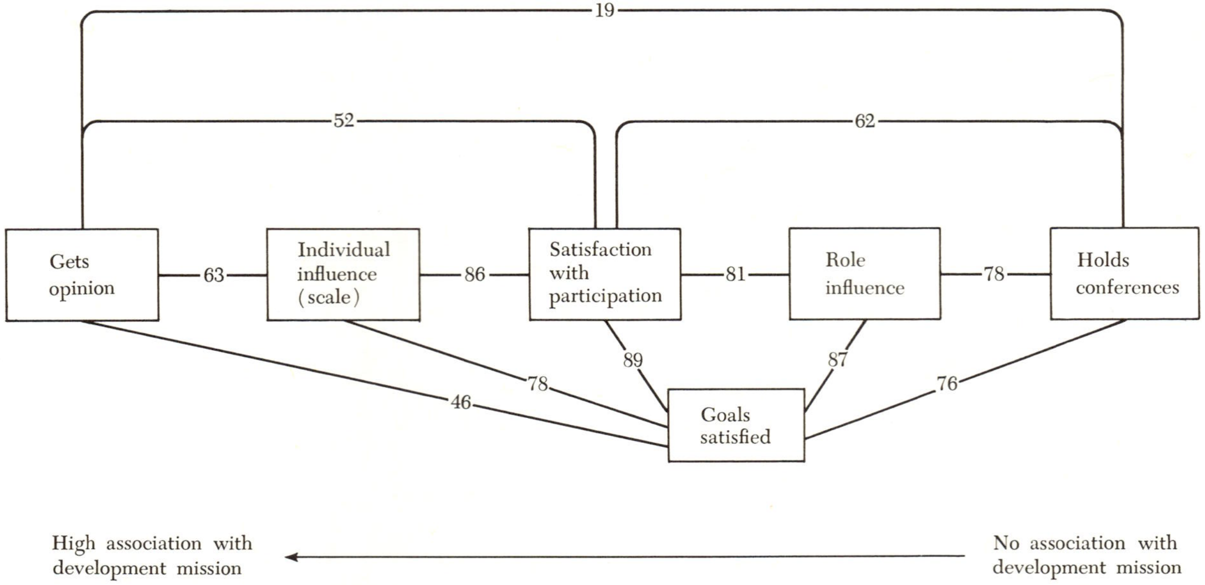

Note: Diagram based on data shown in Appendix D. Decimals omitted.

tudes along rows and columns.[4] This means that the influence variables can be ordered as they are in Figure 8.1 with none out of place; that is, with the highest correlations between adjacent variables and so on.

Now, what Figure 8.1 shows is that the two dimensions of influence implied by the correlations have to do with (1) mission and individual consultation and (2) organizational role and group consultation. Two independent supervisory behavior descriptions serve as indicators of the presence or absence of these factors. As pointed out earlier, getting the opinion of your men before committing the department is an indicator associated with technology emphasis and presumably with opportunity for individual consultation. It is important to understand that it is still possible to get such opinions additionally through group conferences at some locations. The data show only that frequency of conferences bears no systematic relationship to mission.

On the other hand, holding departmental conferences to discuss the course of future activities is an indicator of a satisfactory management environment. Here again we can see that the group conference may be the only way to get the opinion of your men in a laboratory with a high emphasis on schedule. But doing so certainly does not preclude individual consultation where possible.

The point is this: The relative presence of a good deal of individual consultation is more or less an accident of the development mission. Our diagram in Figure 8.1 shows that it has a positive effect on satisfaction of personal goals. The relative presence of departmental conferences, however, is not an accident, and is evidently one indication of a conscious management effort to mitigate the work-force status of the engineer. Thus the high correlation with role influence. Finally, satisfaction with participation—"How satisfied are you with

[4] Geometrically, the vectors representing the variables can be visualized as spanning one quadrant within a two-space. Assuming that the rank order correlations approximate product moment correlations, "technical mission" and "holds conferences" would be set 90 degrees apart and the remaining variables arranged with highest correlations adjacent, and so on. Note that this need not follow for any set of variables. Thus, those variables representing close supervision correlate neither with mission nor with role influence. To include these in our model we would need a three-space.

your present degree of participation in setting the objectives of your department?"—seems to be equally a function of individual influence and role influence; a joint outcome of a mission that provides latitude for technical innovation and a management environment that permits it.

In view of these findings I think it necessary to redefine the notion of management environment to some extent and also to identify a variable that can serve as an index of the concept. Our understanding of management environment is that of mutually shared expectations about appropriate behavior, understandings about who has a legitimate right to determine the course of technical programs. At one point it seemed reasonable to think that the management environment is determined in part by technological constraints. And indeed, some aspects of supervisory behavior are. But our important finding is that certain role-related aspects of the management environment and underutilization are independent of the immediate technical mission. And since role-related expectations are central to the concept "management environment," I shall from this point use the term to refer exclusively to those aspects of the social system of the laboratory which are implicitly or explicitly member-class definitions or policy definitions. I exclude those aspects of organizational behavior, regardless of how uniform, that flow from predictable response to technological factors. In consequence of this more explicit redefinition, the management environment now refers to organizational effects that are directly accessible to modification through management policy.

As the empirical indicator I shall use the "manager holds conferences" survey item. This choice is motivated by the configuration of Figure 8.1.[5] And again, as with the mission index, I want to emphasize its use as but one indicator of a more general configuration of role relationships. That is, I think that this is but one manifestation of a management attitude toward the lower organizational levels which includes the idea that these levels of the organization should be included in setting objectives. The holding of department confer-

[5] I have used this item rather than role influence because it is based more on perceived behavior than on evaluation. This should help minimize association due to over-all "halo" effect. As it turns out, the correlations are much the same regardless of which variable is used as an index of the management environment.

ences, even when individual consultation is difficult because of schedule pressures, is one of a host of small ways in which management communicates by its *actions* its belief in the legitimacy of nonsupervisory participation in the management process.

And *local* management may be no more free to establish a favorable environment than it is to set the development mission. By this I mean that pressures from the division management or top corporate management can force the adoption of programs that run contrary to the judgment of local top management, first-line management, and the nonsupervisory engineers. By way of example, Avondale is the most technology-oriented of the group. In keeping with this, its first-line management is also rated high in individual attention and consideration. But the laboratory ranks last in participation in setting objectives and the role influence dimensions. The reasons are best expressed in a letter I received from a top manager at that location.[6] The intent of his letter was to call my attention to some factors that might have influenced the survey results, and by way of carbon copies to point this out as well to his own top management. He had no desire to be blamed for something beyond his control.

> As a result of replanning, the . . . laboratory has been subjected to substantial changes. Approximately one month prior to the survey date, a series of financial cuts was instituted that had resulted in the termination of several projects and a reduction of laboratory staff [by 40 per cent]. A total of —— people must, therefore be transferred from the laboratory.
>
> This information is known to the laboratory personnel and, in fact, at the time of the opinion survey [20 per cent of these] people had been transferred and approximately [65 per cent] were actively involved in interviews and discussions aimed at leading to transfers.

The reader is left to judge for himself whether or not holding departmental conferences to discuss the course of future events might have remedied the situation.

I want to go back for a minute to an earlier finding. I think it is

[6] Actually there were two laboratories at this location at the time of the survey. The writer of the following letter was the manager of the smaller laboratory. However, due to the fact that the engineers were housed physically in the same building, were doing work with the same type of technical mission, and were under like pressures, I have chosen to analyze the data as one location. In addition, on the variables under discussion in this research the laboratories were very similar compared to other locations.

no accident that the degree of association between the distance from headquarters and the role influence level of the laboratory is extremely high (r=.87). I suspect that the nearer to headquarters laboratory management finds itself, the more it must give the appearance of "strong" management. A management that genuinely seeks the opinions and tries where possible to implement the advice of its lower ranks may be interpreted as being weak or vacillating management. Strong, "responsive" local management should see no need for compromise. And the nearer you are to corporate or division management the more visible your actions.

By way of contrast, the degree of association between distance and the development mission is negligible (r=.17). So it seems that regardless of the development mission, where local management is free to define the nonsupervisory level as being legitimately involved in the management process the amount of participation in setting objectives open to nonsupervisory levels will be viewed more favorably and personal goals are more likely to be satisfied.

INFLUENCE, UNDERUTILIZATION, AND THE MANAGEMENT ENVIRONMENT: A SUMMARY

I now have some summary observations to make about the material presented in this and the preceding chapter. First, about the meaning of the term "decision." In a systems environment, decisions are most certainly not the result of solely individual deliberations. The important characteristic of a systems decision is that it involves a number of people who have their own interests and hold their own opinions. That is the nature of systems design. Furthermore, important systems decisions involve business and economic considerations, as well as intelligence about the activities of competitors. These kinds of information are seldom entirely within the grasp of the nonsupervisory engineer. As a point of policy he may not have access to some of the required items of information.

So the first point about a decision is that it is generally never made by any one person. Technical decision-making is an information-processing procedure. Engineers sort out technical alternatives and select those that seem most promising. The job of management is to ratify a given selection and to act as a focal point for the information-processing activity. There will always be a better technical solution waiting a month or a year or so hence. But to keep things moving, to meet the schedule, someone must select an alternative now. And so there must be someone to put a stamp of approval on one of the alternatives. A decision, thus, is the product of joint consultation and compromise subsequently ratified by a management coordinator. Making the decision means that you are able to insert your judgment or piece of design information into the total systems design.

While discussing technical decisions with engineers I have been struck by the fact that the examples of decisions they give are generally about things that impress me as relatively insignificant. This is because larger issues usually spread over a number of technical areas, and are thus beyond their immediate concern. Even the decisions they do make commonly involve a choice of their way of doing things over that proposed by someone else. And this requires ratification from higher authority.

My conclusion is that decisions are made and influence is exerted indirectly through the existing management mechanisms. Groups of people are involved because they must be. The diverse interests and judgments of all concerned must be represented. But I am not trying to paint a portrait of bureaucratic rigidity. There is always a great deal of informal negotiation and "horse trading."

My second point is that the amount of influence an engineer can bring to bear on technical decisions does not derive from favorable or unfavorable supervisory styles. We have good evidence that both engineers and managers share in an organizational environment. Engineers benefit when their supervisors are relatively more influential. And here again I am not trying to deny that some managers are more persuasive than others, just as some engineers are politically more astute than others, and thus better able to protect their own interests. The fact is simply that the political acumen of individual lower-level managers matters very little in the assignment of a favorable development mission to the laboratory, or in the development of rules and procedures by top management to institute greater control over systems design. From my point of view, supervisory behavior is an outcome, not a determiner, of organizational environment. Differences in the aggregate descriptions of supervisory behavior by engineers can be used to describe the organizational environment.

To characterize our observations, we have been using two concepts: the development mission and the management environment. In Electromech these turn out to have unrelated attributes that are jointly responsible for most of the important organizational effects. For the sake of simplicity I have represented these concepts in a fourfold table as shown in Figure 8.2, and have characterized each as being flexible or inflexible.[7] A development mission with high emphasis on technology and low emphasis on meeting schedules is characterized as a relatively flexible environment, characteristic of advanced development activity. Relative inflexibility is associated with the later stages of large systems development. The pressure is on, and there is little freedom left for innovation. A flexible management environment would be one in which lower-level management is relatively free from arbitrary rules and constraints imposed from the top. Multiple quantitative measurements, inflexible decision rules, and the removal of lower-level power to ratify courses of technical action will produce inflexibility.

Each of these dimensions seems to be associated with its own kind of influence and supervisory behavior. Flexibility in the development mission promotes greater individual influence and an organizational situation in which individual supervisory consultation is more nearly possible. Flexibility in the management environment is related to greater role influence. Role expectations emphasize relatively more participation in the setting of technical objectives at all levels. The indicator we use is the frequency of group meetings in which the entire department discusses the course of future activities. This is, for reasons stated earlier, essential in a systems environment.

[7] It is possible to array the laboratories in this fashion because the "manager holds conferences" variable and the mission variable are uncorrelated. That is, of the six locations ranking highest in flexibility of management environment, three also rank highest in mission flexibility, and vice versa.

In Figure 8.2 I have shown as $\bar{R}$ the average rank of each group of laboratories on satisfaction of personal goals. Type I organizations are most favorable, and Type IV the least. As for mixed types II and III, the summary table shows that the flexible management environment is more important to goal satisfaction than the flexible mission. In addition, ranked levels of utilization are very similar for types I and II, and much higher than those for types III and IV, which are also similar.

Figure 8.2
Typology of Twelve Laboratories
by Management Environment and Development Mission
(Three laboratories in each type)

		Development Mission	
		Flexible	Inflexible
Management Environment	Flexible	Type I $\bar{R} = 9.5$	Type II $\bar{R} = 8.0$
	Inflexible	Type III $\bar{R} = 5.8$	Type IV $\bar{R} = 2.7$

Note: $\bar{R}$ is the average rank of laboratory level of satisfaction of personal goals for the three laboratories in each type.

But these are static descriptions of coexisting states. And while we are limited by the nature of our data, I think it is important to speculate about the process involved. A project flow chart—a PERT network—graphically depicts the complexity of successfully managing a systems development project. This complexity leaves top management with an uneasy feeling. Executive level managers lack positive control over many of the outcomes upon which their success depends. To quiet this uneasiness they set up quantified measurements, control systems, and rational decision rules. I think these executives feel such control procedures will take care of difficulties as they arise, even if no one happens to be looking at the time. Slavish dependence on these rational procedures can mean trouble, however, as shown in the complaint of this engineering vice-president:

> They discount your technical judgment if you can't back it up with figures. This has been personally frustrating to me and I know God damn frustrating to others around here. . . . [The president] has two assistants who have not a smattering of technical background. Don't get me wrong, they're good men, but he has nobody who can read between the lines and see the same things you do . . . you've got to face the fact that to manage a God damn mess like this you need an awful lot of rules, an awful lot of figures. It's the unsympathetic interpretation of those rules that you're fighting.

Thus, my conjecture is that the process leading to the inflexible management environment starts with trouble and is completed by the removal of control up the line. This control may be exercised personally, or remotely through formal rules and procedures.

The comparison between the Avondale and Belleville laboratories is instructive in this respect. In the previous chapter we saw that Belleville has a much more flexible control system than Avondale. Belleville is a success and Avondale a failure. In addition, the Avondale mission is complex, a schedule emphasis mission. There had been a lot of disagreement as to whether a project could be brought off at all. Interestingly, the dispute came about over economic rather than technical feasibility. Now when it became apparent that the Avondale project people were not going to meet their commitments, top management started to apply that "grinding management attention." Top management had lost faith in the ability of local management to do the job. The point is this: When something gets out of hand, one likely management action is to remove control from local levels. I know this is true in Electromech and several other companies with which I am familiar. I suspect it is true in most systems operations. What results at this stage, then, is both inflexible mission and inflexible management environment. My conjecture is that the causal sequence relating role influence and organizational effectiveness runs from lack of effectiveness to lack of influence. This is obviously so in the examples I have cited.

But if this is true, does restriction of control in fact increase the effectiveness of the organization? Is restriction in any way desirable? For the process described also fits the underutilization–role influence link. Trouble means growing overdependence on rational control and management by measurement. As I have tried to point out earlier, juggling projects usually leads to underutilization; it results in engineers doing nothing while they wait for the next directive, and then perhaps doing nothing while the project is canceled and they are reassigned to another. At the very least, removing project control from the lower levels where the immediate facts of existence are known leads to inflexibility and difficulties in matching people to jobs.

An example will serve to illustrate the problem vividly. In this instance an engineering manager is found at midyear to be going well over the budget. That is, at his current rate of expenditure he will exceed his budget by more than the customary allowance at year's end. Headquarters staff informs him of this, and tells him that he must get back in "the ball park." He will have to reallocate a portion of his resources elsewhere. What this means, of course, is that he must reassign some fifty of his men elsewhere. Other company procedures and policies on transfers dictate that these transfers must be permanent.

The project manager responds that this directive is insane. His is a continuing and growing project. Next year he is to be funded for increased manpower. The plans are already approved. It makes no sense to transfer men now only to hire back replacements and additions in four to six months. Still, the directive remains, now with top levels of management involved. Finally, at the conclusion of some months of negotiation, it is mutually decided that only half the original number will be transferred.

The net outcome of all the turmoil, uncertainty, emotion, and confusion generated by this episode is that a number of careers are disrupted and a number of people have nothing to do for several months. I am fond of this example because of its patent absurdity. And yet I recognize also that some capable and intelligent men see the necessity of enforcing the dictates of these control procedures.

Some of the reasons why they do so will be discussed in the next two chapters, but for now they can be summarized as follows. First, the complexity and size of the Electromech systems development organization means that it is almost impossible for executives to have a personal "feel" for the allocation of resources. By this I mean that they cannot know from direct experience whether funds are well used or wasted. However, they are aware of several disasters and near disasters that attended lack of suitable financial controls in other organizations. What is the alternative? It must be some kind of formal control system.

The second reason for our example incident is the existence of the first. Once controls and procedures are instituted, executives are measured by their success in meeting objectives, staying within the budget. This, of course, is but one of the performance characteristics against which they are evaluated. But such is not the case for their staff assistants who actually manage the controls. The success of the procedures is the one most important, perhaps the only, yardstick against which the past performance and future potential of the headquarters financial staff man is judged. Let the other fellow worry about his end of it. The staff assistant wants to know only where the funds are going and where they should be going. That is his job.

And this is where the distance correlation fits in. Remote control has got to be more difficult to exercise than local control. The management environment is more flexible at a distance because problems are easier to hide from direct inspection. While this observation is probably of limited relevance, unique to the way the Electromech Corporation chooses to run its affairs, it does serve to strengthen our explanation of the connection between the management environment, influence, and underutilization.

A final point about group meetings and the flexible management environment. Can we assume that the institution of group meetings will create a flexible environment? Possibly, if local management is free and willing to act on suggested alternatives. On the other hand, my observation is that where lower-level management is under pressure, where local management has little or no influence, these meetings are seen as useless and tend to be avoided. It does not do much good simply to keep repeating that you cannot do anything about the situation. Thus it seems to me that holding departmental meetings for the purpose of overlaying a veneer of participative management will not have much effect. That is why I feel that the presence of group meetings is simply a good indicator of the existing management environment.

With the conclusion of this chapter we are finished with the development and analysis of the problems of the unhappy engineer. What has been achieved is the identification and understanding of the key organizational factors associated with the person-role conflict connected with underutilization and lack of role influence. We have seen as well that problem definitions taken from the viewpoint of individuals within organizations differ from definitions provided by a cross-organizations perspective. By direct extrapolation this suggests that a perspective taken across companies employing different technologies might be different still. In fact, our main thesis has been that the problems we have identified become most acute in systems technology. Thus it seems to me that we are now at the most effective point in this study to enter into a discussion of a systematic body of findings reported by other researchers in the field of organizations. For we can now compare our own results with this knowledge from other organizations in the hope of arriving at a more general synthesis. This is the task we now undertake.

9

Organizations: Form and Function

To my mind one of the most fascinating aspects of the systematic study of organizations is the unexpected orderliness of the data. Unexpected, that is, from the usual perspective on human events, on the "softness" of social data when compared with the "hardness" of physical data. The research reported here thus far has exhibited some of this intriguing regularity.

In this chapter I want to take a look at several other major pieces of research that have in common the discovery of consistent relationships between the productive process employed by an organization and several aspects of its function and structure. The unifying feature of these studies is the viewpoint that many aspects of behavior in organizations and of the management structure of these organizations follow necessarily from the nature of the business they are about.

My reasons for reviewing these research studies are several. First, as indicated in the preceding chapter, Electromech represents primarily one technology. If we can broaden our persective to include different technologies, we may be able to expand and generalize our findings. A second reason is that this broader framework of analysis can help to extend our understanding of the possibilities for corrective action. To look ahead a bit, the key synthesis comes in the appreciation of the fact that successful organizations evolve structures and systems of human relationships that are compatible with their function. What this suggests is that problems arise when management, from a limited perspective, tries to impose the "one best way," when structures and procedures found successful in one function are applied to an alien function.[1] So perhaps the essential feature of the flexible management environment is that it incorporates the means to maintain the necessary compatibility with its technological factors. It is this kind of generalization that is directly relevant to our subsequent chore of attempting to reconstruct the management procedures of the systems development engineering organization. Therefore, it seems to me that we are well advised to spend some time in the review and analysis of the studies that follow.

TECHNOLOGY AS THE INDEPENDENT VARIABLE

One branch of the study of human relations in organizations—now called "Organizational Behavior"—has for some time concerned itself directly with technology or the productive process as a major explanatory factor. Researchers in this tradition who come immediately to mind are William F. Whyte and Leonard Sayles.[2] However, this point of view has probably been stronger in Britain than in this country.[3] In particular, two pieces of research done in Britain have emphasized the role of the productive process—or technology—as an independent variable that determines the necessary management structure. I refer here to the work of Burns and Stalker, *The Management of Innovation,* and that of Woodward, *Industrial Organization: Theory and Practice.* The concern of both these works is somewhat different from our own in that they concentrate on the relative success or lack of it experienced by a firm. The conclusion of both is that successful firms are structured in response to the different technical environments in which they exist. Specifically, Burns and Stalker discover that firms engaged in innovative

[1] This point is made in each of the major pieces of research treated in this chapter. See, for example, Lawrence and Lorsch, *Organization and Environment,* p. 225.

[2] Examples can be found in Whyte, *Human Relations in the Restaurant Industry,* and Sayles, *Behavior of Industrial Work Groups.*

[3] This point of view is connected with researchers at the Tavistock Institute of Human Relations. A relatively early study is Trist and Bansforth, "Some Social and Psychological Consequences of the Longwall Method of Coal-Getting," *Human Relations,* IV (1951), 3–38.

activities will display different management processes from successful firms engaged in routine activities. They posit a continuum of management process running from "organic" to "mechanistic." Organic management is characterized by emphasis on general vs. specific role definitions, lateral vs. hierarchical communication networks, and informal control procedures. Organic management is more successful under conditions requiring innovation. Mechanistic management, the opposite of organic, is found successful for the performance of routine tasks or under stable operating conditions. The message is not that one system is better than another, but that each system is appropriate for a given environment. As Burns puts it, "The utility of the notions of 'mechanistic' and 'organic' management systems resides largely in their being related as dependent variables to the rate of 'environmental' change."[4] There is obviously a relationship between our characterization of flexible-inflexible management environment and the organic-mechanistic system described by Burns and Stalker.

Woodward's findings again emphasize the dependence of management structure. Her key descriptive variable is the productive process—technology—employed by the manufacturing function of the firm. Somewhat arbitrarily, this descriptive dimension runs from unit or prototype production at one end, through large batch and mass production, and on to process production (e.g., chemicals or petroleum) at the other end. There are two major conclusions:

1. Each type of productive process exhibits a typical form of management organization. These forms differ in number of levels of management hierarchy and in typical span of control.
2. Successful firms exhibit a management structure most like that typical for the kind of productive process; unsuccessful firms have structures least like the typical one.

Woodward notes also that organic management systems seem to occur at either end of this technology scale, that is, in unit production and in process production. Thus, a "clear-cut definition of duties and responsibilities was characteristic of firms in the middle ranges, while flexible organization with a high degree of delegation both of authority and of the responsibility for decision-making, and

[4] Burns and Stalker, *The Management of Innovation*, p. vii.

with permissive and participating management, was characteristic of firms at the extremes."[5] Furthermore, at the middle of the technology dimension—the large batch and mass production technologies—Woodward finds firms where "control procedures were most elaborate and sanctions most rigorously applied."[6] Apparently, the reason for this is that control procedures are difficult to apply in unit production and few attempt to do so. But in process production, say, chemical technologies, controls are simple to exercise and are often built into the production process itself. Though it is hard to say at this point how this characterization of productive processes can be directly related to development engineering, it is possible to characterize Electromech manufacturing as large batch production. And to speculate for a moment, it might be interesting to consider how a form of organization, dependent on and appropriate to a manufacturing technology, might be applied inappropriately to other forms of activity in the total corporation.

Now, directly related to these preceding studies is the work of Lawrence and Lorsch.[7] The primary emphasis of their research is on the systematic differences in management structure which are observable among different functions within an organization. These functions are research, applied research, sales, and production. Technology, the productive process typical of an industry, enters as a secondary consideration. As in the previously cited research, emphasis is on management structure as a dependent factor and the success of the firm as the variable to be predicted or explained.

From our point of view, the major finding of this study is that management structure and behavior are dependent upon the type of organizational function being performed. That is, different functions exhibit different characteristics in the following:

1. The formality of management structure. For the management functions studied, the finding is that the more certain the task and the more predictable the outcome, the more formal the structure. Thus, production has the most formal structure and basic research the least.

2. Interpersonal style. Using a directive-permissive characteriza-

[5] Woodward, *Industrial Organization*, p. 64. [6] *Ibid.*, p. 66.

[7] Lawrence and Lorsch, *Organization and Environment*.

tion of management behavior, the authors find that directive or task-oriented behavior tends to occur at the extremes of the certainty scale, that is, at the very uncertain—basic research—or the very certain—production—ends of the scale.

A third finding, related to productive process rather than unit function, is that the characteristic distribution of influence over levels of hierarchy in successful firms depends on the productive process involved. Seemingly the successful firms show patterns of influence that are congruent with the existence of the detailed knowledge necessary to make informed decisions.[8] The levels at which this knowledge exists differ among industries with unlike productive processes.

CORRESPONDENCE OF RESEARCH RESULTS

The first point that seems worthwhile making is that the studies just described are in fairly good agreement with one another, and that they use as key explanatory factors dimensions similar to those emerging from our own research. This is true even though the research reported here is motivated by different concerns and takes quite a different approach to the problems of organizations. In fact, the correspondence did not strike me until the research analysis of the data reported here was essentially complete. To restate those major factors:

1. The organic-mechanistic typology corresponds closely to the flexible-inflexible management environment, with its emphasis on role influence and formal management control procedures. Differences do exist, however, in that Burns and Stalker emphasize additional factors in organic management (e.g., cosmopolitan vs. local concerns).

2. There is a concern with technology, wiith the productive process or the development mission, as a key explanatory variable.

Within this framework both similarities and differences in the findings exist. The consideration of these will lead to a better understanding of how to cope with the problems outlined in this book.

[8] *Ibid.*, p. 142.

Managerial Behavior and Organizational Function. As Sayles has pointed out in his book *Managerial Behavior*, it is often not possible for a manager to pick and choose his style regardless of his organizational function.[9] Supervisory behavior is dependent on the technology and organization of the work that characterizes the function in which the manager finds himself. His behavior is also constrained by the formal controls imposed by the organization, and he must adopt administrative patterns that are to some extent compatible with those with whom he must interact—his superiors and peers in other functions. Our own research indicates that supervisory behavior can be characterized along several dimensions, some of which are related to the technological dimension. Thus, the "manager shows consideration" dimension seems highly related to the technology factor, while closeness of supervision is not. And though there are no direct parallels in the research of others we are discussing here, their work also suggests a connection between supervisory behavior and technology.[10] The finding that spans of control are greater in unit than in process production suggests also that workers will perceive different amounts of individual attention given by their supervisors. Certainly, where supervisors have fewer employees the possibility of giving greater individual attention exists. In agreement with this, Lawrence and Lorsch also find that the task-orientedness of supervisors is related to their organizational function, which in turn is related to structure.

To summarize, then, our finding that individual supervisory behavior relates to the technological dimension—to the productive process—is supported in other research which examines this dimension.

Innovation and Organic Structure. Burns and Stalker find that the management style they characterize as "organic" coexists with task uncertainty. Woodward finds in addition that organic management characterizes the highly certain end of the technological dimension, that is, process production. So there is some disagreement. Different

[9] Sayles, *Managerial Behavior*, p. 256.

[10] This connection is made by Dubin in Dubin *et al.*, *Leadership and Productivity*, ch. 1.

still is our finding that the productive process—the mission—and the management environment are independent of one another within Electromech.

A number of explanations for this lack of relationship in Electromech come to mind, the most likely being that organic or flexible management in Electromech seems to be achieved despite top management desires or directives. I refer again to the correlation between distance from headquarters and role influence. The point is that the management environment has not been allowed to come into natural concordance with mission requirements. Because of top management "attention," because of efforts to impose structures and policies from the top, technologically dependent relationships have been unable to emerge. Yet, I think this is only half the answer. In particular, some broader issues must be examined concerning the use and meaning of the words "uncertainty" and "innovation."

A major theme of this book has been the description and analysis of problems arising from attempts to reduce the uncertainty of systems development engineering through planning and programming innovation—by routinizing innovation.[11] I have tried to point out that there are competitive advantages that flow from this and that planning and routinization are necessary for success in this environment. And Electromech is successful. As for the meaning of innovation, I have also tried to illustrate that programmed innovation, with its consequent specialization and routinization of tasks, ceases to have the essential character of innovation for the working engineer. Routinized innovation ceases to be innovation at all from the viewpoint of the worker-engineer. To put it somewhat differently, though the task of the entire systems development engineering organization is to innovate, the thrust of management efforts is to achieve the predictability, the routineness, and the certainty of the production plant. The character and magnitude of certain kinds of systems development discussed earlier make this necessary. Therefore, if Electromech structures and its management environment are

[11] This point is elaborated in Ritti and Goldner, "Professional Pluralism in an Industrial Organization," *Management Science,* XVI (December, 1969), B-233–B-246.

more characteristic of stable than of innovative tasks, perhaps we should not be surprised.

Formality of Structure, Influence, and Technology. Related to the organic-mechanistic management typology is the concept of formality of structure used by Lawrence and Lorsch.[12] Formal management is characterized by more levels of hierarchy and a higher ratio of supervisors to subordinates. Data for judging performance are readily available and precise, and these data are often used. There is greater reliance on written rules and procedures. Now, what we find is that there is a direct relationship between formality of management and the certainty of the functional task. Thus, if the certainty of task requirements runs from production, through sales and engineering, and on to research, we should find that production has the most formal management structures and procedures, and research the least. This, of course, would directly parallel the results of Burns and Stalker. And, given these findings, we would expect manufacturing engineering to be more formal than development engineering.[13] We would also expect field sales to be more formal than development engineering, to have more levels of hierarchy, fewer employees per level, and more frequent and formal review and control procedures. Yet neither is the case.

Actually, within the twelve Electromech laboratories there is a correspondence between technology emphasis and the number of levels of hierarchy. That is, there is a correspondence between the certainty of the task and some aspects of organizational formality. But I think this has little to do with task certainty. Primarily, it seems to result from the fact that the technology emphasis organizations are smaller over-all and therefore have fewer levels of hierarchy. For development engineering in Electromech is structured in a uniform way. This is partly by design and partly by chance. Electromech management tries to achieve uniformity in salary administration, promotion, and other personnel policies. Similarities in

[12] See Lawrence and Lorsch, *Organization and Environment,* pp. 31–32.

[13] By manufacturing engineering I mean that function responsible for the engineering of production processes or equipment. This is not what is sometimes termed "product engineering," a function subsequent to development and responsible for ease of manufacture, standardization of parts, and the like.

structure help. The chance part results largely by emulation. There is a great deal of managerial mobility from one location to another, and consequently managers try to follow administrative policies learned at previous locations.

In any event, both field sales and manufacturing engineering have fewer levels in the local organization and more employees per level.[14] This is exactly the opposite of the Lawrence and Lorsch findings. These discrepancies are important, I think, because they will help to emphasize the unique nature of systems development engineering and to extend and generalize the findings of the other research.

Why, then, do these differences exist? First, an essential feature of development engineering is that it tends to be structured by the technical task it faces. That is, structure corresponds directly to technological function. The organization is factored out by system, by special function within that system, and so on down to the departmental manager. In fact, the department manager in Electromech, as in many such organizations, is really the lead engineer. He performs managerial functions, yes, but the structure of the task determines the structure of the unit organization, and the lead engineer generally has few engineers reporting directly to him. In a study of the ratio of engineers to managers in several Electromech systems laboratories I found the typical ratio to be 1½ or 2 engineers for every manager. This was within perhaps five or six levels of hierarchy.

Now, manufacturing engineering is quite different. Here, a ratio of 10 or 15 engineers per manager is the usual case. This difference in ratios is a matter of common knowledge in Electromech administration because of the problem it causes in attempting to achieve uniform salary and promotion policies. Yet, why it is this way I cannot say with certainty. However, development and manufacturing are separate organizational functions in Electromech and apparently manufacturing engineering has tried to coordinate its structure and its functional divisions with manufacturing generally. Development

[14] Employees in this case include professionals and professional managers only.

engineering, of course, has more or less evolved in response to the needs perceived by its management. As for the field, it seems clear that the nature of the task does not require the coordinated hierarchy of systems development. And while some of this even as I write is changing in response to changes in environmental demands, the traditional field sales office has been a highly independent operation. Local office managers often speak of satisfaction in their work in terms of its similarity to running a small company. I never heard anything remotely like that in development engineering. The measures and standards in the field are clear, formal, and demanding, but the achievement of high performance is unrestricted and is basically an individual matter.

Therefore, my explanation of the differences in functional structure resides in differences in technology in the sense that Woodward has elaborated. And I suspect that the differences between our observations of Electromech structures and those of Lawrence and Lorsch are rooted in some inherent differences between the chemical plastics business (to cite their largest group) and the electromechanical systems business.

CHEMTECH: DIFFERENT TECHNOLOGY, DIFFERENT RESULTS

By fortunate coincidence I have had some direct experience with chemical plastics development. In fact, I suspect that the development laboratory I studied may be one of those included in the Lawrence and Lorsch sample. At the suggestion of the Director of Development Engineering, I administered my Electromech engineering survey to his Chemtech engineers. The resulting data are very interesting, in fact, quite surprising. First of all, in items such as rating of the company compared to others, rating of salary, and rating of working conditions, the Chemtech engineers compared unfavorably to Electromech. The average rating they gave to these aspects of the job falls well outside, and below, the entire range of the twelve Electromech laboratories I have used here. More interesting are the results with regard to the job itself and influence. Chemtech is again outside the Electromech range, but now much higher! [15] Since the Director of Development Engineering was involved in a relatively long-term program of restructuring laboratory management, my first explanation was that these efforts had produced beneficial results.[16] He had flattened his organization and developed greater interpersonnel competence in his management. The data seemed to speak eloquently of this success. Still more important from my point of view, I now had some comparisons to help in persuading Electromech management to try some modifications of its own.

And yet as I learned more about the Chemtech organization I came to distrust my first explanation. There are very major differences in organizational structure that cannot be so easily dismissed. The most pronounced of these flow from the technology. Specifically, differences in the productive process are reflected directly in project size—the natural unit of organization flowing from technology. Discovering that a total technical program in chemical plastics development might take but five to fifteen professional people came as a shock. For while there is no direct way to compare Electromech structures directly, a parallel total program effort in large systems development might involve thousands, and an autonomous subpart easily hundreds. Thus, I came to realize that I might be very wrong in recommending a program of change based on the favorable comparisons provided by the Chemtech system. I cannot be sure, but it seems to me that fundamental differences between the requirements of chemical plastics technology and those of large systems technology in electronics or aerospace prevent the application of lessons learned in one directly to the other. This, of course, is a major point made by Lawrence and Lorsch. It is also my major point. The problems of organizations reflected in the attitudes of their members cannot be considered independent of the requirements of technology. This is not to say that a favorable technological situation cannot be mismanaged, for it can, and later I will have

[15] In fact I ran two surveys about two years apart. The results from the second showed little or no change over this period of time, indicating at least that the data are characteristic of Chemtech at this period.

[16] This restructuring dated to a time approximately six to seven years earlier. At the time of my surveys the management development program was continuing.

some examples. But it seems clear to me that the productive process constrains the management process. Organizational therapies can be introduced in Chemtech that are simply impossible in Electromech. And so I think that the flattening of the Chemtech structure worked, and may have produced benefits as well, because that structure is compatible with the technological situation.

One final point about Chemtech structure and job attitudes. In Chapter 3 I pointed to the fact that the goals of student engineers change in response to their new work environment, that goals yield to the realities and possibilities of that work environment. My point there was that the high importance accorded to the organizational influence goals by student engineers fell off sharply in both the total Electromech sample and in the sample of Junior Engineers. Given this fact, it is fascinating to find that the two goals dealing with participation in both technical and business decisions remain unchanged in Chemtech from the student level.

This pattern is shown in Table 9.1 [17] While the other goals are quite consistent with earlier findings, it is evident that the process responsible for changing role influence expectations in Electromech is not taking place in Chemtech.

The point is this: Chemtech is a chemical plastics development laboratory that looks just as Lawrence and Lorsch say it should. The Electromech systems development laboratories do not. And I do not think they could. Consistent with the differences in technology and hence management structure are certain differences in the attitudes and expectations of engineers. Not only are these perceptions of the job itself, but they relate to the possibilities of the environment—goals. Furthermore, the differences are not due simply to the fact that Chemtech is a better place to work. It is not. The company, salary, and working conditions all receive relatively low ratings.

Does this mean that the "organization development" undertaken by Chemtech management was unnecessary, that it did not produce

[17] The Electromech and students data are those from the total Electromech group and the student seniors group shown in tables 3.3 and 3.5 respectively. The Chemtech group is comparable in character to the Electromech group and comprises 149 professionals. In size it is like the Avondale laboratory and is comparable to the five smaller Electromech locations.

Table 9.1

Comparison of Work Goals of Senior Engineering Students and Development Engineers in Chemtech and Electromech

	Per cent indicating goal is very important		
	Chemtech (N=149)	Students (N=447)	Electromech (N=4,582)
How important is it to you to—			
have the opportunity to help the company build its reputation as a first-class organization	83	75	72
have the opportunity to help the company increase its profit	76	57	69
participate in decisions that set the direction of technical effort in the company	70	68	38
participate in decisions that affect the future business of the company	69	64	41
establish your reputation outside the company as an authority in your field	39	41	29
publish articles in technical journals	13	20	15

the observed differences in attitudes? Frankly, while I suspect this is the case I have no way of knowing.[18] But one thing of which I am now certain is that while Electromech continues in its current technology, there is no way in the world of its arriving at the Chemtech structure. As we shall discuss shortly, if Chemtech benefited from its therapy, it did so because the changes brought its management structure into congruence with its technological prerequisites.

TECHNOLOGY, ENVIRONMENT, AND STRUCTURE

Our findings do match those of Lawrence and Lorsch on the formality of measures of performance and of controls. I think this is so

[18] While most people at the laboratory are convinced that the program has brought about change, there are few data on which to base before-and-after comparisons. Apparently satisfaction with the effectiveness of the laboratory has gone up, but there are no comparisons on satisfaction with work. However, I do know that no change in work satisfaction took place between my surveys even while the development programs continued.

because this factor is related more to function than to technology. Sales and production generate numbers that just do not exist in development. And if there are numbers we can assume that these numbers will be used and reviewed by management. This is the situation in Electromech. There is no doubt that measures of performance and criteria of program success are much more concrete and more readily available in sales and production.

Therefore, I suppose, I must justify why I have characterized the laboratory as more bureaucratic than sales. One of the features I had in mind, as did Lawrence and Lorsch, is the number of levels of hierarchy characteristic of the organization. The second factor is a less concrete notion of constraints. These constraints are technical, and result from task complexity and the interdependence of functions. But I realize now that the discussions of differences between field and laboratory have not explicitly recognized the differences between technical and administrative constraints in the two situations. Yet I have made this distinction explicitly in the discussion of the concepts of technical mission and management environment. A similar distinction might be made for the field situation.

The field is free of the high degree of role interdependence present in the laboratory and is less constrained by technological factors, but it is also unquestionably burdened by a greater assortment of quantitative measures and controls. So it is more bureaucratic in administrative procedures. Then why the difference in attitudes? I think the answer lies in the congruence between the factors of the productive process and the character of the evolved management environment. This, after all, is the message of the research cited in this chapter. Put differently, the question is not so much one of the absolute degree of formalization or bureaucratization as it is of the degree of compatibility between the task and the structures developed by management to achieve that task. The performance of a field organization is tangible, measurable. Formal measures and the review of those measures seem more reasonable. They fit. They are used for control, to be sure, but control and performance are not in conflict. If controls are used to shift emphasis from selling in one product area to selling in another, it does not necessarily follow that careers are sacrificed and performance impaired. The point is that the measures are current, generally available, and objective. And while there is always room for argument, they are reluctantly but generally acknowledged to be valid indicators of performance.

However, the reverse is more often true in development engineering. Obviously, measures of the performance of individual engineers and managers are more subjective, but I think the important issue is the measurement of project or program performance. The issue is the establishment of numbers controlling schedules, budgets, and project priorities, and the use to which these numbers are put.

Problems start with the fact that these numbers have a misleading appearance of precision in the eyes of division or corporate executives and staff. Engineers commit themselves to a set of figures because they must, but the fact that these figures are jokingly referred to as "guesstimates" tells something about their antecedents. Still, in the future these numbers will provide the basis for measurement and decisions. Success will be measured by how well you do against your forecast. And it does not take too much reflection on this situation to arrive at the correct surmise that success lies as much in rigging the numbers at the start as it does in meeting the numbers at the finish. I recall a situation in which a laboratory manager arbitrarily cut the projected performance of a program by one-half before submitting the program for executive approval. He was much abused for this by a group of lower-level managers who were furious at the way he was "downgrading" their program. Yet the laboratory manager's explanation to me was quite direct. "Even at one-half our projected performance the program will sell, and we look a lot better beating our promise by a million than we do falling short." So it goes.

But most important from our point of view are the critical judgments about project priorities, about the inception and termination of projects. Regardless of the financial numbers attached to projects, these must be "seat of the pants" judgments, for they must incorporate educated guesses about probabilities of success and relative importance to the success of the business. These are the "guesstimates." To the extent these judgments are used to control and shift resources, and to the extent the numbers used have essentially subjective origins, the entire process will appear unjustified. And because of the use to which they are put—killing projects and reallocating manpower—they do interfere with individual performance and the ongoing progress of work.

Let me give an example. Several years ago a new executive brought to Electromech an elaborate control system which he had successfully employed in his previous situation. He soon applied this within one division of Electromech. His reasoning invoked the common justification: the new system would ensure a better, more rational allocation of available resources. The logic of the procedures was stated clearly and in detail, and several innovations proposed seemed at that time to be management breakthroughs. I think it safe to say that top executive management was keenly interested in the system. Unfortunately, after a few years' trial, results did not match expectations. In fact, they were disastrous. The system was heartily detested by laboratory management and engineers. Data from the job satisfaction measure we have used in earlier comparisons showed engineers exactly at the level of Electromech blue-collar workers (19 per cent). Managers gave division management the lowest ratings I have ever seen.

But I think more significant from the company's point of view was the common complaint from managers and professionals that the new procedures were changing their function. More and more they saw themselves drawing away from their stated mission of developing advanced technology, taking on instead projects that were more compatible with the control procedures. For what the control system requires is frequent justification of the right of a project to additional funds. The project manager either demonstrates the potential of the project at specified points or the project is canceled. Furthermore, these justifications are quite specific and quantitative. The response to this system is natural enough; managers select and initiate projects whose potential payoff is easy to demonstrate. And as any engineer knows, those projects are not on the frontiers of technology. They are more commonly found in the quiet backwaters of known techniques.

Thus we have a rather intriguing example of function and structure moving into a compatible relation—this time, however, with function yielding to structure, if only temporarily. This is especially interesting because the research reviewed in this chapter implicitly assumes that structure follows function. In the example I have just given, we can see that the opposite may also be true. The major lesson is that overcontrol is a relative thing. Similar procedures followed in different functional or technological situations produce different outcomes. To sum up, then, excessive control is a relative rather than an absolute phenomenon. The laboratory experiences overcontrol because controls are incompatible with the function. The field experiences relative freedom because the match is appropriate.

MANAGEMENT SOCIALIZATION AND FUNCTIONAL PERSPECTIVE

A final question is suggested by our review and integration of the research findings. The question is this: Since research indicates that different functions can be expected to have different characteristic structures, why do we find the small Electromech development laboratories, especially those involved in advanced technology, run much as the others? Why don't they exhibit flexible rather than inflexible management environments? Put another way, why are inappropriate control systems introduced?

There is no one answer to these questions, but several points are important. First of all, in Electromech we are dealing with one organization, and the various laboratories constitute but one systems development organization. They are parts of a continually shifting puzzle that management is trying to piece together in the best way. Resources needed by high priority projects are found in the termination of low priority efforts. The management chess game is played with all the pieces in combination, not simply with each piece individually. Common management procedures seem reasonable from this perspective. Yet I observe also that an answer lies in a fact suggested both by Sayles and by Lawrence and Lorsch. It is this: The style or philosophy of management practiced by managers seems to be molded by, and thus appropriate to, the organization function that spawns it. Finance people look at things differently from researchers, and not just with regard to finance matters. They differ in a whole range of beliefs about the ways in which organizations should be run, about what makes an organization effective.

I have observed also that companies are likely to be overrepresented in executive management by certain functions. I worked for one organization that was partial to engineers. Yet another favored production men. In general, the overrepresented function is the one that is regarded as the most crucial to success, whether this is true in legend or in fact.[19] Now it is no secret in Electromech that the sales orientation is dominant in executive management. Similarly, it seems that no engineer has been able to remain successfully in a top executive position, though not for want of trying. This is of no little concern to executive management, for it is accompanied by the suspicion that somehow engineers do not have what it takes to become successful executives.

Why? Possibly executive types do not go into engineering, but I suspect the root of the difficulty is in the functional styles learned by engineers, in the difference between styles appropriate to engineering and those appropriate to sales. For if the management style typical of successful sales managers is used by top executives to judge ability, to be a criterion of success, then engineers are going to fail. To put it a bit differently, successful managerial styles and procedures are learned through organizational socialization, by emulating successful role models. The Lawrence and Lorsch study suggests that the dominant role styles of executives will be characteristic of the function that developed them.[20] And the role style of these executives will be generally assumed to be *the* successful role style. If engineers behave differently, if they have been socialized in a different function, then I suppose they will lack the style that marks success. How this relates to the management environment and control procedures should become clear in a minute. The following anecdote may help.

[19] Goldner discusses the power of managers in problematic functions in Fred H. Goldner, "Industrial Relations and the Organization of Management," unpublished doctoral dissertation.

[20] This connection between interpersonal style and organizational function is documented in Lawrence and Lorsch, *Organization and Environment*, pp. 33–36.

From time to time all companies go through periods of readjustment and consequent stress. Electromech is certainly no exception. During such a period a top executive of Electromech called together a large group of development engineering executives and top management for a group work session. I cannot quite describe the atmosphere but the session was a combination pep rally, religious service, and Dutch-uncle talk rolled into one. I thought one speech to the assembled executives to be significant. The executive, let me call him Marsh, started out by pointing to the fine job that had been done. After relating the successes, however, Marsh went on to review matters that he said concerned him. He thought that perhaps some of the problems could be licked if the engineering executives could just get a little bit extra from their technical potential. As an example of what he meant, Marsh pointed to the fact that in his visits to sales offices he always sensed a feeling of "agony" when a big contract had been lost. But somehow he never experienced this in engineering. If technical programs are missing their objectives, might not a little more agonizing help a bit? In the same talk Marsh also pointed to his belief that the incentive commission system in sales is responsible for the high level of motivation and performance in that function. Perhaps something like this in engineering, along with necessarily better measurement of programs and people, might be a key to getting the extra effort needed. Marsh said also, and I duly report it, that he knew it would be no simple thing to apply the sales techniques directly to engineering.

What this story illustrates is that both the diagnosis of the problem—if in fact there was one—and the suggested remedy are rooted in the experience and intimate knowledge of the sales function. If there is no agony, possibly there isn't enough concern. But I can guarantee that there was great concern. It is simply that engineering programs, especially those in complex systems, just don't fail in the way that contracts are lost. Except for a development bid situation (and this was not the case here) you don't wake up in the morning finding that a competitor has won the contract you went after. Rather, there is a slow process in which you come to realize that you will not meet your original objectives, and that these objectives must be redefined and modified in light of the current state of knowledge. If these redefined and modified objectives are sufficiently at odds with necessary systems performance, the program will be scrapped. Engineers know this; they are socialized into this environment. They know also that even programs which are terminated still carry within them a finite probability that they would have been successful if carried a bit further. And thus the clash between perspectives.

I think we are now able to set forth some of the reasons why the laboratories are similarly managed, why there are similar philosophies of control and resource allocation in the face of different technological situations, and why the management environment is most inflexible nearest executive headquarters. First, and best not to forget it, experience has shown that these procedures are necessary in certain sectors of development during the final stages. I suppose it is natural enough to believe that what is necessary for one is good for all. But more important in my view is the fact that key executives have experienced success with this style and philosophy of management. As I have tried to demonstrate, they view problems from a different perspective. Formal controls and quantitative measurements "work" in the field. Energetic, hard-hitting, decisive management is the successful role style of the field. So executives feel uncomfortable with the "iffy" answers tendered by engineers.

What flows from this is predictable. Engineering managers adopting the role style and practices valued by executives are most likely to be put into positions of top responsibility in the laboratory. They know what is expected of them and they know that their performance is judged at least in part from their style. As one executive, currently in organizational limbo, put it, "His eye is on the sparrow, there's not a thing that escapes his notice." What he meant, of course, was that executive management is very attentive not only to results but also to the details of the way problems are handled. Apparently, though, the sparrows at farthest remove from executive headquarters are the most difficult to see. To conclude, if the laboratories show a tendency toward uniformity of management practices it is because local management is part of a social system of role definitions and beliefs that define a management environment for the entire company. So while the management environments of the laboratories vary, they do so not in correspondence with the development mission—the technology—but rather in almost direct correspondence with the likelihood that variant practices and behavior will go unnoticed.

SUMMARY

The first concern of our research was to account for the pattern of low job satisfaction characteristic of the engineering occupation. It soon became apparent that underutilization and low satisfaction accompany one another. Further analysis pointed to lack of influence as a major factor, in particular, lack of what we have termed role influence. My temptation throughout in analyzing the data has been to relate role influence and underutilization causally. I recognize, of course, that the nature of the data precludes any analytical attribution of cause and effect. But it might be appropriate to speculate if such a framework seemed fruitful. The difficulty is that the facts do not fit with a direct cause-effect explanation for the underutilization-influence link. The situation is not so simple as to be readily described by two variable relationships. Our observations constitute an organizational syndrome, a collection of problem symptoms which occur in conjunction with a set of organizational conditions. The task of easing the problems ultimately comes down to one of constructing an organizational system that provides high utilization, high influence, and high satisfaction. The analysis that constitutes this chapter suggests some directions for constructing such a system.

One major point is this: The characteristic productive process, the technology, is the key. It is the key because it sets limits on the form of management structure that is appropriate for a given situation. What I am saying is that technology supplies meaning and form to the term "flexible management environment." Looked at in this way, the procedures, controls, and role definitions that are perfectly acceptable in the field situation are just as unacceptable in the development laboratory. The flat structure and diffuse authority system compatible with chemical plastics technology seem likely to produce chaos in the final phases of large systems development projects. Clearly, the very existence of a project cycle of one, two, or three years' duration complicates the management problem enormously. As described by our engineer in Chapter 2, the management environment changes dramatically in response to the requirements of different phases of the project cycle. And so it is not only technology and function that we must reckon with, but phase within function.

I think nothing is so unsatisfactory to an engineer as avoidable failure. Our discussion has presented numerous examples of the fact that nothing is more frustrating than failing because you were never given the chance to succeed. Thus, it seems to me, the appropriate management environment for the kind of innovation characteristic of systems development is neither organic nor mechanistic. Nor is it necessarily flat rather than hierarchical. The satisfactory environment is one where the probability of project success is greatest. If, as in the final phases of systems development, success is better assured by more controls, by directive management, then that environment is best. I can personally attest to the great frustration and grinding dissatisfaction that result when a project which needs control and direction is managed in a laissez-faire manner. The point is that flexible management is just that—flexible. It has no one prescription except ensuring that organizational roles are appropriate to the situation, and that organizational members understand the definition of those roles. The lesson of this chapter is that a major task for management is role definition, the construction of a management environment that is appropriate for the productive process, satisfactory for the individual, and successful for the organization.

The variables that management has at its disposal in this task are:

1. The type of personnel
2. The nature and extent of resource control and allocation procedures
3. The formal structure of the organization—the "organization chart"
4. The informal structure of the organization—the communications links which affect the distribution and exchange of information

From this base we can now undertake the task of the last chapter, looking at ways in which management has attempted to cope with the organizational problems of systems development engineering, and suggesting some procedures which might work better.

10

Engineers in Systems Development: Problems and Prospects

My chief concern to this point has been the description and analysis of the problems of a systems development organization and the engineers who work within it. I am well aware that such description and analysis, while interesting, is of secondary concern to some readers. They are more interested in the question, "What do I do about the problems?" I will try to answer that query shortly. But first I want to say that the accurate diagnosis of a problem is indispensable to correct treatment, and that truthful prognosis does not always point to complete rehabilitation. So our first step must be to look squarely at the facts, to recognize the limitations inherent in the technological and economic situation of the complex systems development organization. And in looking at these facts we must keep in mind that we are dealing with organizations whose workers are highly educated, whose mobility expectations are those of the college graduate, and whose current social milieu indicates the existence of a well-developed appetite for individual control in membership organizations. These workers become members of organizations possessing certain features which, far from being remediable, serve to define those organizations. To summarize those features:

1. The systems development laboratory is a factory. While it is more complex than a factory, emphasis on deadlines, costs, and reliability in getting out the product all have much in common with the production plant.

2. The complexity of systems development projects and the time spans necessitated by market requirements dictate a micro-division

of labor and consequent task specialization. The work requirements of the resulting tasks limit the need for individual technical sophistication.

3. This also means that coordinative functions will be very necessary. Because coordinative functions are involved in economic and technical trade-offs, and because they are so numerous, some degree of hierarchy is implied. Logically as well as empirically that degree of hierarchy will be greater than in non-systems organizations of comparable size.

4. In this environment technical decisions are inseparable from organizational and economic decisions. That is, the motivation for any particular technical solution is organizational or economic or both. The solution aims at attaining feasibility within the constraints of marketing and the organizational resources available to do the job. Ideas of separating these decision-making functions are illusory.

5. Because the need for technically outstanding engineers is far smaller than the need for capable coordinators, mobility pressures from below can never be satisfied through existing technical positions. Important, influential technical positions exist but they are in proportion to need.

On the societal level certain trends are appearing which serve to make the problems experienced by systems development organizations more acute. I refer to a continuing trend toward overeducation that is the product of both those who require education and those who desire it. For example, after analyzing a considerable amount of data on the attitudes of organizations toward education, Berg finds that there is a consistent trend to require more education than is necessary to do the job.[1] There is also a consistent dissatisfaction on the part of those who are overeducated for the job. Unfortunately, the rule seems to be that the best employment opportunities go to those with the best—that is, the most—education. As one of our M.B.A.'s put it, "A year and a half in school can substitute for six years in the field." Realizing this, the manpower pool available for organizations is also industriously overeducating itself.

The universities and engineering colleges also play a role. I re-

[1] Berg, "Rich Man's Qualifications for Poor Man's Jobs," *Trans-action*, VI (March, 1969), 45–50.

cently attended a session in which engineering executives and engineering educators were discussing what constitutes a proper engineering education. Many of the comments from executives were directed toward the fact that the kind of engineering graduate currently being turned out is not appropriate for their needs. He is overtrained in theory and undertrained in practical application. At this point the dean of engineering in a small college made a rather emotional statement about his problems. He said that he had tried to do what the executives were asking, but it was almost impossible because of certain institutional factors. The things that attract competent faculty and pay the bills are research facilities and research grants. The faculty wants subject matter that reflects their research interests and they want students capable of serving as research assistants. When all this is summed up it amounts to continued pressure for a science-oriented curriculum and a science-oriented student. In practical terms it means the overtraining of engineers for the vast majority of jobs available to them. When this is combined with the important place of the degree in our mobility-conscious society, it means also that the supply of capable technical support people will dwindle.

These factors constitute the constraints which bound the solutions to the organizational problems we face. Our approaches to the development of more satisfactory membership roles must take cognizance of them.

ROLE DEFINITION AND ORGANIZATION DEVELOPMENT

In concluding the last chapter I surmised that a major task of policy-making management is that of providing structures and a management environment whose implied role requirements are compatible with the productive process and with the role expectations of organization members. Let me make this more explicit. Management is defining the engineer's role when, for example, it decides to formalize and quantify controls and procedures for the allocation of resources. Not that role is explicitly set forth in these procedures, for it is not. Rather it is that these procedures set limits or constraints on the activities and interactions among organization members. Specific, formal controls to some extent substitute for individual judgment. They make consultation with lower members of the organization either unnecessary or meaningless. For what must be done in any particular case is spelled out in whatever memo or company directive applies. The necessary information to implement action is contained within the system.

A second kind of example arises from management anxiety, and it is simply bad management. When problems arise, when the going gets rough, there is always a tendency to withdraw control upward and to check on the work of subordinates in more detail. Under these conditions managers are reduced to transmission links in a downward flow of directions and an upward flow of results achieved. Thus it is that the mutual sets of expectations which constitute role are formed. Again, I am not talking about roles of particular individuals but the shared expectations concerning entire classes of organization members. The pervasive, informal character of these shared expectations is such that they commonly go unnoticed by the very executives responsible for their existence. I remember one occasion during which a group of executives were reviewing some rather interesting regularities in the survey data. We saw some large differences between two division groupings accompanied by some remarkable consistencies among the laboratories within each division. At this point the division vice-president turned to me and said, "You know, the one thing I've learned from this picture is that I never realized the impact the decisions we make here have on the people out there."

Coping with problems from the executive point of view means establishing policies that guide decisions at lower levels. These have technical-financial-marketing components: Which areas of technological development seem to promise most for the future? how large should the total development effort be? if it cannot be developed in three years can it succeed in the market? Where policies have explicit organizational content they deal with structural, impersonal problems of specialization, form, and control. Personnel policies regarding pay, promotions, and overtime are handled at lower levels, and in any case are mostly irrelevant. Only occasionally will a policy with important implications for the human organization, such as the dual management hierarchy, be regarded as a fit subject for executive initiative. The point is this: By and large, role definitions with important consequences for the management environment are the accidental consequences of policies intended for other purposes. It is my contention that the possible solutions for the problems we have been reviewing must derive from *explicit* attention to the role consequences of these policies.

Therefore, in the remaining pages I intend to summarize each of the concerns dealt with previously and to inquire into the effectiveness of a typical management policy expected to handle the problem. Where the problem symptoms appear to be misinterpreted, or where the approach is ineffective or misguided in light of our research, I shall try to outline an alternative course of action. In particular I will treat at length problem solutions related to "obsolescence of technical skills" and to the concept of "dual management."

As a final exercise I will try to outline a set of general solutions to the problems of structure and environment inherent in the enterprise of large systems development engineering.

WORK GOALS AND PROFESSIONALIZATION

The complaints of professionals in business organizations are seen as being precipitated by an undesired involvement in business affairs. Engineers and scientists are commonly thought of as unhappily prostituting their professional goals to the service of profit. As I have tried to demonstrate, this is a misunderstanding of engineers and engineering. For in the most general sense, the engineer's satisfaction comes from solving problems within a given set of constraints. These may be economic, or perhaps simply technical. The systems activity involved in space exploration might be an example of the latter. In any event, I would maintain that the criterion of a job well done for any engineer is that of elegance. How well and how simply was it done within the existing constraints? Cost may or may not be a relevant factor. Yet the test is seldom solely technical —most problems can be solved. But if they are solved through sheer "brute force" the resulting solution produces little satisfaction.

In industry the test is whether or not the job is done elegantly enough to justify sales. Is your system better than that of your competitors? While this is not the only test, the positive feedback and feeling of achievement that comes to an engineer from incorporating his ideas into tangible products or systems is a great source of motivation to him. Yet another source of motivation is the opportunity to be responsible for an entire system. For reasons previously pointed out this generally concerns management. It means welcomed power and unwelcomed responsibility for other people.

Now, a widely accepted solution to the "motivational" problems of engineers has been professionalization.[2] Professionalization is actively urged on engineers. It is subsidized by awards of all sorts as well as by direct compensation for expenses incurred at professional meetings. In several large corporations I have listened to management people discuss the desirability of having engineers hold office and receive awards from major professional societies. They actually plan for and attempt to identify those who might be suitable in this role of "professional Stakhanovite."

And what organizational role does professionalization imply? Well, for one thing, it means less involvement in the affairs of the business organization and more in some professional one. It means a substitution of autonomy for power. And this means that the engineer is freer to do his own technical thing, but has less voice in business-related decisions that greatly influence over-all systems configurations. It means a loss of role influence.

Our analyses suggest that this is satisfactory for the minority only. Attempts to treat the ills of systems development engineering by the professionalization of engineers is a mistake. My observation is that removing the engineer from business concerns creates a class of organizational eunuchs. Engineers are effectively removed from participation in the influence processes of the organization by increasing their organizational distance from those who make the important decisions. Since considerable organizational resources

[2] For a discussion of the meaning of professionalization see Goldner and Ritti, "Professionalization as Career Immobility," *American Journal of Sociology*, LXXII (1967), 489–502.

must be brought to bear on any idea to bring it to fruition, the professional who has been emancipated from business concerns is also rendered powerless to pursue the supposedly professional concerns.[3]

Thus the need is for greater involvement and influence in the total affairs of the organization. And this means changes in the structure of the organization and a redefinition of the role of the engineer. Since these suggestions involve correcting some shortcomings of an attempted solution—dual management—I will treat them in detail later in this chapter. But let me point out here that any notion of dual management is illusory. Those who suggest that technical engineers be given decision-making power while leaving management with the administrative and personnel responsibilities are simply redefining what is meant by management. For I am firmly convinced that management is where the power is, and those with power will come also to have the responsibility for making the decisions about other things that count.

SYSTEMS DESIGN, SKILL UTILIZATION, AND SKILL OBSOLESCENCE

Two overriding facts of systems design are the specialization and the interdependence of organizational units. When a large system is broken down into component facets it is necessary to assign a group or unit of the organization to the completion of each component. The interdependence derives from the fact that the system components must fit together and function properly in the over-all system.

These features of systems design impact the engineering organization in two major ways:

1. Because entire unit organizations, rather than individuals, are specialized within the organization, the majority of engineers will be at work in tasks we have described as "formatted."[4] They will be implementing a component task as laid out by the systems design planners.

[3] This point is made in detail in Ritti and Goldner, "Professional Pluralism in an Industrial Organization," *Management Science*, XVI (December, 1969), B-233–B-246.

[4] The role of the unit organization in specialization is taken from Barnard, *Functions of the Executive*.

2. Innovation will be planned and controlled. Resources are allocated to achieve innovations when and as they are planned. It follows from this that allocation of resources means primarily allocation of people. Since the restricted availability of both people and tasks to be done guarantees some degree of mismatch between tasks and skills, this work-force philosophy of allocating resources necessitates the interchangeability of skills on the part of the engineers engaged in systems design.

As pointed out by Thompson, task specialization and personal specialization are quite different things. Task specialization increases with an increasing division of labor. Task specialization attempts to reduce activities to a single "program"—to a single "set of activities of a goal achieving kind." [5] These are the "formatted" tasks. By personal specialization is meant the ability of an individual to perform a number of perhaps interrelated programs, making him in some ways irreplaceable, providing him with "greater function and status." [6] Following from this description must be the conclusion that task specialization results in personal despecialization. Organizational units are specialized, not people. To the extent that engineers are truly specialized, unique in function and irreplaceable, there must be a problem in allocation of resources. In fact, what is wanted in a systems-design engineering work force is unspecialized people who are allocatable to specialized units and who possess interchangeable and common skills. This fact was first pointed out to me by a director of engineering who claimed that his aim was to have 80 per cent of his people able to perform any new task within two weeks of their initial assignment. And so we have a built-in contradiction within the systems engineering organization. On the one hand, the skill level of engineers should be such that any new assignment can be readily handled, and on the other hand, systems design work produces a plethora of formatted tasks.

The consequences of this can best be seen through the situation of the recent graduate—a highly specialized person who can do almost anything in general but nothing in particular. His first few years of work constitute a process of personal despecialization as he is fitted to specialized tasks assigned to his organizational unit. The result of

[5] Thompson, *Modern Organization*, p. 33. [6] *Ibid.*

this in combination with previously described conditions of misutilization and underutilization is observed in the problem of "obsolescence of skills." The symptom of the problem is the existence of engineers who are unaware of recent technological developments and who produce technically inferior solutions. The ill is the "explosive" advance of technology; the cure is continuing education.

Here is one diagnosis of the ill:

> Obsolescence refers not to the individual but to the extent to which he has failed to keep abreast of current knowledge in his field. It is a gradual process—subtle, pernicious and debilitating—in the social sense. . . . It signifies a failure on the part of a previously trained individual to advance with and *at the same rate* as the state of the art in his field.
>
> The problem of keeping pace with changes in professional knowledge and procedures is particularly acute for the engineer. There has been an unprecedented, explosive advance in engineering and scientific technology since the close of the second world war. As a result, it is conceivable that an engineer could go to school every night of his professional life and still fall behind in some areas of the new technology.[7]

Because the obsolescence problem has been interpreted in this way, continuing education is the remedy. This is a very apposite example of Thompson's contention that solutions to organizational problems are more likely to be sought through the remaking of individuals than through changes in organizational policy or structure. So we have an organizationally sanitary explanation—the explosive advance of technology—and an equally sanitary remedy, continuing education. The problem is, of course, that neither the diagnosis nor the remedy bears much relation to the problem. I think the following comment puts the subsequent discussion in context.

> The corporation places too much emphasis on education, just for the sake of exercising one's brain. It's very frustrating to spend many hours on education—at the suggestion of management—only to find in a year's time we've forgotten what we learned.

The facts are that while 41 per cent of Electromech engineers feel they are "only fairly well" or "not at all" up to date, only 7 per cent see a "significant" *problem* in the obsolescence of technical skills among their fellow professionals. And when asked, "If professionals

[7] Raines and Missar, "Engineering Obsolescence: A Challenge to the Training Director," *Training Directors Journal*, XIX (January, 1965), 35.

do allow themselves to become out of date technically, what in *your opinion* might be the main reasons for this?" we see from Table 10.1 that the primary reason given is that assignments do not require knowledge of the latest developments. The fact that developments are rapidly taking place is given about the same importance as lack of interest in technical work.

Table 10.1

Reasons Given by Engineers for Causes of Obsolescence of Technical Skills

Reason	Per cent indicating reason is important
Work assignments that do not require knowledge of the latest developments	51
The press of schedule demands leaves no time or energy for other study	43
Work is so specialized that the broader base of knowledge is unused and forgotten	40
Developments in the field are coming so rapidly that it is very difficult for anyone to keep up	30
Lack of interest in the technical end of their work	26
Managerial duties require little knowledge in depth of new technical developments	20

But I think more to the heart of the issue is a survey of the educational needs of engineers in industry conducted under the auspices of the American Society for Engineering Education. The report of the results covers some 144 companies and over 4,000 respondents, all of whom graduated about 10 years before the time of the survey. Engineers were offered a list of some 123 subjects for which they could indicate a definite need or a probable need. Table 10.2 presents the top ten subjects on this list in terms of the per cent responding in both these categories.[8] This, as stated in the report, is the per cent of engineers indicating that the subject "would be helpful."

[8] American Society for Engineering Education, "Synopsis of the Joint ECAC–RWI Feedback Committee Report," *Journal of Engineering Education*, LV (1965), 254–56.

Table 10.2

Reports by Engineers of Subjects in Which Additional Training "Would Be Helpful"

Subject title	Per cent indicating training in subject "would be helpful"
Management practices	65
Technical writing	64
Probability and statistics	60
Public speaking	60
Creative thinking	57
Working with individuals	57
Working with groups	55
Speed reading	54
Talking with people	53
Business practices (marketing, finance, economics)	51

The fact of this list should lead us to question the burning need for "technological updating." Of the top ten subjects only Probability and Statistics can be classified as technical. But is Probability and Statistics a product of rapidly advancing technology? Only in a remote sense. Modern manufacturing techniques and demands for quality control have made a knowledge of statistics essential for management. That is the point.

The list of the most frequently chosen technical subjects discloses these preferences:

heat transfer, 43 per cent
ordinary differential equations, 37 per cent
vector analysis, 31 per cent
solid-state physics, 30 per cent

Of these subjects only solid-state physics might be characterized as new. Certainly heat transfer and ordinary differential equations are subjects of long standing in the engineering curriculum (the author having taken both himself in the 1940s) and vector analysis is nothing particularly new.

What it boils down to is this: Even technical subjects with considerable generality to all fields of engineering (e.g., mathematics), subjects not ordinarily restricted to advanced graduate study, are dramatically underchosen as compared to the management–human relations skills group.[9]

What useful conclusion can we draw from these data? First of all, given the goals of engineers, if technical subjects would help them get ahead they would be taking technical subjects. Secondly, I think it *is* true that the majority of engineers are not up to date technically; they are not even up to where they were! Technical refreshment rather than updating would be more appropriate terminology. The systems environment wants only a handful of technical superstars. In the face of this the average engineer looks to improve his chances of performing some directive, coordinative function that requires a blend of managerial skills and technical experience. This is his only road toward broader, more interesting, higher status activities. The despecialized engineer is not in the forefront of technology, nor is he required to be. But he does present a problem in the process of "allocating resources."

At this point I have the feeling that the reader is about to ask what all this has to do with management environment and low-influence role definitions. First, as stated earlier, implicit definitions of role derive from the definition of the problem and its assumed solution. The definition of engineer as "worker" masks the real problem. In the extreme, management would like its workers to be a universally allocatable resource, interchangeable engineering bodies who fill the breach when and where needed. This is approximately the view of the factory manager. But engineers are not factory hands. So the perceived problem, technical obsolescence, is a product of management's attempts to apply a structure that is incompatible with the function. The responsibility for obsolescence lies not with engineers as individuals; it follows directly from system development management's definition of what "engineer" means. The problem is

[9] This interpretation depends on the fact that all specialties choose management subjects first. Thus, if the only common choices among the various engineering specialties were management subjects, these subjects would appear to be more popular than technical subjects restricted to one field. But this is not the case. A list for mechanical engineers only shows almost identical figures. See "The Profession: Deficiencies in Retrospect," *Product Engineering*, XXXVI (1965), 33. A second biasing factor might be the presence of engineers with managerial responsibilities. Again, the feedback committee report finds no difference in the results relating to job responsibility.

more one of technical amnesia than of technical senility. And the solution must be found in the organization of work roles rather than in individual updating. The answer lies in redefining what is meant by "engineer" by redefining role requirements. Exactly what can be done must agree with subsequent discussion in this chapter. But for now it can be pointed out that the only compatible role definition is managerial, and the answer lies in redefining the role of engineer from worker to manager.

Beyond this a second set of directions pointing to the solution is already recognized. That is, management does understand that skill obsolescence is the product of misutilization.

ENGINEERS NEED CHALLENGE

Because of this knowledge on the part of management, engineering administrators are exhorted to keep engineers "challenged." And it does not take many interviews with disgruntled engineers to arrive at this solution. Yet the problem persists. Why? The answer again flows from the organizational roles associated with systems development. Systems design activities are group activities and they have built-in tendencies toward misutilization and underutilization of people. The problem persists because the solution is attempted through the exhortation of individual managers. Yet the only solution possible is at the laboratory level.

Misemployment. The problem, our analysis shows, is easily understood. Engineers are doing things that clerks or technical support people could easily do. The problem is one of proper manpower management and has supposedly an equally direct solution—hire more technicians. Yet while the problem and its solution are widely recognized, I have never seen it solved. I think the reasons are the following:

1. Cost. For one thing, an engineer does not cost much more than a technician. The gap in salaries is not great, and when overhead expenses are factored in even this difference diminishes. So it turns out that "head count" is a more important figure than total dollars. A senior man may cost twice as much as a junior man, yet they often do the same type of work. It hardly seems fair to allocate costs

directly. For these reasons there is little to be gained in attempting to minimize salary costs by having more technicians and fewer professionals.

2. Self-protection. A graduate engineer can do more things than a technician—at least in the beginning. Therefore, it is plain to most engineering managers that their flexibility is increased by "requisitioning" more engineers and fewer technicians. And, since they operate under the constraint of total head count, the solution is easy to implement: more engineers and fewer technicians.

3. The project cycle. In fact, the project cycle may really be the most difficult problem. The nature of project work activity changes radically through time, yet the personnel remain the same. When the job nears completion, and clerical or technical support could handle it easily, engineers who were perhaps needed in earlier phases are the only ones familiar enough with the project history to finish it up. Bringing in new technicians or clerks would require a period of training and managers are reluctant to spend this unnecessary time. Engineers plod on with the "grunt" work because it is actually more efficient to do so in the short run.

Then what motivation has the first-line engineering supervisor to cope with the problem of misutilization? Not much. And hence the problem persists. Yet while the cost of this mode of operation in terms of a dollar difference between engineers and technicians is not much, I suspect the cost in terms of motivation and quality of future solutions is fairly great. Therefore it behooves the administrator to find a way of providing a flexible incentive for managers to use technicians. Requiring a fixed ratio of technicians per engineer is a poor solution, another example of inflexible control. Perhaps the answer lies in some differential weighting of the all-important head count. Engineers might "cost" two units while technicians only cost one. This would provide the manager with an incentive to employ technicians, while leaving open the option of using engineers if necessary.

Underemployment. Engineers seem willing to live with misutilization, but nothing is as frustrating or demoralizing as unemployment. Underutilization of technical manpower first came to public attention in terms of the stockpiling of engineers necessary to obtain government contracts. That is, contracts were awarded on the basis of currently existing capacity to do the job. If you wanted a government contract, you went out and hired yourself enough engineers to do the job *if* you got the job. And what did your engineers do in the meantime? Nothing.

Though this is definitely not the situation in Electromech, the problem still exists. It exists, I think, because of the anxieties of executive management. How to keep track of what is going on? How to be sure that resources are being allocated in the best way? One way to cope with these questions is to piece together a framework of approval, evaluation, and control procedures—formal procedures designed to promote a rational best over-all allocation of resources (people) to projects in some known predictable way. I have tried to adduce evidence to support my belief that the inflexibility inherent in these procedures leads to underutilization for the reason that people in direct contact with the situation are unable to act. These management control procedures are analogous in the engineering work force to the time and motion study procedures applied to the factory work force. They draw sustenance from the same informing philosophy—"the one best way"—and they are antecedents of the same emotions: futility, alienation, and demotivation. They also presume the same role for the organization member—the "worker" role.

JOB ENRICHMENT: A SOLUTION TO UTILIZATION PROBLEMS?

That many nonprofessional industrial jobs are inherently unsatisfying and demotivating has been a long-standing matter of concern to social scientists.[10] Their common observation is that the typical job uses but a fraction of the worker's actual or potential skills. The problem is the overspecialization of work tasks and the removal of responsibility for even the most minor decisions. The treatment cur-

[10] For example, Elton Mayo wrote at length on the problems derivative from the monotony of industrial blue-collar work during the 1920s.

rently called for is aptly termed "job enrichment."[11] On the theory that satisfaction and motivation will be increased if skills are better utilized, the job enrichment program calls both for the enhancement of task content and for the broadening of discretionary responsibility. Practitioners of job enrichment techniques are careful to point out that enlarging jobs means more than simply the addition of more duties. They call for filling out the entire job with related responsibilities. Ford uses the term "vertical loading" to signify the addition, as well, of greater control and influence.[12] Furthermore, it is clear from Ford's discussion that job enrichment includes a conscious attempt to shift role definitions in the direction of higher status, away from "worker" to resemble "manager" more (e.g., removing controls without removing accountability).

Now, Ford's evidence is that job enrichment works for blue-collar and clerical jobs. But it is obvious from our research that identical considerations are involved for engineers, though the root problems are in some ways different. His concern is the restructuring of individual jobs within the departmental organization (though he does stress the necessity of involving local higher management). Our research points to the fact that entire organizations are involved, and that the necessary role redefinition involves entire classes of organization members. In addition, the problem of underutilization as it exists in systems development engineering is not the problem that the practitioners of job enrichment have in mind.

I think that the idea behind job enrichment is as much applicable to engineering as it is to clerical work. But the actual methods used in enlarging jobs are fundamentally inapplicable in the systems organization. The situation there requires action that is considerably more complex. For one thing, we can see from our research that local, departmental action is almost impossible independent of the total organization. Job content varies with the development cycle, and there are larger problems of resource allocation. For another

[11] I do not know who should be credited with coining the term, but current advocacy of job enrichment may be found in Herzberg, *Work and the Nature of Man*.

[12] Ford, *Motivation Through the Work Itself*, pp. 28–29.

thing, my guess is that some tasks will not yield to improvement. In this case job enrichment means finding someone else to do the job.

To sum up, I think the philosophy behind job enrichment points toward the same goal as our research; the answer lies in changing role definitions. Yet it seems also that the practical implementation of that answer implies much more far-reaching organizational consequences in systems development engineering. I feel that a department-by-department attempt to modify jobs as they are currently defined is doomed to failure. For we are faced not simply with a matter of additions and subtractions that enhance individual roles but with a matter of the rearrangement of the entire system of interdependent role-sets which constitute the management environment. Our practical task thus remains as previously set down—we must proceed toward the redefinition of the organizational role of the engineer in directions which imply greater role influence and increased utilization.

UNDERUTILIZATION, INFLUENCE, AND CONTROL IN ORGANIZATIONS

Earlier we saw that organizations can be characterized by control curves describing the amount of influence in setting the direction of technical goals felt at each level in the organizational hierarchy. These curves have two major features:

1. Location: the position in the organizational hierarchy perceived to be exercising the greatest degree of control.
2. Amount: the average degree of control perceived to be exercised over all levels in the organization.

Positive attitudes and feelings of productivity are related to the nearness of one's own position to the point of maximum control, and to a greater average level of control throughout the organization. We find also that the perceptions of influence that characterize these control curves are the result of both the technical mission of the organization—the work itself—and the control procedures instituted by management. But the level of underutilization seems to be a function only of the level of role influence characteristic of the entire laboratory organization.

What all this suggests is that the major share of underutilization, and certainly the part which can be dealt with at the policy level, is the result of attempts by executive management to utilize manpower resources better. For these control procedures are followed in an effort to avoid misallocation, to ensure that resources will be applied where they are most needed. From the executive viewpoint better utilization occurs when a questionable project is killed and its funds are transferred to a more promising project. Better utilization occurs when the budgeted funds are allocated by priority to the most promising development projects currently under way.

The problem as I see it is that executive management defines utilization in the abstract, while lower levels experience it concretely. More specifically, the problem of underutilization arises from these differences in the perspectives of executive and lower management:

1. Seeing the big picture. At executive levels there are staff officers who are responsible for the budget and whose careers depend upon realizing cost objectives. When it is decided that a high-priority project needs additional resources, funds must come from somewhere. Where projects run over the budget, they must be brought back under control. Objections will always be raised by those directly affected. And yet it is easy to see why those objections cannot be honored. Executive staff specialists have neither the information nor the time to assume the responsibility of separating the unfortunate from the incompetent. The concern of the executive staff is to ensure that the pieces of the big picture fit together at the end of the year.

2. Knowledge of results. A second difference is that executive management does not see the concrete impact of reassigning individuals. The phrase "allocation of resources" is a nice, antiseptic way of describing a rather messy process of aborting projects and uprooting people. The fact that taking root in new surroundings takes appreciable time does not appear on the balance sheet. Nor is the manager who receives these "resources" likely to complain. After all, he is better off than before.

So it is my opinion that the gains from this sort of shuffling are largely illusory. This kind of top management attention is more likely to result in continual misrepresentation calculated by lower levels to stymie the control systems, and considerable organizational rigidity because upper management is ignorant of the actual facts. Yet I am not saying that no control procedures are needed. I call into question primarily procedures that span many levels of management, guided and enforced by specialists remote and insensitive to local problems, specialists whose organizational welfare is bound up with the appearance of a ledger rather than that of a product.

The solution to this problem is suggested by our observation in the last chapter that the characteristic distribution of influence in successful organizations matches the existence of detailed knowledge necessary to make sound decisions. Our problem, consequently, is that of arriving at some arrangement whereby those levels of organization which experience underutilization as a practical day-to-day matter will have the greatest influence in decisions which bear directly on utilization.

INFLUENCE AND CONTROL IN DUAL MANAGEMENT

One organizational arrangement offered as an answer to this problem is dual management.[13] While it takes many forms, dual management is essentially a setup in which technical professionals make technical decisions or control technical matters, and supervisory management takes care of personnel, budgeting, and the like. This arrangement is usually formalized into parallel hierarchies or ladders of advancement. Each has its set of titles and job descriptions. Therefore, among the presumed benefits that accrue to this system is the recognition of the equal status of technical men and managers. This gives the engineer an incentive to remain on the technical side of things, thus leading directly to improved utilization of skills and incidentally taking care of the career mobility problem. "Management" positions are created for those who otherwise would never have been promoted into management. One truly remarkable feature of this arrangement is that almost every engineer does eventually wind up in management. In Electromech, for example, only

[13] See Shepard, "The Dual Hierarchy in Research," *Research Management,* I (1958), 177–87.

15 per cent of the engineers who have been with the company over ten years are not in the dual hierarchy.

Now the logic of dual management is supplied by an ideology of professionalism based on the local-cosmopolitan distinction already described. Supervisory management actively defends these beliefs, and points to true professionalism as a preferred career for an outstanding engineer. Yet we know that the local-cosmopolitan distinction is inappropriate for most engineers, for it maintains that the professional should be free from involvement in organizational affairs and should look to his peers for recognition. Thus we must ask whether a dual hierarchy can work and whether it provides an answer to the questions we have posed concerning control and utilization. I am about to suggest that the answer is no.

Dual management presumes the separability of technical and administrative duties. Yet our description of the systems development environment must make it plain that such a separation is not possible. Systems development is not a matter for individual contributors —at least not many of them. The complex factoring of large development projects means that people providing the coordinative function are essential. And where coordination is necessary so is hierarchy. Some system must necessarily evolve that will restrict formal control to a limited number of individuals. Those individuals—whoever they may be and whatever they may be called—are members of management. And they will be higher-status organizational members than those in nonmanagement. Yet it is not necessary to argue that nonmanagement members will have no influence, for they will. What I am saying is that a formal separation of decision powers between technical and administrative management will not exist for long. The group with formal responsibility for technical decisions of any consequence must eventually have responsibility as well for manpower and other resources.

I think this fact is responsible for the results shown in Table 10.3. Nonsupervisory engineers were asked to rate the two types of position on the dual hierarchy with respect to thirteen different attributes. They could indicate that the staff technical position had more of the attribute, that the managerial position had more, or that they thought the positions had about the same amount of the attribute.

Table 10.3

Judgments of the Extent to Which Managerial and Staff Technical Positions Differ on Selected Attributes

Attribute	Per cent saying: Managerial position has more of attribute	Per cent saying: Staff technical position has more of attribute
Power to initiate programs	80	6
Prestige	78	5
Potential for advancement	75	5
Potential for getting action on your ideas	73	10
Salary	64	3
Recognition of your contributions	50	22
Effort required	46	16
Chance to make important technical decisions	44	38
Excitement	42	27
Ability required	22	26
Interesting work	23	52
Offers opportunity to follow your own interests	22	60
Utilization of skills	15	61

The picture that emerges is quite clear. Electromech engineers are almost unanimous in their agreement that attributes related to status and influence are more characteristic of the managerial than the staff technical positions. On the other hand, the attributes dealing with autonomy and skill utilization are seen as being more characteristic of the staff technical positions.

However, when the data are broken down by current position level, as shown in Table 10.4, another fact emerges. These data show responses from all first-line managers, staff technical engineers on the other side of the dual hierarchy, engineers (those beyond the entry grade but not yet on either side of the dual management hierarchy), and Junior Engineers (those who have been in the business for less than two years).[14] What we see is that judgments bearing on

[14] For computational convenience I have used only the Darby and Ferndale groups of nonsupervisory engineers in this table and in figures 10.1 and 10.2. The group sizes are: managers, 787; staff engineers, 328; engineers, 779; Junior Engineers, 154.

the influence and status of staff positions become increasingly less favorable as one progresses up the staff side of the dual hierarchy. Engineers currently holding staff positions view their own positions less favorably than do their managers. This organizational learning effect is especially dramatic in the "chance to make important technical decisions" attribute. Young engineers presume this to be the prerogative of the technical professional. Yet by the time they reach the staff technical positions their opinion has been reversed.

Table 10.4
Judgments of the Extent to Which Managerial and Staff Technical Positions Differ as a Function of Current Position of Respondent

Attribute	Current position level	Per cent saying: Managerial position has more of attribute	Per cent saying: Staff technical position has more of attribute
Power to initiate programs	Manager	85	4
	Staff	90	1
	Engineer	78	8
	Junior	67	14
Potential for getting action on your ideas	Manager	78	7
	Staff	81	6
	Engineer	71	10
	Junior	66	12
Salary	Manager	52	5
	Staff	73	1
	Engineer	62	3
	Junior	37	5
Recognition of your contributions	Manager	43	24
	Staff	57	16
	Engineer	50	24
	Junior	38	28
Chance to make important technical decisions	Manager	54	27
	Staff	54	27
	Engineer	41	41
	Junior	33	48
Interesting work	Manager	49	26
	Staff	19	54
	Engineer	26	53
	Junior	20	60

But such a change does not take place in judgments with regard to autonomy and interesting work, and the pattern for the "utilization of skills" attribute is the same.

On this basis one might be tempted to draw the conclusion that while the dual hierarchy fails to meet its aim of providing professional influence, it does succeed in achieving greater utilization of skills. Yet I wonder. The attributes that show no effect from organizational learning are essentially subjective, intra-individual comparisons. They reflect judgments on such questions as "Is my work more interesting to me than managerial work?" On the other hand, attributes that show the greatest effect are defined mostly by organizational transactions. Power to make decisions, recognition, and prestige are not questions of subjective preference. Experience in the process of decision-making informs the staff professional on the possession of power. But in skill utilization the question is open as to which *kind* of activity best utilizes skills. Project managers do not use their technical knowledge directly on design problems. They also "waste" a certain amount of time in "political" activity and administration.

Engineers on the staff side of the dual management hierarchy come to view their positions in consonance with the ideology of professionalism through a process of cognitive adjustment. Cognitive dissonance results from a clash between the desire to be "management" and a manifest lack of formal power. Professionalism, with its emphasis on cosmopolitanism and autonomy, provides the needed framework in which the engineer can bring into balance his cognitions of what should be and what is.[15] The process I am referring to is displayed in figures 10.1 and 10.2. These figures present data on the aspirations of pre-management engineers as they change over a period of time. I have tried to control for career potential by including only those engineers with bachelor's degrees who have already advanced beyond the Junior Engineer level. It is possible, of course, to view the trends in two ways. That is, the trend could be produced because engineers change their viewpoint as they learn more about themselves and the organization. Or the trend might simply

[15] These points are elaborated in Goldner and Ritti, "Professionalism as Career Immobility," *American Journal of Sociology*, LXXII (1967), 489–502.

Figure 10.1

Attitudes about Promotion as a Function of Length of Service (B.S. degree only, Engineers 1 and 2 only)

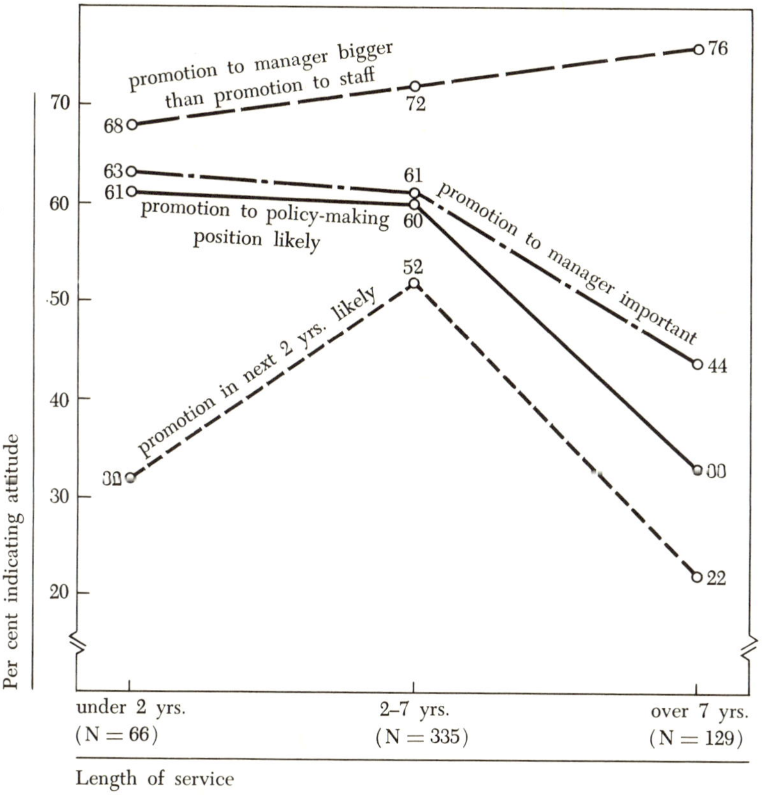

be the result of the removal of engineers with a similar outlook from the nonmanagement group, leaving behind an equally similar group. While the change in attitudes by organization level seems to favor the former interpretation—as do I—there is no difference in the conclusion. For whether it is selection, or change, or both that is responsible, the fact remains that the probability of goal achievement decreases as the preference for the staff technical position increases. And this happens in conjunction with a trend in the direction of the managerial promotion being seen as the bigger promotion. Finally,

Figure 10.2
Attitudes about Staff Position
and Achievement of Important Career Goals
as a Function of Length of Service
(B.S. degree only, Engineers 1 and 2 only)

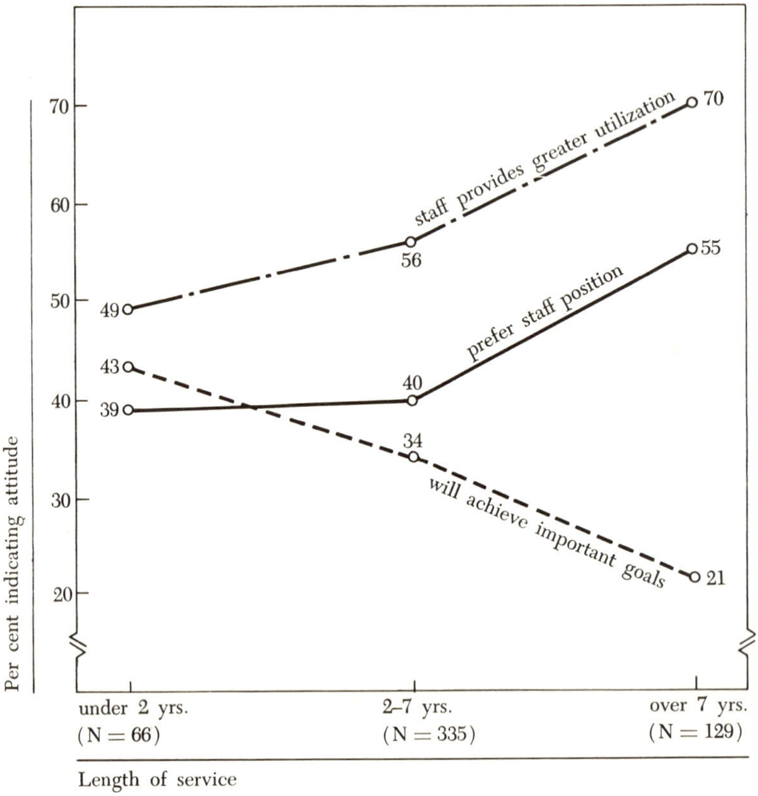

accompanying a decreasing likelihood of being promoted to an influential position is the professed belief that the staff positions provide greater skill utilization.

To summarize, if dual management were to improve utilization in the Electromech environment it would have to do so through increasing the role influence of the staff professional. This would be consistent with our earlier research findings. But far from increasing role influence, dual management actually serves to formalize the powerlessness of the staff professional by creating a second-class management without management influence. Proof of this contention can be found in the common management practice of moving middle management failures from the supervisory side to a high-level position on the nonsupervisory side of the hierarchy.[16] Thus management honors in its actions what it denies in its statements. For these managers are most certainly not moved because it has been belatedly discovered that they are better technically than they are at "handling men." Such middle management jobs contain more executive than supervisory tasks. No, these ex-managers have been put away on the staff side of the hierarchy to get them out of the way, and to allow them to save a certain amount of organizational "face" while ensuring that they can do no further damage. That all this is generally known in laboratory folklore serves to define organizationally the role of the nonsupervisory specialist. As one engineer put it:

> The person is or isn't qualified for management. To offer them staff-professional with the statement that it is equal is considered by many to be an attempt by high management to avoid the unpleasant task of telling some men there isn't room for all of them.

Thus the actual function of dual management is to create an alternative definition of success legitimated by notions of professionalism. And this success is manipulated and granted by management. What remains for the majority of staff engineers who for one reason or another have not been deemed to possess supervisory abilities is an assortment of specialized tasks rather similar to those performed by junior colleagues.

I think I heard the best critique of the notion of dual management from an administrator in a research laboratory. As we discussed the idea he said, "Yes, I think it would probably work out all right here. But, you know, I don't think we really need it." His point was that the researchers in the laboratory were basically independent opera-

[16] A friend of mine in engineering management made an informal survey of the job history of engineers in the top staff technical category. While there are far fewer of these engineers than equivalent managers, he found that over 50 per cent of the top technical people had previously held managerial jobs. This is not true of the lower staff levels.

tives. The need for coordinated effort was small and the management structure consequently flat. Status was based on scientific reputation and the top performing scientists became the first-level managers, in fact, research leaders. Laboratory administration handled all other matters relating to personnel. There was no need for dual management because in many ways it already existed. To put it another way, the failure of the dual hierarchy in the development laboratory is not so much because it does not accomplish its objectives within the existing system. It is because it fails to change the system. Dual management is fated from the start because it is based on misplaced ideas and is overlaid on an existing system of role definitions with which it is incompatible.

SOME GUIDELINES FOR ENGINEERING ADMINISTRATION

My perspective has been that of trying to understand the problem rather than that of providing prepackaged solutions. In fact, it would be counter to the evidence presented here to outline detailed solutions to the general problem. These must be generated by management from a comprehensive knowledge of the individual situation. Keeping this in mind, let me take an organization like Electromech and see what might be done to treat the symptoms of engineering distress it presents.

Keep in mind that our focus is primarily at the policy level. This is because the research evidence clearly shows that the central tendencies of the behavior of lower-level management are dependent on the total management environment and the technological situation. Individual tasks are dependent on the technologically determined division of labor and are supported by executive-level schemes for managing the allocation of resources. A second reason for this focus is my personal belief that exhortation and training cannot be effective in themselves. Structures must be provided which make the desired activities or behavior possible. For example, flatter management structures provide opportunities for greater role influence.

Flattening the Organization Pyramid. For a number of reasons management structure tends toward increasing hierarchy. For one thing, there is a need to provide room for managerial mobility. But the most basic reason seems to be the increased need for coordination that accompanies increasing organizational size and complexity. In the development of complex systems this need for coordination evolves from the factoring out of development tasks along technological lines. The more complex the system, the more detailed the factoring. Multiple levels of management are needed to perform the tasks of coordination and system integration. They serve also as focal points in the information retrieval system used by higher management. In my view this retrieval function serves mainly to transmit detailed (and often faulty) information about particular programs rather than about general conditions. Top management uses this information to audit and control technical program activity. Removing levels of intermediate management has the function of reducing this upward flow of detailed information. Remaining levels are incapable of gathering and transmitting equivalent detail. Obviously, more responsibility for auditing and coordination must devolve to lower levels.

From this discussion it must be obvious that management structure and management environment are related in a systems sense. "Steep" structures make possible the detailed control procedures characteristic of the inflexible management environment. Conversely, managements that subscribe to this philosophy will eventually find steep structures necessary. Flattening the organizational pyramid will increase role influence at lower levels as a result of shifting downward the point where the knowledge necessary to make decisions exists. But it will be effective only to the extent that management is prepared to operate this way. Furthermore, I think it worthwhile to repeat that different technological situations have different structural requirements related basically to the need for the coordination and integration of development activities. Exploratory technology can be relatively flat; big systems must be steeper. Still, any specific arrangement must be tailored to the given situation. Experimentation and evaluation are necessary.

Laboratory Specialization and the Management Environment. Earlier I made a point that management desire for control and task specialization are related. Routine activities are more predictable, more easily controlled. And routinization is achieved through specialization. Now, this is true not only of lower levels in the organization but for entire laboratories. Specialization at the laboratory level means that executive management knows where resources are going, who is directly accountable for what. This is especially true of exploratory or advanced development activities. For executive management knows that exploratory development activities in unspecialized laboratories can be hidden by local management and supported by funds supposedly going to other projects. The paper work will be in order, but the actual activity will have little to do with the funded activity.

This kind of "bootlegging" is more difficult to carry on in a specialized laboratory, especially if the entire laboratory is devoted to exploratory development or some similarly specialized function. For it follows from the definition of the responsibility of the laboratory that any activity being carried on must be exploratory development or something similar. Control-conscious executive management likes this arrangement, for both budget and technical program are open to direct scrutiny.

Now, my point is that this kind of laboratory specialization and the inflexible management environment are directly related. For just as task specialization at the individual level requires more levels of coordinative function, so does laboratory specialization necessitate the removal of control farther up the management structure. With laboratory specialization the level of coordination of various activities is not at the local laboratory level, but rather at division or corporate level. What this means for flexibility and consequent underutilization is that local management is less able to reallocate resources within the laboratory. Transfers of personnel or programs must be made between locations, and this is always resisted. Large systems laboratories tend to come to a standstill at the end of large development projects. And the frequent practice of borrowing resources from advanced technology programs keeps projects in these laboratories in a state of uncertainty. To state the problem directly, control gained by specialization is obtained at the expense of management flexibility. However, where each laboratory has a balance of activities, local control is possible. This in turn means potential for greater role influence. If this is exploited by local management, we have as well the potential for increased utilization.

Control and the Management Environment. In concluding the last paragraph I used the phrase "potential for greater role influence." I did this to recognize explicitly the fact that the removal of some executive-level controls does not guarantee that the local management will act appropriately. So now let us see what might be done at the local level in the unspecialized laboratory.

The first thing is to recognize that the necessity for formal control varies with the technological function and the project cycle. For example, it seems to me that work in exploratory or advanced technology must be taken almost on faith. Projects are small and generally do not require the level of coordination necessary in final systems development. Formal controls are difficult to devise; they do not fit and consequently are mistrusted. Am I advocating that laboratory management abdicate its responsibility? Not at all. I am saying that once a program is agreed upon the control procedure must be to fund and hope.

Then what is to prevent engineers and managers in exploratory engineering from "playing in the sandbox," as once I heard it graphically described? Nothing, I suppose, except what we have seen over and over again in these pages. Engineers want to be successful and contribute to the success of their organization. This desire should not be underestimated. So I think that the job of top laboratory management is the critical assessment of results, not the day-to-day manipulation of means. After all, the assessment of results is difficult enough.

But if exploratory engineering is a fund-and-hope proposition, the final stages of the development of large systems require a high level of formal control. The reason for this is the critical necessity for bringing all development components together into a functioning entity. These control procedures must recognize the conflicting tendencies of each project group to go its own way, to resist "finalizing" the design, never to be satisfied. And this need for control is especially true in Electromech where large projects may span several laboratories. The answer? Arbitrary restrictions and "edicted" answers are part of it. Deadlines, specifications, and budgets are part of it, but not all. For while lack of control may produce chaos, rigid adherence to arbitrary control specifications leads to much the same result. Each in its way robs the engineer of his opportunity to exert informed influence over the technical outcome. The flexible management environment is characterized by high role influence, by the ability to adapt procedures and controls to the current needs of the productive process.

Role Definition and the Management Environment. A management that is aware of this need will seek ways to provide the necessary adaptive mechanisms. Our research suggests group meetings as the key—"When your manager receives new information he holds departmental conferences to discuss the course of future activities." But let me say again that I think it incorrect to interpret this research finding in terms of managerial style, in terms of desirable supervisory behavior. We are talking about a characteristic of an *entire laboratory,* not a characteristic of highly rated individual managers. This means in turn that the indicated action involves more than urging individual managers to hold periodic meetings. It means the development of an entire management environment in which engineers and lower-level managers have the opportunity to confront issues—technical, financial, procedural, or whatever—and to work out solutions based on the most relevant knowledge available.

Where this has been tried it apparently has been successful. For example, after the Project Apollo fire which took the lives of several astronauts, the project manager of that complex system initiated a series of meetings between representatives of the various cooperating agencies.[17] These were so successful as to be termed a "sociological breakthrough." Though the writer of that phrase was apparently unaware of it, the idea was not novel, for it is one of the key aspects of Burns and Stalker's organic management, and has otherwise been described in detail by Likert as an interaction-influence system.[18]

Finally, to those who feel that such a scheme is unrealistic, I must

[17] Alexander, "The Unexpected Payoff of Project Apollo," *Fortune,* LXXX (July, 1969), 114 ff.

[18] See Likert, *New Patterns of Management,* ch. 12.

point out that this is not a model for a conflict-free organization. There are and presumably always will be conflicts of opinion and interest among engineering groups. The point is rather one of providing an arrangement that will bring conflict into view where it can be dealt with and resolved. There is no reason to presume that conflict will be counterproductive unless it is suppressed and hidden from notice. Nor is it necessary to assume that the resolution will at all times be satisfactory to all.

To sum up, the flexible management environment is characterized by high role influence and by the existence of control procedures that "fit." They will fit when there is a management feedback system that provides the information necessary to make the proper adjustments. This feedback system is keyed to group meetings of members from interdependent functions. And it must be appreciated that more than form is required. Executive management must do its part, and laboratory management must be convinced that the lower members of the organization can really do their job. Ultimately it comes to that. But what is the alternative?

Job Enrichment and the Development Mission. We are now at a point where we can talk about the work task itself. For without taking account of the other factors there is probably not much that can be done about task structure. Earlier we discussed the possibilities of job enrichment. And while I admit to being put off a bit by the phrase, our research data make it plain that something of this kind is necessary. What then?

The first thing to recognize is that job enrichment must mean different things in systems development from what it means in exploratory technology. So the problem is not one of finding a universal prescription but one of finding ways to enhance role influence in different settings. Now, the problems of exploratory technology are easier to handle than those of systems development. Misutilization is less pervasive. There are fewer technicians needed. Underutilization due to overcontrol is the greatest problem. So in line with earlier points about role influence in advanced technology, job enrichment here means doing away with day-to-day accountability and giving lower levels in the laboratory a more direct voice in the over-all process of resource allocation. Not so easy, you say? No, it is not.

And that is why the key job of management is the structuring of an appropriate management environment.

The development of large systems is another matter. The project cycle is involved, technicians are necessary, and the task content is determined by the technical factoring of the development program. Since this is the situation of first interest here, my subsequent discussion of job enrichment is aimed at that kind of development mission.

Job Enrichment: Technicians as Engineers. Since I assume that the technologically determined division of labor is more or less beyond manipulation, there seems little opportunity for changing task content. Thus, where the task content implies misutilization, as at the final stage of the project cycle, the solution is in having people with different role expectations do the job—technicians. Actually, as things now stand technicians are as unhappy as engineers. And the reasons are about the same. First, they are misutilized on clerical or on submarginal technical tasks. Second, they can see no opportunity for advancement to higher-level jobs. And this in the face of the realization that they believe they could do what they see engineers doing.

This situation prompts a common argument against the use of more technicians. Managers point out that they would not be better off. Instead of engineers being dissatisfied, the technicians would be dissatisfied. Furthermore, they say, technicians only think they can do what engineers do. Now, these objections are based on the assumption that the job of the engineer will remain the same. But it cannot. The work of both engineer and technician must be upgraded. Nevertheless, technicians do have different role expectations. I think it reasonable to expect technicians to be happier with a given job than engineers. And yes, it is probably true that technicians can do only 90 per cent of what the engineer does. But there is no reason why the engineer cannot fill in that 10 per cent. What is called for, then, is upgrading the role of the technician and changing the role of the engineer to that of technical manager. And evidence does exist that this is successful.[19]

[19] One such instance of the upgrading of jobs is described in National Society of Professional Engineers, "Success Story," *Professional Engineer in Industry Newsletter*, XIII (May, 1968), 4.

Job Enrichment: Engineers as Technical Managers. If technicians are to do the work now being handled by engineers in systems development, then what of the engineer? In accordance with the prescription of job enrichment, our problem is to increase the scope and influence of the engineer's position. The organizational role of the engineer must be redefined. This means that the work of the engineer must become technical and managerial. Now we know from research evidence that there is nothing antithetical between technical and managerial functions. The majority of engineers expect to take on some kind of managerial responsibility anyway. And it is not only the influence problem that is met, but other difficulties as well. Engineers become obsolete because they forget what they once knew, or because their tasks are so specialized that they are not required to keep up with broader developments. In the role of technical leader, however, an engineer would be able to deal with a broader class of technical problems and at the same time exert more influence on the over-all design configuration. What I have in mind is an organization in which engineers are trained for, and are rapidly upgraded to, positions of technical leadership over groups composed of technical and clerical support. Thus, educational requirements for lower-level personnel would be dropped and, over-all, far fewer engineers would be needed. This has the additional advantage of easing the problem of providing upward mobility in the organization, for fewer engineers will be competing for the same number of positions.

Finally, the combination technical-managerial role suggests a way of coping with the changing nature of the task as it evolves in the project cycle. In the stages of initial planning and preliminary design, few technicans are required. The project starts out with a small management team of engineers. Necessary expansion is taken care of by adding technicians, not engineers. Additional flexibility can be gained through use of temporary clerical help.

But, you say, not all engineers want managerial responsibility. And what of the minority of technical superstars admittedly necessary? Engineers are not people-oriented, they make poor managers.

My answers to such remarks are these. I would not waste time worrying about outstanding technical individuals. They are special people and they are treated in special ways. Furthermore, they are usually involved in the early stages of any program and seldom participate in the large systems activities of concern here. Secondly, I have never seen evidence to support the myth that engineers make poor managers—at least no poorer than anyone else. Obviously, if we expect every engineer to become a good manager there are going to be mistakes. This means that engineers for the development of large systems must be picked carefully. Not every engineer belongs here. As before, there is no reason to think that this is an easy plan of action to put into effect, but that is why it is a top-priority management function.

Recognizing Role Style. In the previous chapter I speculated that one of the pressures to manage in a style inappropriate for the function is a desire to emulate the role style of top executive management. Whether or not this is unique to Electromech I do not know, but I doubt that it is. The problem is especially acute where measures of success are subjective, where the final success of a program may not be known for four or five years. Thus it seems to me that something must be done to help executive management come to recognize the biases derived from organizational socialization within a given function, to help executives arrive at an appreciation of the role styles of managers from other functions. Therefore, while my own bias is toward structural manipulation and policy-level change, it seems clear to me now that some sort of problem-oriented interpersonal training is necessary. This training would focus not so much on the characteristics of individual personalities as it would on typical responses to problem situations. It would be an attempt to demonstrate to executives that managerial role styles tend to be flavored by the functional necessities of sales, engineering, and so forth.

The Measurement of Organizational Effectiveness. Finally, the most difficult and in some ways the most important issue, effectiveness. The plain fact of the matter is that top management in engineering development has no formal way of determining the relative effectiveness of various organizational arrangements. Projects and problems tend to be one of a kind, or change over a period of time. Judgments tend to be binary—they did it or they did not—and they tend to be anecdotal—"When Joe Smith had the lab . . ." Generally, these judgments are unreliable and highly personal. The criteria against which the judgments are made are those of cost, time, performance characteristics, and sales. And while the criteria are quantitative in themselves, the process of comparing the quantities from projects A and B is highly qualitative and subjective because A and B are different in many ways. The net result is that there is no incentive for a manager to grapple with problems of underutilization and organizational inefficiency. He really has little idea how much more effective he could be.

Recently some questions were raised about the C-5 air transport program. The program has exceeded its original contract cost by about 100 per cent. A senator wants to investigate because "there is some evidence that poor management on the part of the contractor may be a significant cause."[20] My guess is that, rather than poor management, the problem is management inexperience with a system this large. I suspect that management has no idea of the degree of underutilization that can be generated in such a program. And there seems to be no formal way to find out.

Thus I think that the most likely road toward improved effectiveness in such organizations is the opposite of the one commonly taken. For what is usually done in such cases is to institute additional controls and to create new organizational units to apply these controls. I suggest instead the development of some systematic way of assessing the effectiveness of an organization indirectly through the perceptions and attitudes of organization members, both supervisory and nonsupervisory. Data of this kind, collected periodically, can provide management not only with a different kind of effectiveness measure but a means as well of assessing the extent of change produced by its efforts at organization development. The end in view would be neither the reduction nor the addition of controls, but the tailoring of the management environment for increased effectiveness and member satisfaction consistent with the nature of the enterprise.

[20] Blair, "Congress to Investigate Increase in Cost of C-5A Plane," New York *Times*, December 1, 1968, p. S–15.

APPENDIX A

Additional Description of the Laboratories

Electromech development engineering activities are to some extent specialized within several operating divisions of the company. Thus, while most of the resources of development engineering are allocated to what I characterize as typical of systems development engineering, a few of the laboratories are engaged in somewhat different kinds of activity. In general, the development missions of the laboratories can be characterized as follows:

1. Main-line systems development. These are the complex systems that constitute the backbone of the Electromech business, the standard lines of equipment. This mission is centered in the divisions coded D and F, and accounts for roughly two thirds of the population of the laboratories.

2. New business systems development. This mission is primarily the investigation of new business opportunities for systems applications, and the development of prototype systems to demonstrate feasibility. If these prototypes are sufficiently promising, the designs, and in many cases the personnel, will be transferred to one of the main-line laboratories. Divisions in this activity are coded A and C, and account for 10 per cent of the population.

3. Specialty business applications and systems development. The remaining laboratories make up about 25 per cent of the population. Garwood and Hammond (about 5 per cent) are working on special applications which have few of the characteristics of systems development. Beverly has capabilities for large systems but is unique for the fact that it depends on a variable flow of contract business. This differs from the main-line activities where programs are planned and developed in advance. Easton also has systems characteristics but the work is quite different from that described in Chapter 2.

Other significant characteristics used in later analyses are presented in Table A.1. Rank orders are used to show the characteristics of the laboratories relative to one another and to some extent to protect the anonymity

Table A.1

Ranks on Selected Variables for Twelve Laboratory Locations Ordered by Level of Underutilization

Location	Size[a] (Rank no. of engineers)	Education (Per cent of M.S., Ph.D. degrees)	Technical support (Technical to-profes-sional ratio)	Rank distance from headquarters[b]
Centerville	10	18	03	4.5
Avondale (A1)	9	52	17	1
Easton	5.5	39	74	2
Beverly	5.5	23	45	7
Darby (D1)	1	23	57	3
Hammond	12	16	93	7
Danville (D2)	3	12	73	4.5
Garwood	7	41	79	9.5
Fargo (F3)	4	32	47	11
Ferndale (F1)	2	22	63	7
Aurora (A2)	11	44	40	12
Foster (F2)	8	25	73	9.5

[a] Rank no. 1 is largest in size. Includes all engineers and engineering managers.

[b] Rank no. 1 is closest to headquarters. Ranks based on convenience of travel rather than absolute distance.

of Electromech. Beyond these descriptions, three significant situations exist in the laboratories:

1. Avondale (A1) is going through the process of decommitting an entire function within the laboratory. It is, in fact, dissolving a sub-laboratory devoted to a new systems specialty.
2. The Centerville laboratory is being rethought as a mission by top management. Activity is almost at a standstill and several months after the date of this study the mission was to be phased out.
3. The engineers at Hammond have recently been told by their division chief executive that their current development function has no future. Far-reaching modifications of the mission are now being considered. Transfers and relocations will be forthcoming.

APPENDIX B

Methodology

This appendix provides both additional detail for the research-oriented reader and additional explanation for the curious layman. It is not intended as an exhaustive methodological description of the research reported here.

ITEM RELIABILITY

The basic survey instrument used in this study contained some 330 items and took about one hour to complete. While the respondents for the most part were committed to the purposes of this work, questions must arise as to the reliability of the responses. I will try to answer the questions in two ways. First, individual items showing consistently large correlations with several other items indicate that they must be sufficiently reliable to produce these correlations. All of the items used here have been factor-analyzed at least once prior to their use. Low communalities or ambiguous factor patterns were taken as indications of unreliability in a general sense. I have not used an item to demonstrate a lack of relationship where it has not shown a strong relationship in another situation. A second point is that we have estimates of a kind of split-half reliability between items measuring the same content. For example, the ratings of salary "considering your duties and responsibilities" and "considering what you could get for the same work at other companies" show correlations around .80 within the various laboratories. This is a good single-item reliability for a 5-point scale even though the items measure somewhat different things. The composite scales show better values. The correlation of the 4-item goal-satisfaction scale with one of its components—"Do you feel that your personal goals are being satisfied in your present position with Electromech?"—is .88 in both Darby and Ferndale. The single item comes at the end of the survey booklet. Granted that the correlation is somewhat inflated by the presence of the single item in the composite scale, the fact that the goal-satisfaction scale correlates .73 and .77 with a different work-itself scale indicates a reliability in the .80s.

The rank order correlations present a somewhat different problem. Geographical differences among locations change the reference points of some items. Hence, the rank correlation between the salary items described previously is a disappointing .81. This almost certainly reflects some east to west differences. However, for items that should mean the same thing—"In general, would you say that the work description you have just given represents a satisfying kind of job for you?" and "In general, would you say that the work you are presently doing is helping you to achieve your more important goals?"—the rank correlation over the twelve laboratories is a very satisfactory .99. The two questions are about fifty items apart in the questionnaire format. Finally, the rank correlation between two rate-your-manager items appearing at the very beginning and the very end of the questionnaire, one in 5-point format and the other in 11-point format, is .95. Again the result is very satisfactory for this kind of statistic.

USE OF RANKS

As just mentioned, I have used rank correlation instead of product moment in the analysis of differences among the locations. There are several reasons for this. First, it was a simpler procedure given the setup of the data. But more important, with only twelve observations "outliers" can seriously distort the product-moment correlation. A relatively large correlation can be generated by the presence of one or two points falling well outside an otherwise random scatterplot. Since the relationship between the two statistics is close (for our purposes), and since tests of significance are not the issue, I have chosen to use the rank order statistic.

In two instances I am guilty of the use of averaged ranks. I recognize that the procedure is technically indefensible, but it seemed to make sense in each instance. In the two cases what I wanted was a general index of the variable being considered, and rank averaging seemed to be the most straightforward approach. I did, in fact, want to combine the component variables in the nonmetric sense.

FACTOR ANALYSIS

In the descriptive chapters of this book I use factor analysis to derive dimensions of goals and work characteristics which are more basic than the individual items. Each item has a core of common meaning shared with several others, and one way of uncovering this is through an analysis of the items' statistical interrelationships. Presumably these more basic constructs will give our explanations greater generality and produce more stable estimates of interrelations with other dimensions because the unique aspects of each item have been submerged beneath the common. This is not "shotgun empiricism." The item pool used in constructing the several sections of the questionnaire is based on a conceptual framework developed for each section. The work goals, for example, had been under development for four years prior to the survey, and are the product of many interviews and at least three previous surveys and factor analyses.

In computing individual scores, items were chosen to represent a dimension if they showed a strong relationship to one of the general dimensions and little or no relationship to all the remaining dimensions. This was taken as an indication of dimensional purity. Scores of individuals were the simple arithmetical sum of the scores on the items chosen to represent the dimensions. I did not use factor scores ("best" weights to estimate the factor) for several reasons. First, they tend to vary wildly from sample to sample when the analysis is based on individual items. Frankly, it should be cause for considerable joy if the investigator is able to replicate his general factor structure. A second reason is simply the pragmatic observation that the weighted scores correlate very highly with the unweighted sum, so little is lost with the simpler, more reliable procedure.

Factor analysis and its derivative scales have some weaknesses. One of these is that the unique character of a survey item is lost. It may be this unique content that gives the item its explanatory power. Such an instance occurs in my use of the underutilization item and the role influence item. There is the risk that these special meanings may go unnoticed. This risk must be balanced off against the advantages of the composite scale and its greater reliability. One other complaint is that the factor analytic scales are "incestuously derived" from the very data they are meant to explain. I think I have taken care of this in part by replicating individual findings in at least two laboratories. One of these is unstained by the proscribed relationship.

The program procedure is a maximum-likelihood routine developed by Rolf Bargmann. An advantage of it is that the investigator can tell how many statistically reliable dimensions are contained in the data. The rotation is a variant of the Thurstone single-plane procedure and produces an oblique solution. Thus, the dimensions as general constructs are related to one another though they are conceptually separable. The best example of this is the scientific and the technical goals. They are different constructs and show very different "popularities," but the engineer who finds one set relatively important tends to find the other set relatively important as well.

MULTIPLE REGRESSION

I have used multiple regression here primarily as a statistical accounting procedure. The question is one of the total extent to which the six work characteristics account for the level of goal satisfaction. The lay reader can think of the procedure as one in which an individual's level of goal satisfaction—his score on the goal satisfaction scale—is predicted from his scores on the work characteristics. The correlation coefficient indicates the extent to which this prediction is successful. A value of 1.00 means that the prediction is perfect—no error. A value of zero means that on the average knowing the scores on the work characteristics does not help us account for the scores on the goal satisfaction scale. Now since the work characteristics are themselves interrelated, the multiple correlation coefficient provides us with a measure of the extent to which all our information in linear combination will account for goal satisfaction—a measure of the importance of the work itself. The partial coefficients indicate the extent to which a given characteristic contributes uniquely to the prediction of goal satisfaction. Low values indicate that the dimension contributes little that is not accounted for by a composite of the remaining five. Large values inform us that something unique is being contributed, though how much cannot be directly ascertained without reference to other numbers. That is, large values may indicate that a large proportion of very little remaining to be unaccounted for is related to the given variable.

CLASSIFICATION ANALYSIS

The technical name for classification analysis would be discriminant function analysis. I used the term "classification" at the behest of a friend of mine who claimed that "discriminant" confused him so badly he could not understand what followed. The problem here is one of finding some procedure to account for a two-valued nonmetric response using a multiple set of related variables. As in the regression procedure, the aim is to find a way to measure the total extent of our knowledge of the characteristic in question. In the first case we want to know how well we can account for the "prefer more" response. However, as in the case of multiple regression, problems arise in the interpretation of the function itself. Where the variables in the function are themselves highly interrelated and where different numbers of similar variables mirror common content, we can use the classification function itself only as a best linear predictor of the characteristic we wish to account for. However, since interpretation seems important I have used a suggestion by Rolf Bargmann to correlate the scores on the original variables with the function scores. Since the function itself is a best composite predictor it seems intuitively reasonable that the variables most correlated with it should be useful in describing the underlying situation. Actually, this final step is accomplished within the program by one additional matrix manipulation.

The variables included in the analysis are as follows:

1. The work characteristics described in Chapter 2 with the exception of *Utilization of Skills,* which seemed redundant in this context.
2. The work goals described in Chapter 3.
3. The conflict dimensions of Chapter 4.
4. Seven composite scales reflecting decision-making problems of management (e.g., Unpredictability of management).
5. Thirteen additional measures:

   time demands of the job
   intellectual demands of the job
   manager's emphasis on commitments of schedule and performance
   manager's emphasis on development of new technology
   role influence
   conflict in work goals
   involvement in work
   participation in goal-setting for department
   misutilization
   manager's responsiveness to complaints
   opportunities to move to a better job
   rating of own productivity
   level of education

APPENDIX C

Measuring the Development Laboratory Mission

The mean response of professionals to the following question has been used to characterize the development mission of the laboratories.

> "While work groups have many basic objectives in common, different managers place different amounts of emphasis on these objectives. How much emphasis would you say your manager actually places on each of the following as demonstrated in his day-to-day manner of directing your project activities?"
> —Meeting schedules
> —Building a backlog of technical discoveries toward future product developments

Both engineers and their managers responded to this question on a five-point scale running from "Utmost emphasis is evident" to "No emphasis is evident." As might be expected, there is a correlation between placing heavy emphasis on schedules and not placing emphasis on technology ($r = .59$). That is, laboratories which had missions emphasizing the development of a backlog of technology showed less emphasis on meeting schedules. (See Figure C.1 for the range of laboratory levels on three mission variables. Only the two extremes are used in the mission index, however.) Since the ranks are correlated, a new average rank can be formed by combining the ranks on emphasis on schedules and on technology. Thus, at one end of the continuum we have laboratories in which emphasis on meeting schedules is relatively high and emphasis on new explorations in technology relatively low. At the other end of the continuum are laboratories in which the emphasis on developing new technology is relatively high and emphasis on meeting schedules relatively less important.

Now if the laboratory is a system of management and if this system of management can be characterized uniformly, then the managers of the professionals should take a similar view. When this ranking procedure

Figure C.1

Engineers' Reports of Emphasis Placed by Managers on Schedules, Utilizing Technical Advances, and Building a Backlog of Technical Discoveries

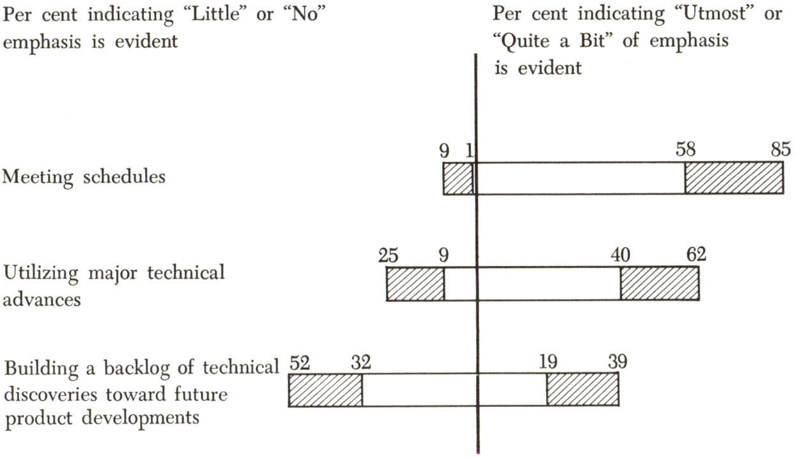

Note: Shaded area shows range for twelve laboratory locations.

is repeated using responses of the first-line managers in these development laboratories about what *their managers* emphasize, the composite ranks for the professionals and those of the managers are in good agreement (r = .89). This check from a different population indicates the reliability of this characterization of the laboratory mission. Both professionals and their managers agree in certain laboratories that the environment emphasizes meeting commitments at the expense of advancing technology. Two other pieces of reinforcing evidence are these:

1. The laboratory mission thus characterized is associated with the per cent of master's and Ph.D. degrees in the population (r = .74).

2. Subjectively, the rank order list of the laboratories agrees with the known mission of the laboratories. Thus laboratories 1, 2, and 3 in the composite rank were highly involved in the development of large systems at the time of the survey. There was considerable overtime being applied in those laboratories and there was no question but what meeting the schedule was being emphasized as the primary criterion of success. On the other hand, the last three laboratories in the rank order were all heavily involved in advanced development activity. Two of the three had missions explicitly described as advanced development, and the

third laboratory had a substantial component of advanced development activity.

Note that emphasis on schedules does not necessarily mean the same thing as time pressure. To be sure, emphasis on schedules does produce time pressure but, as we have seen earlier, there are good reasons why laboratories within which maximum emphasis is being placed on meeting schedules will also contain scattered groups of professionals who have no work to do. The laboratory that ranked first in emphasis on schedules actually ranked below the median (seventh) on time demands. That is, professionals in that laboratory reported that their managers placed the highest emphasis on meeting schedules but also reported the time demands as being below average relative to the other laboratories. Thus it is that for our twelve laboratories the association between the schedule emphasis reported by professionals and the time demands they report is far from perfect (r = .67).

A final point is that laboratory size is to some extent associated with laboratory mission (r = .55). This is a result of the fact that the advanced development laboratories are in general smaller, and the big systems laboratories larger.

APPENDIX D

Degree of Association[a] among Five Measures of Influence, Goal Satisfaction, and Development Mission

	Mission[b] (1)	Gets opinion (2)	Individual influence (3)	Partici-pation (4)	Goals (5)	Role influence (6)
(2) Gets the opinion of his men before committing department to goal or schedule	87					
(3) Individual influence (scale)	49	63				
(4) Satisfaction with participation in setting objectives of department	39	52	86			
(5) Work satisfies important goals	32	46	78	89		
(6) Role influence	08	25	58	81	87	
(7) When receives new information holds conferences to discuss the course of future activities	19	19	54	62	76	78

[a] Rank order correlations for twelve laboratory locations. Decimals omitted.
[b] Positive association is with low schedule emphasis.

Bibliography

Alexander, Tom. "The Unexpected Payoff of Project Apollo," *Fortune*, LXXX (July, 1969), 114 ff.

Allen, Thomas J. "Sources of Ideas and Their Effectiveness in Parallel R&D Projects." Alfred P. Sloan School of Management, Working Paper #13065. Cambridge, Mass., M.I.T., 1965.

American Society for Engineering Education. "Synopsis of the Joint ECAC–RWI Feedback Committee Report," *Journal of Engineering Education*, LV (1965), 254–56.

Andreas, Henry J. "Cooperation among Professional, Technical and Non-professional Organizations in the Electrical Industry," in Collective Bargaining for Professional and Technical Employees. Conference Report of the Institute of Labor and Industrial Relations. Urbana, University of Illinois, 1965.

Bambridge, James J., Albert A. Blum, and Hermine Zagat. Unionization among American Engineers. New York, National Industrial Conference Board, 1956.

Barlow, Walter O. "Discontent among Engineers," *Journal of College Placement*, XXV (1965), 24 ff.

Barnard, Chester I. The Functions of the Executive. Cambridge, Mass., Harvard University Press, 1938.

Becker, Howard S., and James Carper. "The Elements of Identification with an Occupation," *American Sociological Review*, XXI (1956), 341–48.

Berg, Ivar. "Rich Man's Qualifications for Poor Man's Jobs," *Transaction*, VI (March, 1969), 45–50.

Blair, William M. "Congress to Investigate Increase in Cost of C-5A Plane," New York *Times*, December 1, 1968, p. S–15.

Blauner, Robert. Alienation and Freedom. Chicago, University of Chicago Press, 1964.

Burns, Tom, and G. M. Stalker. The Management of Innovation. London, Tavistock, 1961.

Campfield, William L. "Motivating the Professional Employee," *Personnel Journal*, XLIV (1965), 425 ff.

"Career Comments," *Machine Design,* xxxv (June 6, 1963), 114.

Coch, Lester, and John R. P. French, Jr. "Overcoming Resistance to Change," *Human Relations,* xi (1948), 512–32.

Dalton, Gene W., Louis B. Barnes, and Abraham Zalesnik. The Distribution of Authority in Formal Organizations. Boston, Harvard Graduate School of Business Administration, 1968.

Danielson, Lee E. Characteristics of Engineers and Scientists. Ann Arbor, Bureau of Industrial Relations, 1960.

Dubin, Robert, George C. Homans, Floyd C. Mann, and Delbert C. Miller. Leadership and Productivity. San Francisco, Chandler, 1965.

Edwards, Allen L. The Social Desirability Variable in Personality Assessment and Research. New York, Dryden, 1957.

Festinger, Leon. A Theory of Cognitive Dissonance. Stanford, Stanford University Press, 1962.

Fleishman, Edwin A. "Leadership Climate, Human Relations Training and Supervisory Behavior," *Personnel Psychology,* vi (1953), 205–22.

Fleishman, Edwin A., Edwin F. Harris, and Harold E. Burtt. Leadership and Supervision in Industry. Columbus, Ohio State University, 1955.

Ford, Robert N. Motivation through the Work Itself. New York, American Management Association, 1969.

French, John R. P., Jr. "The Social Environment and Mental Health," *Journal of Social Issues,* xix (October, 1963), 39–66.

Galbraith, John Kenneth. The New Industrial State. Boston, Houghton Mifflin, 1967.

Glaser, Barney G. Organizational Scientists: Their Professional Careers. Indianapolis, Bobbs-Merrill, 1964.

Goffman, Erving. "On Cooling the Mark Out: Some Adaptations to Failure," *Psychiatry,* xv (1952), 451–63.

Goldner, Fred H. "Industrial Relations and the Organization of Management." Unpublished Ph.D. dissertation, University of California, Berkeley, 1961.

Goldner, Fred H., and R. Richard Ritti. "Professionalization as Career Immobility," *American Journal of Sociology,* lxxii (1967), 489–502.

Hansen, A. J., and Donald G. Marquis. "Can Creativity be Predicted in Research Professionals?" Alfred P. Sloan School of Management, Working Paper #73-64. Cambridge, Mass., M.I.T., 1964.

Herzberg, Frederick. Work and the Nature of Man. Cleveland, World Publishing Co., 1966.

Herzberg, Frederick, Bernard Mausner, and Barbara B. Snyderman. The Motivation to Work. New York, Wiley, 1959.

Hirsch, Irving, William Milwitt, and William J. Oakes, Jr. "Increasing the Productivity of Scientists," *Harvard Business Review,* xxxvi (March–April, 1958), 66–76.

Kahn, Robert L., Donald M. Wolfe, Robert P. Quinn, J. Diedrick Snoek, and Robert A. Rosenthal. Organizational Stress: Studies in Role Conflict and Ambiguity. New York, Wiley, 1964.

Katz, Daniel, Nathan Maccoby, and Nancy C. Morse. Productivity, Supervision and Morale in an Office Situation. Ann Arbor, Institute for Social Research, 1950.

Kornhauser, William, with the assistance of Warren O. Hagstrom, Scientists in Industry: Conflict and Accommodation. Berkeley, University of California Press, 1962.

Lawrence, Paul R., and Jay W. Lorsch. Organization and Environment. Homewood, Ill., Irwin, 1969.

LeBold, William K., Robert Perrucci, and Warren Howland. "The Engineer in Industry and Government," *American Society for Engineering Education Proceedings,* LXXIII (1966), 237–73.

Likert, Rensis. The Human Organization. New York, McGraw-Hill, 1967.

—— New Patterns of Management. New York, McGraw-Hill, 1961.

March, James G., and Herbert A. Simon. Organizations. New York, Wiley, 1958.

Mayo, Elton. The Human Problems of an Industrial Civilization. Boston, Harvard Graduate School of Business Administration, 1933.

Mecklin, John. "The C-5: The Ordeal of the Plane Makers," *Fortune,* LXXII (December, 1965), 158 ff.

Moore, David G., and Richard Renck. "The Professional Employee in Industry," in Charles D. Orth III *et al.,* Administering Research and Development. Homewood, Ill., Irwin, 1964.

Morse, Nancy C. Satisfactions in the White Collar Job. Ann Arbor, Institute for Social Research, 1953.

National Society of Professional Engineers. "Success Story," *Professional Engineer in Industry Newsletter,* XIII (May, 1968), 4.

—— "Utilization of the Engineer," *Professional Engineer in Industry Newsletter,* xiv (May, 1969), 1.

Northrup, Herbert R. Unionization of Professional Engineers and Chemists. Industrial Relations Monograph #12. New York, Industrial Relations Counselors, 1946.

Nussbaum, Frederick L. A History of the Economic Institutions of Modern Europe. New York, F. S. Crofts, 1933.

Opinion Research Corporation. "The Complex Problems of Engineers in Industry." Mimeographed report, 1964.

—— "The Conflict Between the Scientific Mind and the Management Mind." Mimeographed report, 1959.

Patchen, Martin. "Labor-Management Consultation at TVA: Its Impact on Employees," *Administrative Science Quarterly,* x (1965), 149–74.

Pelz, Donald C., and Frank M. Andrews. Scientists in Organizations: Productive Climates for Research and Development. New York, Wiley, 1966.

Peter, Hollis W. "Human Factors in Research Administration," in Reusis Likert and Samuel P. Hayes, Jr., eds., Some Applications of Behavioral Research, pp. 124–59. Paris, UNESCO, 1957.

"The Profession: Deficiencies in Retrospect," *Product Engineering*, xxxvi (1965), 33.

Raines, Irving I., and Joseph C. Missar. "Engineering Obsolescence: A Challenge to the Training Director," *Training Directors Journal*, xix (January, 1965), 35–42.

Raudsepp, Eugene. "How Well Are Engineers Utilized?" *Machine Design*, xxxv (December 19, 1963), 100–2.

—— "Improving Engineer Productivity," *Machine Design*, xxxvi (January 2, 1964), 83–86.

—— "Money Isn't Everything," *Machine Design*, xxxvi (March 12, 1964), 132–34.

Raudsepp, Eugene, and the Editors. "Why Engineers Change Jobs," *Machine Design*, xxxv (January 31, 1963), 70–74.

Riegel, John W. Administration of Salaries and Intangible Rewards for Engineers and Scientists. Ann Arbor, Bureau of Industrial Relations, 1958.

—— Collective Bargaining as Viewed by Unorganized Engineers and Scientists. Ann Arbor, Bureau of Industrial Relations, 1959.

Ritti, R. Richard. "Control of Halo in Factor Analysis of a Supervisory Behavior Inventory," *Personnel Psychology*, xvii (1964), 305–18.

—— "Engineers and Managers: A Study of Engineering Organization." Unpublished Ph.D. dissertation, Cornell University, 1960.

—— "The Purdue Engineering Graduate: His Background, College Experiences and Expectations." Unpublished Master's thesis, Purdue University, 1957.

—— "Work Goals of Scientists and Engineers," *Industrial Relations*, vii (1968), 118–31.

Ritti, R. Richard, and Fred H. Goldner. "Professional Pluralism in an Industrial Organization," *Management Science*, xvi (December, 1969), B-233–B-246.

Sayles, Leonard R. Behavior of Industrial Work Groups. New York, Wiley, 1958.

—— Managerial Behavior. New York, McGraw-Hill, 1964.

Shepard, Herbert A. "The Dual Hierarchy in Research," *Research Management*, i (1958), 177–87.

—— "Nine Dilemmas in Industrial Research," *Administrative Science Quarterly*, i (1956), 298–309.

—— "Patterns of Organization for Applied Research and Development," *Journal of Business*, xxix (1966), 52–58.

Smith, Clagett G., and Oguz N. Ari. "Organizational Control Structure and Member Consensus," *American Journal of Sociology*, LXIX (1964), 623–38.

Stevens Institute of Technology. "Stevens Alumniletter," Vol. I (February, 1960).

Tannenbaum, Arnold S. Control in Organizations. New York, McGraw-Hill, 1968.

Thompson, Victor A. Modern Organization. New York, Knopf, 1961.

Trist, E. L., and K. W. Bansforth. "Some Social and Psychological Consequences of the Longwall Method of Coal-Getting," *Human Relations*, IV (1951), 3–38.

Weber, Max. The Theory of Social and Economic Organization. Trans. A. M. Henderson and Talcott Parsons. Glencoe, Free Press, 1947.

Whyte, William F. Human Relations in the Restaurant Industry. New York, McGraw-Hill, 1948.

Wolfe, Donald M., and J. Diedrick Snoek. "A Study of Tensions and Adjustments under Role Conflict," *Journal of Social Issues*, XVIII (1962), 102–21.

Woodward, Joan. Industrial Organization: Theory and Practice. New York, Oxford University Press, 1965.

Index